EXPANDING THE DONOR BASE IN HIGHER EDUCATION

Traditionally, institutions have relied on wealthy White men to reach their fundraising goals. But as state investment in public higher education lessens and institutions look to philanthropy to move from excellence to eminence, advancement officers continually need to engage all populations, including many that have historically been excluded from fundraising strategies. Based on theory, research, and past practice, *Expanding the Donor Base in Higher Education* explores how colleges and universities can build culturally sensitive fundraising and engagement strategies. This edited book presents emerging research on different communities that have not traditionally been approached for fundraising—including Lesbian, Gay, Bisexual, Transgender, and Queer (LGBTQ) alumni, African Americans, Latinos, graduate students, young alumni, women, and faculty donors. Chapters discuss and analyze successful programs and provide practical suggestions and strategies to create and implement fundraising programs that engage these new donor populations. *Expanding the Donor Base in Higher Education* is an essential resource for any institution looking to expand their pool of donors and cultivate a more philanthropic mindset among alumni and students.

Noah D. Drezner is Assistant Professor of Higher Education and a faculty member in the Center for Philanthropy and Nonprofit Leadership at the University of Maryland, College Park, USA.

EXPANDING THE DONOR BASE IN HIGHER EDUCATION

Engaging Non-Traditional Donors

Edited by *Noah D. Drezner*

NEW YORK AND LONDON

First published 2013
by Routledge
711 Third Avenue, New York, NY 10017

Simultaneously published in the UK
by Routledge
2 Park Square, Milton Park, Abingdon, Oxon OX14 4RN

Routledge is an imprint of the Taylor & Francis Group, an informa business

© 2013 Taylor & Francis

The right of Noah D. Drezner to be identified as the author of the editorial material, and of the authors for their individual chapters, has been asserted in accordance with sections 77 and 78 of the Copyright, Designs and Patents Act 1988.

Library of Congress Cataloging in Publication Data
Expanding the donor base in higher education : engaging non-traditional donors /
    [edited by] Noah D. Drezner.
    pages cm
    Includes bibliographical references and index.
    1. Educational fund raising—United States. 2. College benefactors—United States.
    I. Drezner, Noah D., editor of compilation.
    LB2336.E95 2013
    378.1'06—dc23
    2012044228

ISBN: 978-0-415-53398-0 (hbk)
ISBN: 978-0-415-53400-0 (pbk)
ISBN: 978-0-203-11371-4 (ebk)

Typeset in Bembo and Stone Sans
by EvS Communication Networx, Inc.

Printed and bound in the United States of America by Publishers Graphics, LLC on sustainably sourced paper.

In Memory of
Irene Greenhall (1934–2012)
Who inspired me, made me laugh, loved me,
and I continue to love
and
Donald Greenhall (1928–2013)
Whose quiet support
is already missed.

CONTENTS

ACKNOWLEDGMENTS

Thinking about all of the people in my life that have influenced and helped me both directly and indirectly in being able to edit *Expanding the Donor Base in Higher Education: Engaging Non-Traditional Donors* was a daunting task. I am very fortunate to have so many people supporting me. To begin with I have a number of students that I work with formally and informally at the University of Maryland who inspire me as a faculty member in and out of the classroom. First and foremost, I thank Jason C. Garvey for not only joining me on our Queering Philanthropy research project, of which we report some of our findings from the first phase of our research, but also for reading and commenting on this manuscript at various stages from the writing of the proposal through its final versions. Jay is a great research partner, mentee, and friend.

Beyond Jay, I must thank my other wonderful Ph.D. advisers, Rebecca Villarreal, Steve D. Mobley, Jr., Michael Puma (another chapter author), and my newest additions to "Team Drezner," Nina Daoud and Candice Staples. I continue to be excited to see prior students excel in their philanthropy scholarship and practice. It is a pleasure and honor to include three chapters from such students in this volume, Luke Greeley, Ryan Merkel, and Kozue Tsunoda. I benefit from their work every time I read it.

Additionally, my colleagues at Maryland provide me with a supportive work environment in which I thrive. Special thanks to Tom Davis, a colleague and friend since starting at Maryland together, for reading this manuscript and giving it an outsider's eye. Thank you especially to Sharon Fries-Britt, Alberto Cabrera, KerryAnn O'Meara, Marvin Titus; those who have left Maryland, Susan Komives, Connie North, Stephen Quaye, Susan Jones; and my newest colleagues, Kimberly Griffin and Michelle Espino, who have made my tenure track both a continuing learning and growth experience and—dare I say it—pleasurable.

In addition to my higher education and student affairs colleagues, I am lucky to have found others with the passion for philanthropy scholarship and teaching. Thank you to Robert Grimm, Jr. and Jennifer Littlefield for their support and opportunity to help create the University of Maryland's Center on Philanthropy and Nonprofit Leadership. I never thought that I would be part of creating a center for scholarship and teaching devoted to creating future philanthropists. This experience is simply inspiring.

From a scholarly and career perspective, I would not be where I am today without the continued support of my mentor and close friend, Marybeth Gasman. Marybeth is an inspiration as a scholar, teacher, parent, and friend. She has supported me, challenged me, and given me opportunities for which I will continue to be forever indebted to her.

I am so lucky to have family and friends who support me daily—even in the smallest ways. Thank you to my father, David, for his endless love, confidence, and support. I am also blessed with an extended family that not only supports me but brings me joy—a special thank you to my Aunt Judy and Uncle Steve Lippard, my cousins Sandra, Josh, and Alex Lippard; Audrey Greenhall and George Chressanthis, and Diana and David Newby. Beyond the traditional family, I am privileged to have some people in my lives who are family in the truest sense of the word, even though not by blood or law. Thank you to Alan Baldridge who is not only one of my best friends but is the brother I never had.

Everyone who knows me knows that children give make me smile, inspire me, and give me a strange energy that feed my work. Thank you to some of those children that give me that energy: Chloe Epstein, Philip, Matthew, and Christopher Baldridge, Emily and William Chressanthis, and Lucy and Annie Lippard.

Finally to Oren Pizmony-Levy, whose support and love bring a smile to my face and a confidence to my work—I am so lucky to have met you.

1

INTRODUCTION

Noah D. Drezner

During the closing plenary session of the 2011 Association of Fundraising Professionals (AFP) International Conference on Fundraising, conference chair Andrea McManus, CFRE,[1] charged those in the audience to take the profession beyond fundraising and to engage ourselves and our donors in philanthropy. This call was more than semantics. She challenged the field to engage *all* potential donors in their giving and their reasons they wanted to support others by moving beyond merely "closing the gift" and working with the "usual suspects."

Within a context of American higher education, as with fundraising at many other nonprofits, for too long institutional advancement officers have relied on wealthy, White, heterosexual men to reach their fundraising goals (Drezner, 2011). As campaign goals grow and the economy recovers slowly, the base of the campaign pyramid, the smaller and medium size gifts, is becoming more and more important to successfully raising the dollars needed (Grenzebach, Glier, and Associates, 2010). The small and medium sized gifts not only help reach current campaign goals, but are important in the cultivation of future campaign leadership gifts.

Therefore, there is an increased importance to engage all populations in advancement strategies, many that have historically been excluded from fundraising strategies (Drezner, 2010). As such, *Expanding the Donor Base in Higher Education: Engaging Non-Traditional Donors* looks at the emerging research on different communities that are often excluded from the focus of institutional advancement offices. Before going into how this book is organized, the significance of the research disseminated in the chapters, and their implications for practice, it is important to understand the context of fundraising and voluntary support of American higher education at the time of writing this book.

Where We Are Today: An Overview of the Landscape of Advancement in American Higher Education

Since the "great recession of 2008," advancement programs at colleges and universities across the country have been wondering how to continue to provide the necessary voluntary support for their institutions in order to simply meet their budgetary needs. As fiscal year 2011 ended, there was hope that voluntary support and endowment returns had begun to recover to pre-2008 levels. In August 2011, the confidence from the philanthropic giving recovery led the University of Southern California to announce a $6 billion campaign. USC's campaign was the largest announced fundraising goal for any higher education campaign to date. Within a few months of USC's announcement, three universities, Case Western Reserve University, Georgetown University, and the University of Rochester, launched campaigns of at least $1 billion, which the institutions had been holding off during the recession.

According to the Council for Aid to Education's annual Voluntary Support of Education (VSE) survey, colleges and universities raised 8.2 percent more in fiscal 2011 than the prior year. The $30.3 billion in giving is only $1.3 billion less than higher education's record for voluntary support of $31.6 billion reached in fiscal year 2008, just prior to the economic downturn. To place this increase in context, colleges' and universities' fundraising dropped 12 percent in 2009. This was the largest one-year decrease in giving that the Council for Aid Education has recorded since they began conducting the VSE in 1969. The following year, giving to higher education only increased by one half of one percent (Council for Aid to Education, 2012).

While the increases in giving were significant, not all institutions fared as well as others. The top 20 institutions, in terms of gifts received in 2011, a group consisting mostly of elite private and public research universities, raised a combined $8.24 billion, accounting for 27 percent of the funds raised by all institutions. While this concentration of fundraising success is not new, giving was more concentrated in 2011 than in the past. For example, the top quartile of institutions raised 11.3 percent more in fiscal year 2011 than in 2010. However, the rest of the higher education sector raised 9.6 percent less in fiscal year 2011 than in 2010. Looking at this another way, the top quartile of institutions raised 86 percent of dollars raised, leaving 13.7 percent, or $4.15 billion dollars for the rest of American higher education (Council for Aid to Education, 2012).

Additionally, after taking a huge hit in fiscal year 2009, almost half of all college and university endowments are still worth less than they were in 2008. Yet, in fiscal year 2011 overall college and university endowment returns reached near-pre-great recession levels. According to the National Association of College and University Business Officers (NACUBO)/Commonfund annual endowment survey, investments returned an average of 19.2 percent. However, like the fundraising results, these high returns were not distributed equally across all sectors of American higher education (NACUBO/Common-fund, 2012). Between 2008 and 2010, institutions with smaller endowments outperformed the wealthiest institutions. However, in fiscal year 2011, like prior to 2008, institutions with large endowments, which are able to invest in alternative investment strategies such as hedge funds, venture capital, private equity, and private real estate, due to their size, saw the highest returns. Those institutions with smaller endowments, which tend to be invested more in domestic equities and fixed-income investments, saw lower returns (NACUBO/Commonfund, 2012). Therefore, there continues to be a growing gap in endowment values between the wealthiest elite institutions and the rest of higher education. This gap can be narrowed by institutions looking beyond their traditional donor bases.

A Need to Expand the Donor Base

As a result of the current economic situation and decreased funding for higher education, institutions, private and public alike, are turning more and more to private giving in order to meet budgetary demands. As external support of higher education from both state governments and donors decreases and the cost to educate a student rises, the need for alumni support to maintain higher education's eminence and to increase access heightens. There is a need for more research on philanthropic giving patterns as institutions expand their focus to new donor communities.

A greater understanding of philanthropy within the higher education setting is critical because of the greater reliance on voluntary giving at all colleges and universities since the recent economic downturn as well as the imminent intergenerational "great wealth transfer" (Schervish & Havens, 1998). With the higher education endowments plummeting in 2008 and 2009, retrenchment of state appropriations at public institutions, and the possibilities of engaging a broader range of donors, it is imperative that intuitions understand the theories, motivations, dynamics, and ethics of philanthropy. It was with this aim that I endeavored to bring together this edited book.

Further, as colleges and universities move into continual campaign modes, where as one large campaign ends the next one begins its planning phase, institutional advancement officers should not only think about the larger donors of today, but must engage those who might be able to give the leadership gifts in future campaigns. While expanding the donor base and thinking about how to engage in more donor-centric advancement strategies is important for *all* institutions, it is particularly important at many public institutions.

In the grand scheme of things many state-supported colleges and universities have only just begun to fundraise from alumni in concerted efforts. Until the mid-1990s, many public institutions did not have the large, sophisticated advancement offices that were commonplace at large private universities for decades and in some cases over a century. Setting up sophisticated advancement offices and employing donor-centered cultivation and solicitation strategies that aim to expand the university's donor base will continue to allow the universities to further increase their fundraising ability. Therefore, there are a number of chapters in this book looking at a variety of research and programs that engage different constituencies that are often not the focus of the cookie-cutter fundraising strategies that institutions employ. These new strategies are designed to expand the university's pool of donors and cultivate a more philanthropic mindset among alumni and students.

Brittingham and Pezzullo (1990) believe that fundraising is often "thinly informed by research" (p. 1). The vast majority of philanthropic literature within higher education is atheoretical (e.g., Burnett, 1992/2002; Ciconte & Jacob, 2001; Connors, 2001; Dove, 2001; Flanagan, 1999; Greenfield, 2001; Worth, 2002). Although existing research offers some guidance for practitioners, the implications are limited by the failure to ground the research in any theoretical or conceptual framework. In this volume, each chapter examines the existing literature and introduces the reader to new research and fundraising practice that not only helps fill the theoretical void in the literature, thereby improving future research, but also informs current fundraising practice.

Organization of the Book

Creating a fundraising strategy that takes into account a person's interests is not a new concept. "Donor centric" fundraising has been the hallmark of major gifts programs from their inception. However, identity-based fundraising is more recent. The authors of a 2012 *Cultures of Giving* report by the W. K. Kellogg Foundation and funded by the Rockefeller Philanthropy Advisors found that

> identity-based philanthropy is a growing movement to democratize philanthropy from the grassroots up by activating and organizing its practice in marginalized communities, particularly communities of color. Simply described, it is the practice of raising and leveraging resources by and from a community on its own behalf, where "community" is defined not by geography but by race, ethnicity, gender, or sexual orientation.
>
> *(2012, p. 2)*

Higher education for too long has defined its prospective individual donors simply by their alumni, parent, or "friend" status. It is time that practitioners and philanthropy scholars make concerted efforts to engage their work not only by these traditional definitions but through new ones, including race, ethnicity, gender, or sexual orientation.

This book is organized into three sections, each based on different social identities of potential donors to higher education. The first section explores giving among racial minority groups with chapters on giving within the African American, Latino/na, and Chinese American communities. The second examines giving behaviors and motivations among other alumni constituencies that are often not traditionally segmented for special engagement strategies. In this section chapters look at giving from women, the lesbian, gay, bisexual, transgender, and queer communities, Ph.D. alumni, and young alumni who have graduated in the past decade. The third and final section looks at on-campus constituencies and future donors. Here the authors explore faculty and staff as potential donors, how to engage students, members of fraternities and sororities, and how to build partnerships between student affairs and institutional advancement. Finally, the book closes with a call to think about how fundraisers operate in order to further engage future donors.

Racial Minorities

Marybeth Gasman and Nelson Bowman's chapter, "Engaging and Soliciting African American Alumni," builds off their experiences as both researchers and as fundraising practitioners. Their chapter highlights the prevailing literature on Black giving, including historical and current giving patterns, differences in giving based on socio-economic status, and gender differences. Finally, they discuss practical ways to engage African American alumni giving at both predominantly White and historically Black institutions.

José A. Cabrales, in his chapter: "An Approach to Engaging Latina/o Alumni in Giving Initiatives: Madrinas y Padrinos" uses community cultural wealth theory to explore the interconnectedness between careers, community, and giving from Latina/o alumni. Building off of prior philanthropic research on Latinas/os, where researchers find that three informal media of philanthropy, extended family networks, church involvement, and mutualista organizations, provide social services and social justice supports, Cabrales reports the findings from his phenomenological study. He finds that Latina/o alumni employ different forms of capital through their occupations and community engagement to give back to students and their communities, both financially and through mentorship.

Kozue Tsunoda looks at the philanthropic contributions of the largest ethnic group among Asian Americans. In her chapter, "Chinese American Philanthropy: Cultural Contexts behind Major Gifts in Higher Education," she highlights the historical, cultural, and contemporary trends of Chinese American giving to higher education. Using in-depth interviews of Chinese American mega-gift donors, Tsunoda reveals donor motivations to give philanthropically. She finds that donors often give for reasons of racial uplift wanting to help Chinese American and Chinese international students and scholars within American higher education. By integrating existing research and her own study, Tsunoda provides a holistic view of Chinese American educational giving and suggests ways advancement officers can better foster and harness philanthropic giving by Chinese Americans.

Other Alumni Constituencies

In their chapter, Sara Kaiser and Amy Wells Dolan explore women's philanthropic contributions to higher education. Building off the work of other scholars, Kaiser and Wells Dolan explore the unique giving philosophies and interests that often compel women to give. They note that women are participating in higher education as students, faculty, staff, administrators, and friends at the highest levels in history and therefore not engaging in fundraising practices that engage women potentially leaves a large market of prospective donors untapped.

In my chapter with Jason C. Garvey, "Alumni Giving in the LGBTQ Communities: Queering Philanthrophy," we explore the motivations of LGBTQ alumni to give to their alma mater. Prior to our study, the scholarship and practice involving LGBTQ philanthropy, towards any part of the third sector, was scarce. Therefore, we look at how LGBTQ communities think about giving to higher education. Using a constructivist case study analysis, we found unconscious influences of LGBTQ identities on giving, importance of campus climate for LGBTQ individuals, and LGBTQ alumni affinity group involvement. We draw implications from our findings, discussing the need to create a warm campus climate for current students, increase and encourage involvement within LGBTQ affinity groups, systematize data collection to include LGBTQ identities, and develop culturally sensitive solicitations.

Relatively little alumni giving is generated from Ph.D. graduates. Building on her study looking at Ph.D. alumni donors at the University of Pennsylvania, Anita Mastroieni challenges institutions to look at their alumni beyond those who received their undergraduate degree at their institution. She finds that Ph.D. alumni have distinct motivations in their philanthropic giving. Using social exchange theory, Mastroieni found that Ph.D. graduates donated to their alma mater in gratitude for their training and for the graduate funding they received. As such, Mastroieni gives suggestions to universities on how they can design fundraising appeals that take these different interests and motivations into account.

Meredith Billings reminds us that although young alumni often have lower participation rates and lower giving capacity than alumni further from graduation who might be more established and have greater disposable income to donate, recent graduates should not be ignored in institutional advancement strategies. In her chapter "Examining Young Alumni Giving Behavior: Every Dollar Matters," Billings examines young alumni giving behavior at one university. She describes the university's approach to target those graduating in the past decade after she developed a logistic regression model to predict young alumni giving behavior. In addition to her predicative donor model, Billings compares the institution's young alumni donors from non-donors in the same age group, in terms of their demographics, academics, and attitudinal characteristics. From her findings, Billings offers several strategies for fundraisers to consider when identifying, cultivating, and ultimately soliciting young alumni.

On Campus Constituencies and Future Donors

Genevieve G. Shaker challenges institutional advancement offices to not overlook the potential of faculty and staff in their annual and comprehensive campaigns. In her chapter, "Faculty and Staff as Prospects and Donors: Giving on Campus," Shaker explores faculty and staff giving through data from the Voluntary Support for Education (VSE) survey, existing literature, and exploratory research by her and her colleague Megan Palmer that focuses on faculty major donors. Based on her findings, Shaker shows that faculty and staff are worthwhile prospects and that colleges and universities should enhance annual and major gift fundraising efforts "at home," where faculty and staff—especially long term members of the community—are personally and professionally invested.

In Lori A. Hurvitz's chapter, "Building a Culture of Student Philanthropy," she cautions advancement officers that they must actively engage and cultivate their students in order for them to be generous alumni in the future. Grounded in social psychology and student development theories, Lori's research study explores nine student philanthropy initiatives at different Ivy-plus institutions. Her findings indicated that students should be taught about how to be an active alumnus or alumna. She concludes that informing students about how philanthropy is used at their alma mater should be considered part of a long-term fundraising strategy that begins as students and continues throughout the life of the alumnus or alumna. Finally, she points out how institutions can reinforce an environment where altruistic and prosocial behavior is developed through a program geared toward student satisfaction with his or her overall experience.

Prior scholars have shown that student involvement greatly impacts alumni philanthropic decisions. Student activities such as fraternity and sorority involvement are particularly indicative of alumni giving. Ryan E. Merkel, in his chapter, "The Influence of Sorority and Fraternity Involvement on Future Giving," extends this research. Using relationship marketing theory, he explores how members of Greek organizations make meaning of the relationships between alumni and their alma mater. Merkel includes student perspectives from different fraternities and sororities but focuses on those from Black Greek letter organizations and multicultural Greek organizations, as he found that these students presented unique perspectives on alumni relationships. Merkel explains that students' experiences in fraternity and sorority life substantially influenced how they view their future alumni relationship with their alma mater. As such,

Merkel suggests that alumni relations and development offices should explore how they might be able to use student and alumni Greek experiences to further engage their alumni in the university after graduation.

Michael Puma's chapter, "Fostering Student Affairs and Institutional Advancement Partnerships," looks at the need to build long-term collaborations between fundraising offices and those working with current students. In response to campus budget crunches, student affairs divisions are compelled to find alternative funding sources for their programmatic initiatives. Puma explores various ways in which institutions are creating these partnerships. He finds that through new positions, trainings, and collaborations these partnerships have both spanned and expanded the traditional divisional boundaries. Puma argues that future success in these partnerships depends on mutual understanding and support for both importance of fundraising and student affairs activities in a manner that engage alumni, parents, and even students as future donors.

The book closes with Luke Greeley's "Creating an Engagement Model of Advancement for Young Alumni" in which he calls for a shift in operating paradigms among university fundraisers in order to expand the donor base of their institutions. He points out that traditionally philanthropy and fundraising scholars have operated primarily from objectivist and rational paradigms. Additionally, Greeley shows that practitioners are mostly focused on institutionally self-centered goals, such as persuading wealthy donors to give to serve the purposes of the university. In a shift in perspective, Greeley points to emerging scholars and practitioners who adopt a constructivist paradigm in their work. Here the scholars and practitioners view universities as part of a larger community in which they engage others to reach the goals of the university. Drawing on student development, alumni relations, and donor motivation theories, Greeley's chapter proposes a way in which institutional missions, volunteer solicitations, and university programming might be altered to adopt an engagement model for fundraising. His discussion focuses on how community residents, students, faculty, staff, and alumni can interact as equal partners in promoting the simultaneous advancement of the institution.

A Call to Action in Research and in Practice

When I began my career as a development officer, as a privileged Jewish-gay-White man, I often felt a lot of discomfort with the fact that the vast majority of donors, volunteers, and leaders were older White wealthy men—almost all married and straight. While I was able to see myself within many of those who were deemed as the university's leaders, I felt that something was wrong. To deal with my discomfort, I began to ask why we were not engaging more people who did not look like me. After many professional conferences, where I was not getting answers, I decided to return to graduate school to find answers myself. While beginning my research and reflecting on my experiences as a practitioner, I realized that as fundraisers much of our engagement and solicitation strategies were due to stereotypes, in particular, that people of color, were less generous. Therefore, we approached most prospective donors with the same strategies. This did the university and fundraising, more generally, a disservice and renders people of color with wealth and giving in communities of color invisible. This is not acceptable.

While the majority of wealth in the United States is held by the White majority, that is beginning to change. There is an increase in the number of people of color in the middle class; however, that is a reflection of income rather than wealth. Wealth is accumulated, and a wealth gap continues to exist. Sociologists and economists have looked at the racial wealth gap of individuals in the United States. Conley (2003), Adelman (2003), and Shapiro (2004) argued that past forms of institutional racism have put communities of color, particularly Black families, at a continual disadvantage in the accumulation of lifetime wealth.

These social structures and institutional racism, both historical and contemporary, that impede the ability for the accumulation of assets in communities of color contribute to the stereotype that people of color are less generous than the majority. When we, as practitioners or scholars of philanthropy, operate based on this stereotype, the consequences for our institutions are extraordinary. We can no longer operate like this, when fundraising is so important for colleges and universities to make their annual budgets. In fact the W. K. Kellogg Foundation contends:

> Identity-based philanthropy is transforming the way that generosity flows through and to communities of color—and creating new philanthropic resources, new forms of community empowerment, new leading actors, and new methods to tackle complex problems in the process. As a result, this emerging field is influencing and invigorating the way that philanthropy across all communities gets practiced at a time when many of our old forms are crumbling.
>
> *(2012, p. 20)*

Therefore, advancement offices must engage in culturally sensitive fundraising practices that honor prospective donors' different social identities.

Beyond looking at race, it is important to think about engaging others in the fundraising process. It is too easy to only focus on those who are wealthy now. While current students, young alumni, and most university faculty and staff might have less disposable income than other donors, we should not use this as a reason to wait until they accumulate wealth to fully engage them. A number of scholars find that establishing a habit of giving among young alumni is important in increasing the potential of major gifts in the future (Meer, 2011; Monks, 2003; Turner, Meserve, & Bowen, 2001). In fact, Meer (2011) found that those alumni who gave frequently in their first five years from graduation, on average, gave 5.6 times more when older than an alumnus or alumna who did not give regularly in their first five years out of college. Therefore, it makes sense to invest in engaging our students and most recent alumni in philanthropy, even if their giving in the short-term is small.

Expanding the donor base of our institutions by thinking of how to engage those that we have not gone to in the past is definitely needed for higher education to continue to survive in our current economic context. This approach requires long-term investment and commitment, but in the end, we will have a more engaged donor base and better institutions. I hope that this book not only furthers our understanding of non-traditional donor groups, but that it also pushes advancement offices to look within their own practices and think about how to create more culturally sensitive engagement and solicitation strategies.

Note

1. CFRE is a professional accreditation, Certified Fund Raising Executive.

References

Adelman, L. (2003). A long history of racial preferences—for Whites. Retrieved from http://www.pbs.org/race/000_About/002_04-background-03-02.htm

Brittingham, B. E., & Pezzullo, T. R. (1990). *The campus green: Fund raising in higher education. ASHE-ERIC higher education report no. 1.* Washington, DC: The George Washington University, School of Education and Human Development.

Burnett, K. (1992/2002). *Relationship fundraising.* London: White Lion Press.

Ciconte, B. K., & Jacob, J. G. (2001). *Fund raising basics: A complete guide.* Sudbury, MA: Jones & Bartlett.

Conley, D. (2003). Interviewed in *Race: The power of an illusion* [PBS transcript]. Retrieved from http://www.pbs.org/race/000_About/002_04-background-03-03.htm

Connors, T. D. (2001). *The nonprofit handbook* (3rd ed.). New York, NY: John Wiley.

Council for Aid to Education. (2012). *2012 voluntary support of education.* New York, NY: Author.

Drezner, N. D. (Ed.). (2010). Fundraising in a time of economic downturn: Theory, practice, & implications [Special issue]. *International Journal of Educational Advancement, 9*(4).

Drezner, N. D. (2011). *Philanthropy and fundraising in American higher education.* San Francisco, CA: Jossey-Bass.

Dove, K. E. (2001). *Conducting a successful fundraising program: A comprehensive guide and resource.* San Francisco, CA: Jossey-Bass.

Flanagan, J. (1999). *Successful fundraising: A complete handbook for volunteers and professionals.* New York, NY: McGraw-Hill Trade.

Greenfield, J. (2001). *The nonprofit handbook: Fund raising.* New York, NY: John Wiley.

Grenzebach, Glier, and Associates (2010). *Implications of the economy on development practices: Adjusting Long-term strategy.* Retrieved December 15, 2010, from http://www.grenzebachglier.com/files/webfm/ABALawSchoolPresentation2010.pdf

Meer, J. (2011). *The habit of giving* [Working paper]. Retrieved from http://econweb.tamu.edu/jmeer/Meer_Habit_of_Giving_FINAL.pdf

Monks, J. (2003). Patterns of giving to one's alma mater among young graduates from selective institutions, *Economics of Education Review, 22,* 121–130.

NACUBO/Commonfund Institute, (2012). *2012 NACUBO-Commonfund study of endowments.* Washington, DC: National Association of College and University Business Officers.

Schervish, P. G., & Havens, J. J. (1998, Summer). Money and magnanimity: New findings on the distribution of income, wealth, and philanthropy. *Nonprofit Management and Leadership, 8*(4): 421–434.

Shapiro, T. M. (2004). *The hidden cost of being African American: How wealth perpetuates inequality.* New York, NY: Oxford University Press.

Turner, S., Meserve, L., & Bowen, W. (2001). Winning and giving: Football results and alumni giving from selective private colleges and universities. *Social Science Quarterly, 82*(4), 812–826.

W. K. Kellogg Foundation. (2012). *Cultures of giving: Energizing and expanding philanthropy by and for communities of color.* Battle Creek, MI: Author.

Worth, M. (2002). *New strategies for educational fundraising.* New York, NY: Praeger.

SECTION 1

Racial Minorities

2

ENGAGING AND SOLICITING AFRICAN AMERICAN ALUMNI

Marybeth Gasman and Nelson Bowman III

Since the passing of the 1964 Civil Rights Act, African Americans have had an increased presence on historically White college and university campuses. In fact, between 1984 and 2009, there has been a 240 percent increase in the number of African American students on majority campuses (National Center for Education Statistics, 2012). Yet, college fundraisers tend to ignore these students once they become alumni in terms of engagement and solicitation. Too often Blacks are seen as the recipients of philanthropy rather than givers—even college-educated African Americans (Gasman & Bowman, 2011). This chapter focuses on ways to cultivate, engage, and solicit African American alumni. We highlight the prevailing literature on Black giving, including historical and current giving patterns. We identify common mistakes made by majority institutions in terms of their efforts (or lack thereof) to reach out to Black alumni. Lastly, we suggest practical strategies for increasing giving among African Americans (see Table 2.1).

Although disparities in income and assets between Blacks and Whites still remain, African Americans have increased access to wealth. In 2009, for example, Blacks had $9 billion in buying power, and that number is expected to grow substantially by 2015 due to trends in education and a rising numbers of African American women in the work force (Nielsen Report, 2011; Selig Center for Economic Growth, 2009). This buying power can be tapped, but only if colleges and universities are ready, educated about African American giving, and ask. As with all giving, the main reason that individuals do not give is that they are not asked. In the case of African Americans this is entirely too true. One first needs to understand the roots of African American philanthropy, which are based on a communal notion of giving. When individuals in the Black community support others, the community as a whole benefits, not merely the immediate recipients. This practice originates from a time when social and economic services for Blacks did not exist on any level—national, state, or local and the fact that their treasure was far less in abundance than their time and talent (Gasman & Bowman, 2013). Given this history and as a result of cultural differences, we think that attempting to a measure the depth and variety of African American philanthropy using traditional methods, e.g., *Giving USA*'s annual report, gives a false reading of Black philanthropy or even worse, much of Black philanthropy may not register at all. This results in Blacks being viewed on the demand side rather than the supply side of the philanthropic equation when in reality African Americans give 25 percent more of their discretionary income to charity than do Whites (Gasman & Bowman, 2012; Kellogg Foundation, 2001).

As mentioned, all but a few majority institutions of higher education overlook African American alumni. However, we are starting to see a sea change, more so at majority institutions where the country's demographic predictions are beginning to manifest themselves on campus. Educational powerhouses like Brown University, Cornell University, Emory University, and the University of North Carolina-Chapel Hill are all experiencing record numbers of students of color among their in-coming freshmen (Gasman & Bowman, 2013). Gone are the days of historically White institutions with 100 percent White populations. These changes translate into alumni that are now, and will continue to become, more racially and ethnically diverse. At some point, majority institutions will see the economic potential of this neglected segment of the population. With these ideas in mind, we offer this chapter as a preliminary guide to campus efforts to understand African American philanthropy and the engagement and solicitation of Black alumni.

Overview of African American Philanthropy

African American philanthropy began in the 1600s when free Blacks in the North set up self-help circles to organize their communities and fight against slavery in the South. Blacks were focused on harnessing volunteerism for the greater good and because, even in the North, they were shut out from most social services offered by communities and churches; they had to provide for each other as a people (Gasman & Sedgwick, 2005). Even in the South, under the horrors of slavery, African Americans were giving to one another. For example, in her beautifully written book *Self-Taught*, Heather Williams (2005) discusses how Blacks taught each other to read in order to better the race despite the fact that learning to read and teaching someone to read was illegal in all Southern states (Wallenstein, 2008).

By the 1700s, Black philanthropy started to take shape as formal mutual aid societies from Underground Railroad organizations to civil rights organizations (Gasman & Sedgwick, 2005). Many of these organizations were affiliated with or coordinated thru churches; others were affiliated with fraternal organizations such as the Prince Hall Masons. Eventually these mutual aid organizations resulted in organizations such as the National Urban League and the United Negro College Fund—organizations dedicated to raising money for and empowering African American communities (Gasman & Sedgwick, 2005; Gasman, 2007).

By the 1800s, the Black church was very active in the North, especially in cities like Philadelphia and New York. Churches such as the African Methodist Episcopal Church and the African Methodist Episcopal Zion Church were instrumental in providing services, goods, and counsel to Blacks throughout the North (Gasman & Bowman, 2012; Gasman & Sedgwick, 2005). In addition, after the Civil War, they sent missionaries South to educate former slaves (Anderson, 1988). Most of these missionaries taught in historically Black colleges and universities or makeshift primary schools. In most cases, these small Black colleges refused to take monies from White philanthropists and only relied on the philanthropy and volunteerism of African Americans. Also during the 1800s, Black fraternities and sororities were created (Gasman, 2005, 2011a; Gasman, Louison, & Barnes, 2008). These organizations, although initially social in nature, began to provide services to Black communities. Their efforts included mobile libraries, civil rights advocacy, voter education, and leadership training for youth. They also raised substantial scholarship funds for students to attend college (Gasman, 2005; Gasman & Sedgwick, 2005).

The mid-1900s saw the rise of civil rights–oriented philanthropy (Garrow, 1987). Not only did Black churches raise money and fund civil rights activities, but individual African Americans banded together to support civil rights leaders, including students at the nation's Black colleges. For example, Black citizens of Greensboro, North Carolina, came together to support the Bennett College for Women and North Carolina A&T University students in their fight to desegregate eating establishments in the area (Chafe, 1981; Gasman, 2011b).

Today, there is an emphasis on bringing together funds in an organized way in the form of family foundations (Gasman, 2010). Many African Americans do not trust banks and other formal organizations. As such, they are less likely to deposit their funds in community foundations and instead have chosen to establish family foundations aimed at making changes in education and health care. These foundations range in assets from $425,000 to $40,000,000 (Gasman, 2010).

Where Blacks Give and Why

There are five major areas to which African Americans give philanthropically: emergency assistance, religion, education, civil rights causes, and health-related issues (Gasman & Bowman, 2012). All of these issues touch Blacks personally and, as a result, they are close to the hearts and minds of African Americans.

First, Blacks give to their family and friends in cases of emergency. As many Blacks have little access to quality health care and good nutrition, family members often come to the rescue of one another when in need.

Among all racial and ethnic groups, religion is the largest recipient of charitable giving (*Giving USA*, 2010). However, for most African Americans, the Black church has been a one-stop shop for generation after generation, providing faith, education, entertainment, and social networking needs (Drezner, forthcoming; Gasman & Bowman, 2012; Holloman, Gasman, & Anderson-Thompkins, 2003; Lincoln & Mamiya, 1990). The church provided social services when the government and communities excluded Blacks (Lincoln & Mamiya, 1990). Due to this close and influential relationship, African Americans are very likely to give to the church and, in fact, give 60 percent of their discretionary income to churches across the nation (Gasman & Bowman, 2012).

Another area that is particularly important in terms of African American giving is education. Blacks see education as a necessity to advancement in society and as such it is concrete in nature. Blacks tend to give to concrete causes such as scholarships. In fact, at times, within the education setting, African Americans will often only give to scholarships as they see this type of giving as tangible (Gasman & Anderson-Thompkins, 2003). The monies go to a specific cause or student and the giver knows that a check was issued. It takes time to move scholarship donors to endowment giving and can only be done through education (Gasman & Bowman, 2012).

African Americans have long supported civil rights causes as mentioned above and continue to do so today. Because racism is still a viable problem in America, there continue to be civil rights issues and social causes that have an impact on the daily lives and rights of Blacks. In recent years, Blacks have rallied around issues such as unfair treatment in the judicial and criminal justice systems and education, in particular. African Americans are heavily inclined to give to civil rights initiatives that are closely tied to their communities (Gasman & Bowman, 2012; Gasman & Sedgwick, 2005).

The last area to which African Americans pay particular attention is health-related causes. They tend to focus on those health-related issues that affect Black communities most, such as high blood pressure, diabetes, heart disease, HIV/AIDS, and the disease that Blacks hold the exclusive rights to—sickle cell anemia (Gasman & Bowman, 2012). Because so many family members pass away at the hands of these diseases, Blacks are likely to give to both research and practice related to these health issues.

Motivations for Black Giving

African Americans give in small increments (Gasman & Anderson-Thompkins, 2003). The main reason for this strategy is that there is a lack of trust around giving to mainstream organizations due to past injustices (Gasman & Bowman,

2012). Blacks typically give in small amounts at first and then increase their giving as they become more comfortable with an institution. Among more affluent African Americans, it is typical to give in larger amounts. However, most Blacks begin giving in smaller amounts (Carson, 1993).

Although receiving a tax deduction is not the main reason White Americans give philanthropically, it is one reason and it plays a significant role (*Giving USA*, 2010). Moreover, Whites, by and large, deduct charitable giving on their tax returns. Among African American first time donors, especially those who are low or middle income, earning a tax deduction is not of importance. In fact, in terms of church-related giving, many African Americans consider it wrong to receive something in exchange for their giving (Gasman & Bowman, 2012). For example, consider the following story about one of our mothers (Nelson's mother):

> After my mother's death in 2008, I had the opportunity to comb through her papers and records and came across her annual giving statements to the church. One year she gave $2,300 ,another year, $3,000, and then the largest amount of all, $4,500. My mother never made more than $21,000 in salary during a calendar year, so those charitable gifts to the church represented roughly 11 to 22 percent of her annual income. Researching a bit further, I discovered two things: her other charitable gifts within a given year never exceeded $1,000, and her tax returns throughout the years never reflected any deductions for these donations.

This example supports the research that shows that within African American households, tax benefits are not as important to women as they are to men. Women tend to be more involved in the church, including the choir, mission society, and the usher board and as a result, they feel more strongly about tithing and giving back (Lincoln & Mamiya, 1990).

One of the main reasons that African Americans give is that they have a commitment—almost a sense of obligation—to racial uplift (Carson, 1993; Gasman & Anderson-Thompkins, 2003). Black alumni, specifically, want to provide the same opportunities to future generations that were provided to them. Often times, Black alumni will use the phrase, "reach back and pull someone up" referring to their commitment to racial uplift (Gasman & Anderson-Thompkins, 2003). For centuries, African Americans had to rely on only themselves to make change in Black communities and this sense of commitment has not changed despite the end of legalized segregation and the progress of integration (Wallenstein, 2008).

As mentioned earlier, trust is a key issue with regard to giving among African Americans. Because Blacks were mistreated and taken advantage of by mainstream organizations such as banks and the legal enterprise, they are less inclined to trust initially if unfamiliar with an organization (Gasman &

Sedgwick, 2005). Trust is essential in all giving situations but for Blacks extra time and effort needs to be invested in order to put donors at ease.

African Americans, especially newer givers, prefer to give to more concrete causes. They prefer to give to causes that they can see and touch such as scholarships or building funds (Gasman & Bowman, 2012). Scholarships are tangible. They go directly to a student and often times that student can personally thank the donor demonstrating the impact of the philanthropic gift. Because of their inclination to give to concrete causes, it tends to be difficult to convince Blacks to give to endowment campaigns. This type of giving is nebulous and often needs to be explained. By and large, most alumni in general do not understand how endowment giving works. One of the best approaches to explaining it with any audience, but especially with first time, African American givers, is to compare an endowment to a savings account. We recommend discussing gifts to the operating budget as putting money in the checking account and giving to the endowment as putting money in a savings account. The endowment sustains the institution like savings sustains a family during difficult financial times (Gasman & Bowman, 2012).

African Americans are also moted to give by their peers and family (Gasman & Anderson-Thompkins, 2003). Because of this influence, giving circles or giving within social organizations is particularly successful. For example, giving challenges among Black alumni who are close friends (or were in college) are often successful as there is a healthy amount of competition among these alumni (Gasman & Anderson-Thompkins, 2003). In addition, giving that takes advantage of fraternity or sorority membership is often quite successful because of the fraternal bonds established among members of these organizations. There is a sense of positive peer pressure among these organizations that can be used as the impetus for giving on a regular basis (Gasman & Anderson-Thompkins, 2003; Gasman et al., 2008).

Mistakes Made by Colleges and Universities

Giving to education is a major thrust of African American giving. However, many colleges and universities do not reach out to Black alumni, assuming that they will not give (Gasman & Bowman, 2013). Only more education on the part of development officers will dispel this myth. There are several major problems with colleges and universities in terms of their relationships with African American alumni. We discuss these below. First, as mentioned, Black alumni are often not asked to give nor are they engaged in any substantial way by colleges (Gasman & Bowman, 2013).

Second, many colleges and universities do not see a return on investment when it pertains to Black alumni (Gasman & Bowman, 2013). Development officers are not convinced that the work needed to engage Black alumni will pay off in terms of future giving. Many times these individuals (and their supervisors) want to see numbers in terms of the potential for giving among Black alumni and until then they are not convinced of the value of pursuing them. That said, it is impossible to gather data on Black giving at the institutional level if colleges and universities do not reach out to Black alumni (Gasman & Bowman, 2013).

The third problem is that colleges and universities do not ask Black alumni how they would like to be engaged when they finally do reach out. Rather, they assume the ways that Blacks want to be involved with the institution. It is important to ask Black alumni specifically how they would like to work with the institution; close and meaningful connections lead to greater engagement and increased giving (Gasman & Bowman, 2013).

Fourth, colleges and universities rarely involve Blacks in alumni leadership positions (Gasman & Bowman, 2013). This is particularly off-putting, as most African Americans do not want to give to or engage with an organization that does not see them as a potential leader within the organization. From time to time, we hear development officers say, "But we can't get the prominent Black leaders to be on our boards." The problem with this statement is that colleges and universities need to be grooming leaders and asking a diverse group of Black leaders to engage with their institutions. Too often, the same African American leaders are tapped over and over while there are many other leaders with the potential to contribute (Gasman & Bowman, 2013).

Fifth, most colleges and universities fail to realize that African Americans have often had negative experiences while on campus and harbor negative feelings toward their alma mater as a result of these negative experiences (Gasman & Bowman, 2013). It is vital that these experiences be acknowledged and that Black alumni be brought up to date on the experiences of current Black students—which are hopefully vastly improved. If an alumnus is disgruntled, the best way to reengage him is to ask him to help with the very issue that may have made him angry or caused him to severe ties with his alma mater. Addressing the problem shows the alumnus that the institution is serious about making change.

Sixth, often African American alumni do not see themselves depicted in university publications. The majority of fundraising publications depict scenes of majority students and events that are important in the lives of White students, ignoring the events and experiences that resonate with African American alumni (Gasman & Bowman, 2013). For example, at Indiana University, fundraising brochures have long depicted Little 500, a historic bike race that takes place on the campus every year. When the bike race began, Black students were not included and as such created their own event—a Black Picnic in a meadow on campus. To this day, these events take place separately on the same day. However, only one of the events is celebrated by the institution and highlighted in publications. Institutional advancement professionals need to work with communications professionals to engage multiple audiences with their publications. In addition, it is important to have targeted publications that speak only and specifically to African American audiences. The secret to successful engagement is to include African Americans in general publications and to provide them with a venue of their own (Gasman & Bowman, 2013).

A final mistake is a lack of knowledge on the part of advancement staff. Although knowledge of African American motivations for giving on the part of staff is important on Black college campuses, it is downright crucial on historically White campuses. The majority of White America knows little about Black America, and the majority of advancement staffs are White. Unlike African Americans colleagues, Whites are not forced to operate in a nation that is steeped in another race's cultural values. Thus, sometimes White advancement professionals do not understand cultural differences in giving; they do not understand what is important to various members of the Black communities affiliated with their institutions. For this reason, it is important that advancement staff find out as much information as possible—survey alumni, hold focus groups (and be willing to listen to what people have to say), and become educated by reading books and articles on philanthropy in communities of color and African American giving specifically. One very practical suggestion is to read materials as a staff and then have a conversation, design strategies, and make changes to the institution's approach (Gasman, 2002; Gasman & Bowman, 2013).

The Overall Campus Experience and Its Connection to Fundraising

Although most fundraising professionals do not consider themselves part of the inner workings of the lives of students on campus, they are nonetheless. In order for African American alumni to feel connected to campuses and engaged enough to give back to campus, it is imperative that they have positive experiences while on campus. Advancement vice presidents have the ear of the president and bring in financial resources that sustain the campus, as such they can play a substantial role in institutional change. Unless historically White campuses are more inclusive—beyond just recruiting African Americans—Black alumni and African Americans won't give. They want to see change. They want to see more Black faces among students, administrators, and faculty. And, they want to see the accomplishments and efforts of people like themselves recognized on campus. Those in institutional advancement can play a part in making this kind of systemic transformation by being vocal about the changes that need to take place in order to garner African American alumni support (Gasman & Bowman, 2013).

We conclude this chapter with several questions that advancement staff members need to ask themselves. These questions will lead to a more serious discussion around African American alumni giving: (a) What percentage of your alumni do African Americans represent? (b) What are the current levels of giving from African American alumni? (c) What staff positions support your work targeting African Americans? (d) Which African American affinity groups do you currently target through your fundraising efforts? (e) What have

TABLE 2.1 Recommendations to Engage and Solicit African American Alumni

Recommendation	Strategies for Implementation
Areas Blacks Give and Why	• Family and friends for emergencies • Church as it's always been a welcoming place (60% of their giving) • Education as a necessity for advancement • Civil Rights and Social Causes tied to their community • Health issues that affect Black people
Black Giving Motivations	• Racial uplift and/or advancement of the culture is a giving motivation, not tax benefits • Trust for the organization as mainstream organizations have not always treated Blacks fairly in the past • A preference to give to concrete causes—ones they can touch and feel, like scholarships • Giving by other family members and peers tends to create a greater desire to engage • Organizational membership (fraternity and sorority) stimulates giving because of the fraternal bonds established among members
Avoidable Mistakes	• Stop assuming Blacks will not give and begin asking them to give. People give when they are asked • Why Black alumni are worth the investment: 1) Blacks attending college has increased 25% since 1984 2) Blacks give 25% more of their disposable income to charity than do Whites • Ask Black alumni about their area of interest just like you would any other alum • Grow and groom your own Black leaders rather than picking the usual/popular choices • Acknowledge that racism and racial incidents happened at your institution as older Black alumni still remember • Include all cultures segment in university publications. Everyone enjoys being a part of the fabric • Make the effort to find out about Black culture as one size does not fit all
Connecting to African Americans as Students	• Purposely build-in culturally diverse opportunities and events on campus for the entire student population to experience. Be just as willing to highlight Kwanza and Juneteenth as you would Memorial and Labor Days

you done so far to reach and engage African American alumni? (f) What student programs on campus are geared toward African Americans? (g) Does your institution's marketing include African Americans? (h) In the last 15 years, have there been any racial incidents on your campus? Answering these questions will prepare any development office for the future influx of students of color who will very quickly become alumni of color.

References

Anderson, J. A. (1988). *The education of Blacks in the South, 1865–1930.* Chapel Hill: University of North Carolina Press.

Carson, E. (1993). *A hand up: African American philanthropy and self-help in America.* New York, NY: University Press of America.

Chafe, W. (1981). *Civilities and civil rights: Greensboro, North Carolina and the Black struggle for freedom.* New York, NY: Oxford University Press.

Drezner, N. D. (forthcoming). The Black church and millennial philanthropy: Influences on college student prosocial behavior at a chuch-affiliated Black college. *Christian Higher Education.*

Garrow, D. (1987). *Philanthropy and the civil rights movement.* New York, NY: Center for the Study of Philanthropy.

Gasman, M. (2002). An untapped resource: Bringing African Americans into the college and university giving process. *The CASE International Journal of Educational Advancement. 2*(3), 13–20.

Gasman, M. (2005). Sisters in service: African American sororities and the philanthropic support of education. In A. Walton (Ed.), *Women, philanthropy, and education* (pp. 194-214). Bloomington: Indiana University Press.

Gasman, M. (2007). *Envisioning Black colleges: A history of the United Negro College Fund.* Baltimore, MD: Johns Hopkins University Press.

Gasman, M. (2010). A growing tradition? Examining the African American family foundation. *Nonprofit Management & Leadership,* 21(2), 16-47.

Gasman, M. (2011a). "Passive activism?: African American fraternities and sororities and their role in the Civil Rights Movement." In M. W. Hughley & G. S. Parks (Eds.), *Empirical studies of Black Greek letter organizations* (pp. 116-147). Oxford: University of Mississippi Press.

Gasman, M. (2011b). Perceptions of Black college presidents: Sorting through stereotypes and reality to gain a complex picture. *American Education Research Journal, 48*(4), 836–870.

Gasman, M., & Anderson-Thompkins, S. (2003). *Fundraising from Black college alumni: Successful strategies for supporting alma mater.* Washington, DC: Council for the Advancement and Support of Education.

Gasman, M., & Bowman, N. (2011). Cultivating and soliciting donors of color. *Advancing Philanthropy,* 6-10.

Gasman, M., & Bowman, N. (2012). *A guide to fundraising at historically Black colleges and universities: An all campus approach.* New York, NY: Routledge Press.

Gasman, M., & Bowman, N. (2013). *The essential guide to fundraising among diverse college alumni.* New York, NY: Routledge Press.

Gasman, M. Louison, P., & Barnes, M. (2008). Giving and getting: A History of philanthropic activity among African American fraternities and sororities. In T. Brown, G. Parks, & C. Phillips (Eds.), *Black Greek letter organizations in the twentieth century: Our fight has just begun.* (pp. 235-258). Louisville: University of Kentucky.

Gasman, M., & Sedgwick, K. V. (Eds.). (2005). *Uplifting a people. Essays on African American philanthropy and education.* New York, NY: Peter Lang.

Giving USA. (2010). Indiana University Center on Philanthropy. Indianapolis: Indiana University Center on Philanthropy.

Holloman, D., Gasman, M., & Anderson-Thompkins, S. (2003). Motivations for philanthropic giving in the African American church: Implications for Black college fundraising. *Journal of Research on Christian Education, 12*(2), 137–169.

Kellogg Foundation. (2001). *Cultures of giving: Energizing and expanding philanthropy by and for communities of color.* Battle Creek, Michigan: Author.

Lincoln, C. E., & Mamiya, L. H. (1990). *The Black church in the African American experience.* Raleigh, NC: Duke University Press.

National Center for Educational Statistics (2012), www.nces.ed.gov

Nielsen Report. (2011). *The state of the African American consumer.* New York, NY: Author.

Selig Center for Economic Growth. (2009). *The multi-cultural economy.* Athens: University of Georgia.

Wallenstein, P. (2008). *Higher education and the civil rights movement: White supremacy, Black southerners, and college campuses.* Gainesville: University Press of Florida.

Williams, H. (2005). *Self-taught: African American education in slavery and freedom.* Chapel Hill: University of North Carolina Press.

3

AN APPROACH TO ENGAGING LATINA/O ALUMNI IN GIVING INITIATIVES

Madrinas y Padrinos

José A. Cabrales

Latinas/os play an integral role in the fabric of civic engagement and giving practices in the United States. In order to gain a better understanding of Latina/o
alumni, it is important to first understand Latinas/os in terms of population and
educational attainment in the United States. Latinas/os now account for 16.3
percent of the United States population and comprise its largest minority group
(Pew Hispanic Center, 2011; U.S. Census, 2008). In addition, more Latinas/
os are graduating from four-year colleges and universities each year. Between
1996 and 2006, the number of Latinas/os earning bachelor's degrees from U.S.
institutions rose 84 percent while the proportionate increase of Whites (19%),
African Americans (56%), and Asians (59%) rose at lower rates (Excelencia in
Education, 2008). Furthermore, Latinas/os are becoming wealthier and can
leverage greater monetary donations to university programs (Anft, 2002).
The Latina/o population in the United States alone controlled $978 billion in
spending power in 2009, and that number is expected to reach $1.3 trillion in
2014 (Humphreys, 2009). Now more than ever, it is imperative for colleges and
universities in the United States to understand how they interact with Latina/o
alumni once they have graduated from their respective institution and provide
intentional opportunities for Latina/o alumni engagement.

Over the past several years, researchers have used a number of frameworks
to predict alumni engagement. Yet, many frameworks do not take into account
differences among student experiences or students' motivations to give back
to their respective communities upon graduation. This chapter examines
alumni giving from a community cultural wealth (Yosso, 2005) perspective
and explores the interconnectedness between careers, community, and giving
from Latina/o alumni.

Challenging Assumptions of Latina/o Alumni Giving

Alumni of color, particularly Latina/o alumni, are oftentimes disregarded due to the assumption that they do not give (i.e., monetary gifts). Rivas-Vásquez (1999) argues that many nonprofit organizations dismiss the cultural framework where giving has a different meaning and expression than it does in Anglo culture; therefore, few nonprofits have been successful at developing effective strategies to reach Latina/o donors. Hence, many institutions of higher education have not completely examined how Latinas/os give in the broader context of Latina/o philanthropy.

A number of scholars have explored Latina/o philanthropy and how Latinas/os enact philanthropy in the community (e.g., Cortés, 1991, 1995; Diaz, 1999; Gallegos & O'Neill, 1991; Ramos, 1999). These researchers generally agree that Latinas/os enact philanthropy through three different and frequently informal media: support for extended family networks, involvement in the church, and through *mutualista* organizations that provide basic social services and social justice activities. In addition, Latinas/os find that personal connections are important, particularly when making a charitable donation (Cabrales, 2011; Rivas-Vásquez, 1999). Therefore, many Latina/o alumni oftentimes prefer to give to a targeted fund where they can be involved.

Another assumption for not engaging Latina/o alumni in giving initiatives is the fact that institutions of higher education perceive that alumni who have a negative student experience will be unenthusiastic about participating in programs after graduation (Hay, 1990). Consequently because of this perception, many colleges and universities are not proactive in efforts to engage Latina/o alumni with different advancement activities. However, over the last two decades, many Latina/o alumni and institutions of higher education have formed affinity groups at their college/university to be more inclusive and to engage alumni of color (Cabrales, 2011).

Many of these affinity groups have woven fundraising and other sponsorship activities as a way to maintain ties with the university while assisting students through different giving practices, such as mentoring and networking opportunities. For example, at the University of Arizona (U of A), the Chicano/Hispanic Student Affairs (C/HSA) in collaboration with the University of Arizona Hispanic Alumni Association (UAHA) has awarded scholarships to more than 100 local undergraduate students. As a form of recruitment and retention, the scholarship requires students to participate in the C/HSA programs and events.

> Throughout their four or more years at college, students form mentoring relationships through Entre Familia activities, which include meeting targeted alumni, interacting with the Center's designated abuelitos/as (grandfathers or grandmothers) and a faculty fellow, taking leadership classes, and joining a Hispanic graduation convocation to which the entire Tucson community is invited.
>
> *(Francis & Ousley, 2006, p. 2)*

In a nine-year period, the UAHA raised $300,000 through annual black-tie events. Other Latina/o alumni chapters also focus on the recruitment and retention of students at their alma maters. The Hispanic Alumni Council at the University of Michigan was founded in 1988 with the goals of recruiting, retaining, and reciprocating. These activities, aligned with these goals, include recruiting Hispanic students, faculty, administrative, and academic support from staff members. In addition, they help develop and administer scholarship programs and activities to support Hispanic students and their programs at the university (University of Michigan, 2008).

Although there are a number of ways in which giving to colleges and universities can occur, monetary gifts are typically synonymous with "giving," therefore other forms of giving can be minimized and ignored. Using community cultural wealth (Yosso, 2005) as a conceptual framework helps us understand other ways to engage and recognize Latina/o alumni giving.

Community Cultural Wealth as a Framework for Latina/o Alumni Giving

Yosso (2005) applied the community cultural wealth model to provide a broader understanding of Chicana/o educational pathways; challenging Bourdieu's traditional assertion of social capital, which considers the knowledge of the upper and middle classes as valuable capital. Yosso concluded that communities of color nurture six different forms of capital:

1. *Aspirational capital* refers to the ability to maintain hopes and dreams for the future, even in the face of real and perceived barriers.
2. *Linguistic capital* includes the intellectual and social skills attained through communication, experiences, and more than one language and/or style.
3. *Familial capital* refers to the cultural knowledge nurtured among *familia* (kin) that carry a sense of community history, memory, and cultural intuition.
4. *Social capital* can be understood as networks of people and community resources.
5. *Navigational capital* refers to skills maneuvering through social institutions.
6. *Resistant capital* refers to knowledge and skills fostered through oppositional behaviors that challenge inequality. (pp. 77–80)

Working together, these forms of capital constitute community cultural wealth that benefits community members, such as students in K-12 settings (Yosso, 2005). Community cultural wealth can improve our understanding of how Latina/o alumni give in a higher education context (Cabrales, 2011). Latina/o alumni may use different knowledge and forms of capital (aspirational, linguistic, familial, social, navigation, and resistant) to challenge how many colleges and universities value and define giving.

Using Yosso's (2005) definitions of each form of capital, we can explore how community cultural wealth can be used in the context of alumni engagement (Cabrales, 2011):

Aspirational capital: Latina/o alumni likely share the similar hopes and dreams of parents for their students to successfully complete college. Whether or not the student attends the alum's alma mater, the general hope is to carry on the legacy of giving back to the community. One example of how Latina/o alumni may illustrate aspirational capital is through attending scholarship dinners to support and raise funds for student scholarships.

Linguistic capital: The storytelling tradition in the Latina/o community plays a significant factor in linguistic capital. Latina/o alumni may utilize this form of capital to share the stories they experienced as undergraduates. Additionally, many of the struggles and successes of Latina/o alumni can be shared with undergraduates through oral history. For example, the history of the development of different resources that exist on campus that support Latinas, such as cultural centers, campus organizations, and scholarships, can be shared through this form of capital.

Familial capital: Latina/o alumni may demonstrate this form of capital through contacts with student organizations that supported them like family throughout their undergraduate experience. This time can serve as a way to mentor students—academically and professionally. Alumni can also be instrumental with providing emotional support and showing concern for the well-being of the community.

Social capital: In this capacity, Latina/o alumni can provide students with instrumental information, including scholarships and graduate school options. Alumni can also utilize their social capital to assist students with securing internships related to their major or area of study. Much like Latina/o parents learn about available resources and communicate them with their community, Latina/o alumni can serve as resource vehicles for students (Center of Philanthropy and Civil Society, 2003; Yosso, 2005).

Navigational capital: Latina/o alumni may revisit their alma maters and participate in panels regarding their student experience or their career path. Alumni can utilize this time to guide students through the institution and point to resources (e.g., scholarships, campus services, faculty, administrators, etc.) that were beneficial to them as undergraduates. This would also serve as an opportunity to share their experiences about their participation with student organizations and other Latinas/os on campus.

Resistant capital: Like the characteristics of linguistic capital, Latina/o alumni can share their experiences combating racial and social injustice as undergraduate students. This is a critical resource for students since alumni can provide an oral history of student movements, protests, and demonstrations that occurred and the resources they fought for during that period of time.

The combination of these forms of capital, as they apply to Latina/o alumni, can be illustrative of Yosso's (2005, 2006) model of community cultural wealth. Latina/o alumni may bring rich cultural wealth that can complement and enhance financial capital that alumni and development offices are tasked to seek, but have heretofore been unexplored through systematic research. Traditional alumni research literature has not taken into account the different ways Latinas/os give to their respective communities.

Study Overview

This chapter is based on the results of a larger qualitative study that took place at a predominantly White, Jesuit institution in California. The study included nine Latina/o participants (5 female and 4 male) who represented diverse class years, areas of study, and occupations. Phenomenology was used as the methodological framework, which is "generally seen as a study of people's subjective and everyday experiences" (Crotty, 1998, p. 83). This study examined the everyday experiences of Latina/o alumni and explored how they enacted giving and how they perceived their alma mater framed giving. Each participant was interviewed three times over the period of six months using Seidman's (2006) three-interview series, which concentrated on three areas: focused life history (i.e., childhood, college choice, student experience, and charitable activities), details of experience (i.e., experience as an alumnus/alumna, alma mater interactions, and social, civic, and religious activities), and reflections on the meaning (i.e., how giving is practiced and university benefits of their giving). A central theme in this study was how the interconnectedness between careers, community, and giving provided relevance to how colleges and universities could engage and attract Latina/o alumni donors (Cabrales, 2011).

Careers, Community, and Giving

Latina/o alumni worked with their communities and college students in different capacities through their occupations. The participants of the study held diverse occupations (e.g., attorneys, educators, community developers, etc.) and in the end involved helping people in their respective communities (Cabrales, 2011). In fact, their giving practices resulted in interconnectedness between their occupation and their community engagement (see Figure 3.1).

For example, Dolores, one participant in the study, knew that as a young child she wanted to help people. On her summer breaks she would help her father, who worked in the agricultural industry, make identification cards for

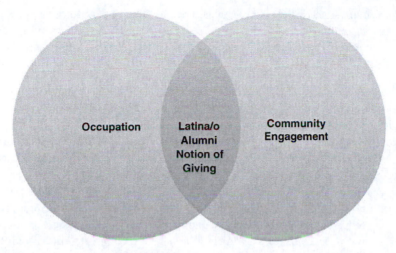

FIGURE 3.1 Latina/o notion of giving.

farm workers. She remembered that the farm workers worked long hours and worked hard. She stuck to her goals and once she acquired her undergraduate degree, she enrolled in law school. Upon completion of law school, Dolores worked for a community rural legal assistance agency that assisted mostly farm workers in the areas of housing, employment, education, and environmental justice issues. While in the process of becoming a lawyer, her intention was not to become an attorney for the sole purpose of the title, rather it was to help people, and particularly the farm workers she remembered as a child. As time progressed, Dolores began working with an Equal Opportunity office for a local community and continued her civic engagement through serving on community boards and planning commissions. Her experience in advocacy led her to pursue a career in politics, where she ran for city council and ultimately became a city mayor.

Dolores's life experiences as a young child and goals of helping people came to fruition through her advocacy as an attorney and a community leader. She continues to give her time and community involvement. Her notion of giving paralleled with those defined by research literature on Latina/o philanthropy: extended family, church, and mutual assistance organizations:

> So I've heard many times where people will say, "Well you're not partici-
> pating or giving in your community," but in fact they [Latinas/os] are.
> They are participating in church activities and they're giving their time
> with youths or senior activities or they're helping at soup kitchens or
> they're just in different areas giving their time to improve the part of their
> world that they are in. And especially if you are kind of newer to this
> community ... you are not going to jump over to unknown groups that

you are not familiar with. But you are going to be giving in your own [community] whether it's your family or your extended family or your schools or your church or you know similar smaller community groups.

(Cabrales, 2011, p. 122)

Although Dolores focused her giving within her local community, another participant, Chato, focused his giving practices through fundraising for scholarships and founding a Latino Role Model Conference. Chato learned about giving through elders in his community. He asserted that his parents had a personal philosophy of helping extended family, the neighborhood, and the community—including the church. However, his parents not only verbalized this philosophy, they lived it. Chato also learned about giving practices through observing the actions of many community activists in his community. He reflected that these were the people who kept him and his classmates engaged with the community and mentored him through his undergraduate and law school days.

Those are the individuals that guided us, that mentored us into becoming Latino activists and as I've mentioned we still are Latino activists. We have just taken the fight from the streets into the boardroom, from the protest line into the board of education, from the picket lines that we had at Santa Clara University to our level of community activism where we are now creating systemic change and lasting change. So we're still in that respect we're still homeboys and homegirls. We just now wear a suit and tie.

(Cabrales, 2011, p. 128)

Learning giving practices from elders has fueled a fire within Chato and other participants of this study to uplift their communities. Chato has in turn used what he has learned from his mentors to advocate for people in his community as a successful attorney. Additionally, he developed a Latino role model conference, which is in its 20th year of existence, where local Latino professionals attend and encourage students to pursue a higher education. As the organizer, he provides monetary support toward scholarships and seeks monetary gifts from other professionals in the community. In 2010, Chato was able to raise $8,000 in scholarships to give at the Latino role model conference to defray college costs. In all, he practices giving through service and his work, crediting the teachings of his parents, mentors, and graduating from a Jesuit institution that had a philosophy of service to humanity.

The Latina/o alumni participants' careers and community engagement were essential to their giving practices in the community. These actions are reminiscent of another common practice in the Latina/o community of sponsorship or *compadrazgo* that mostly revolves around religious practices (i.e., baptisms, *quinceañeras*, weddings, etc.). *Compadrazgo* or the system of co-parenthood, *comadres* and *compadres,* "serves to extend family relations and loyalty to a larger pool of individuals who are not kin but who become quasi-kin as a result of participating in the children's baptism or other rituals" (Melville, 1991, p. 106). This type of relationship, similar to that of a godparent, establishes a family-like bond and trust between parents and godparents so that if the parents unexpectedly pass away, the godparents could step in and raise the children. Typically, a *madrina* or *padrino* (sponsor) is asked to assist the family with sponsorship of cultural or religious relic. For a wedding, a couple may ask family members or extended family to be *padrinos* (sponsors) of different religious symbols that are used during a wedding ceremony, such as *el lazo* (rope), *las arras* (coins), and *el libro y rosario* (bible and rosary). *Padrinos*can also be sponsors to non-religious activities like sponsoring food, entertainment, and/or photography in order to assist the couple with the cost of the wedding reception.

It is evident that Latinas/os often provide monetary support to their respective family and extended family networks through the system of sponsorship/*compadrazgo*. As noted, this type of giving also involves personal relationships or what Melville (1991) describes as *personalismo*, which is the sanctity that is attributed to personal relationships. In addition, *compadrazgo* is often a mutual relationship in the Latina/o community. *Compadrazgo* can also be used to frame giving in higher education along with community cultural wealth.

Madrina and *Padrino* Capital: An Approach to Giving in Higher Education

Cabrales (2011) found that Latina/o alumni played similar roles as *madrinas/padrinos* (godparents/sponsors) would if they were sponsoring a religious celebration. Extending Yosso's (2005, 2006) community cultural wealth model, *madrina/padrino* capital was added to the model to better represent Latina/o alumni giving in higher education. *Madrina/padrino* capital refers to sponsorship that enables students and/or the community to explore and navigate different social institutions. All of the forms of capital in community cultural wealth (familial, linguistic, aspirational, social, resistant, navigational) and *madrina/padrino* capital interact with each other to represent the essence of Latina/o alumni giving. Latina/o alumni in this study employed *madrina/padrino* capital to contribute monetary gifts toward targeted scholarships and sponsor or organize events that would allow students and the community access different social institutions like higher education and different career paths. In essence, Latina/o alumni became *compadres* to the social institution (e.g., university, nonprofit organizations, etc.) and *madrinas/padrinos* (sponsors) to the students and/or community members they supported.

For example, Teresa, a participant in the study, was able to sponsor students in different ways through paying for their meals for professional networking luncheons or through giving monetary gifts toward transportation costs for different Latina professional events. In addition, she asserted that if she were to give toward a university scholarship, it would be targeted toward students who were in her situation as a college student.

> Now that I'm financially able to do that, I want to know that my money is going to something that is important to me. So what I want to do is give back to students who were in my situation.... I want my money to go toward those students ... to go towards those scholarships that helped me, because that is important to me because I know that that money is put to good use. I mean I'm living proof of that and I didn't just graduate and get married. I went on, I've done other things, and those things have been to help other people.
>
> *(Cabrales, 2011, pp. 156–157)*

Teresa is involved with a women's professional organization and has been a resource for undergraduate and high schools students who would like to pursue law careers. Her sponsorship has allowed many Latinas to network with other Latina professionals in different career fields. Similarly, Mateo, another participant, started a non-profit organization whose mission is to improve the quality of life of at-risk youth, young adults, and low-income families. The organization offers mentorship, educational scholarships, and leadership development and over the past five years he was able to raise over $125,000 to sponsor and benefit youth in his community to further their education.

Implications for Practice

Provide Targeted Giving Opportunities.   Researchers have found that Latinas/os, like African Americans, tend not to be unrestricted givers and give to causes that are particularly meaningful to them (Scully, 2008). Latina/o alumni are more likely to give monetary gifts toward a cause and/or scholarships for a population of students that they identify with, such as Latina/o first-generation college students. In addition, they may be more apt to give to campus cultural centers or student organizations. Colleges and universities should find a culturally relevant approach to targeted giving. Pedro, a participant in the Latina/o alumni giving study stated:

> Money is important, but I think that if you look at history and you look at the Latino community, money is no problem if it has to deal with family. So take a quinceañera or take a boda [wedding] or take all those things into consideration. I mean we pour out thousands of dollars for those things, pero [but] the key center part of it is family and if you can make a campaign around. [For example], let's create a family with the Multicultural Center. Can you donate to it? Yes. Let's make a family of incoming freshman from Watsonville. Are you willing to donate for their scholar-

ships? Yes, pero [but] don't say I want you to donate to me [the university] period, because it's just going to Santa Clara University—I mean that's just too vague. It's like saying can you donate to all the quinceañeras in Watsonville without them being your family.

(Cabrales, 2011, p. 134)

Pedro makes the important connection of being a *madrina/padrino* for a specific cause such as a campus center like the Multicultural Center or finding solace or giving toward a scholarship for a specific student from Watsonville, which is a community that is predominantly Latina/o. He also compared donating to all the *quinceañeras* in Watsonville without them being family to the vagueness of donating to general unrestricted funds that are typically solicited by colleges and universities. Given the shift in Latina/o demographics, educational attainment, and buying power, it is important for colleges and universities to explore which targeted funds are available to engage Latina/o alumni donors. Institutions must be responsible for creating the vehicles that provide Latina/o alumni the opportunity to give.

Ethnicity-Based Affinity Group Development.   Affinity groups are a great way to engage alumni, particularly alumni of color. Latina/o alumni chapters provide ample ways for Latinas/os to become engaged with the university and its student community. Comparable to the community cultural wealth model (Yosso, 2005), Latina/o alumni can employ different forms of capital to assist students with navigating through institutions by participating and advising within different mediums, such as alumni panels, networking events, career exploration, and student organization programming. For example, Isabel, a study participant, recalled how Movimiento Estudiantil Chicana/o de Aztlán MEChA alumni would come back to their undergraduate meetings to talk about different struggles they had on campus and how they were able to persevere. Given the opportunity, Isabel would do the same for the Multicultural Center and students of color. She said, "For myself it would be you know, being able to come back and to speak to those students from the Multicultural Center or other students of color, generally about how we made it" (Cabrales, 2011, p. 149). Isabel reflected on her intense experience, but also noted how those experiences prepared her for different spaces and her ability to thrive in those spaces (Cabrales, 2011).

Although over 20 years ago ethnicity-based alumni chapters were vilified for being separatist, they are slowly making their way onto American college campuses because they have proven to increase involvement amongst alumni of color and are necessary for recruitment and retention of students of color, particularly Latina/o students (Cabrales, 2011; Hay, 1990). In addition, many ethnicity-based alumni chapters also raise funds for targeted scholarships, which inevitably increase alumni participation rates and supports students at the institution.

Cultivate and Recognize Latina/o Alumni. Many Latina/o alumni are engaged with their communities in some way, shape, or form. Cabrales (2011) found that the participants in the study were civically engaged through local politics, role model conferences, and/or fundraising efforts to support student scholarships. Though they indirectly represented the university as ambassadors, the institution rarely recognized their community achievements and advocacy. In some respect, this is positive public relations and ambassadorship for the university. It would benefit the institution to develop a mechanism where these achievements could be publicly recognized. In addition, recognition of their achievements can provide opportunities for Latina/o engagement with undergraduates and the campus community through the many forms of capital described in community cultural wealth. For example, navigational capital refers to the skills maneuvering through social institutions (Yosso, 2005). Latina/o alumni can be invited back to the university and talk to a classroom or a student organization to share their student experiences at the university and how they navigated through the challenges and opportunities in order to graduate. This is also an opportunity for alumni to share their involvement with the community post-graduation and share how they have navigated through their own careers.

Targeted Communication. Latina/o alumni are interested in receiving correspondence that will relate to their experience at the university. Latina/o alumni are likely to pay closer attention to a "targeted ask" letter rather than a "stock unrestricted fund" letter. *Personalismo* or a personal connection is important to Latina/o alumni, especially when asking for a monetary gift. In addition, most colleges and universities publish a magazine that is sent to their respective alumni and friends. It is important to cover stories and/or events where the Latina/o community, including its alumni, is represented.

Lastly, colleges and universities should explore the development of a one-stop website where alumni and friends could access anything and everything pertaining to Latinas/os at the institution (e.g., campus events, student organizations, Latina/o alumni chapter information, statistics, Latina/o scholarship funds, etc.) from one location. Oftentimes there is not one location where Latina/o alumni could find information pertaining to Latinas/os at their respective institution. For example, many alumni could have an interest in supporting the student organizations that they were involved with as undergraduates; however, it would be difficult to support those organizations because alumni do not know where to begin. It would be beneficial for public relations or the alumni association to develop a site or location where Latina/o alumni could read articles and stay up to date with information pertaining to Latinas/os at their alma mater. Table 3.1 reviews these implications for practice.

TABLE 3.1 Implications for Practice

Recommendations	Strategies for Implementation
Provide targeted giving opportunities.	• Publicize and provide Latina/o alumni with a list of scholarships that are of interest (e.g., Latina/o 1st generation, cultural centers, undocumented students, etc.). • Establish a Madrina/Padrino program in which alumni can engage with students and sponsor different activities to further their academics and career.
Ethnicity-based affinity group development.	• Create a Latina/o alumni chapter at your institution. • Become familiar with the where Latina/o alumni live geographically. • Target programming where there are large concentrations of Latina/o alumni. • Engage local alumni with panel and speaking opportunities with current students. • Develop joint-programming between the Latina/o alumni chapter and undergraduate students (e.g., New Latina/o student receptions, senior ceremonies, etc.). • Provide networking opportunities amongst Latina/o alumni.
Cultivate and recognize Latina/o alumni.	• Recognize Latina/o alumni who are civically engaged through local politics, role model conferences, and/or fundraising efforts to support student scholarships. • Provide senior Latina/o college students an opportunity to engage with alumni from similar professional interests. • Appoint Latina/o alumni on national alumni association executive boards. • Provide targeted ambassador opportunities and engage Latina/o alumni as featured speakers/volunteers (e.g., Leadership Institutes, Raza Day, etc.).
Targeted communication.	• *Personalismo* is key to engaging with Latina/o alumni. Send targeted communication with information that involves Latinas/os (e.g., enrollment statistics, Latina/o-centered ask letters, etc.). • Develop a one-stop website where alumni and friends could access anything and everything pertaining to Latinas/os at the institution (e.g., campus events, student organizations, Latina/o alumni chapter information, statistics, Latina/o scholarship funds, etc.). • Feature Latina/o alumni and topics affecting Latinas/os in university communications, such as the university magazine or alumni updates.

Conclusion

Community cultural wealth and Latina/o philanthropy research contribute a culturally relevant approach to expanding the Latina/o alumni donor base in higher education. Using community cultural wealth as a framework for giving allows Latina/o alumni to employ different forms of capital via their occupations and community engagement to give back to students and their communities, financially and through mentorship. Additionally, attention to the three tenets of Latina/o philanthropy: support for extended family networks, involvement in the church, and through *mutualista* organizations are also essential to Latina/o alumni giving because relationships are cultivated and cultural and giving practices are maintained through these tenets, to include *compadrazgo*. Awareness of issues, such as recruitment and retention, university policies, and activities that affect Latinas/os is relevant to Latina/o alumni giving because more often than not Latina/o alumni need a pulse on where their engagement is needed the most. Lastly, as evident through the involvement and giving through *compadrazgo*, Latina/o alumni have the capacity to give monetarily. Hence, the institution should be responsible for developing the vehicle (i.e., targeted funds, undergraduate engagement, board of trustees, alumni boards, etc.) in which Latinas/os can become engaged.

References

Anft, M. (2002). *Tapping ethnic wealth: Charities pursue minority giving as incomes rise among blacks, Hispanics, and other groups.* Retrieved March 20, 2010, from http://philanthropy.com/free/articles/v14/i06/06000401.htm

Cabrales, J. A. (2011). *Conceptualizing Latina/o philanthropy in higher education: A study of Latina/o undergraduate alumni from a predominantly white Jesuit institution* (Unpublished doctoral dissertation). Iowa State University, Ames.

Center of Philanthropy and Civil Society. (2003). *Latino philanthropy literature review.* Retrieved April 20, 2010, from http://www.philanthropy.org/programs/literature_reviews/latino_lit_review.pdf

Cortés, M. (1991). Philanthropy and Latino nonprofits: A research agenda. In H. E. Gallegos & M. O'Neill (Eds.), *Hispanics and the nonprofit sector* (pp. 139–160). New York, NY: The Foundation Center.

Cortés, M. (1995). Three strategic questions about Latino philanthropy. *New Directions for Philanthropic Fundraising, 8,* 23–40.

Crotty, M. (1998). *The foundations of social research: Meaning and perspective in the research process.* London, England: Sage.

Diaz, W. A. (1999). Philanthropy and the case of the Latino communities in America. In C. T. Clotfelter & T. Ehrlich (Eds.), *Philanthropy and the nonprofit sector in a changing America* (pp. 275–292). Bloomington: Indiana University Press.

Excelencia in Education. (2008). *Latinos in undergraduate education.* Retrieved September 16, 2009, from http://www.edexcelencia.org/images/latinosundergraduate-2008

Francis, L. C., & Ousley, M. D. (2006). *Using a comprehensive strategy to retain Hispanic students.* Retrieved September 20, 2009, from http://nrc.fye.sc.edu/esource/pdf/pdfES03/3(6).pdf

Gallegos, H. E., & O'Neill, M. (Eds.). (1991). *Hispanics and the non-profit sector.* New York, NY: The Foundation Center.

Hay, T. M. (1990). Common ground: Catering to alumni who share similar interests. *Currents,* *16*(4), 26–32.

Humphreys, J. M. (2009). The multicultural economy 2009. *Georgia Business and Economic Conditions, 69*(3), 1–16.

Melville, M. B. (1991). Latino nonprofit organizations: Ethnic diversity, values, and leadership. In H. E. Gallegos & M. O'Neill (Eds.), *Hispanics and the nonprofit sector* (pp. 97–112). New York, NY: The Foundation Center.

Pew Hispanic Center. (2011). Hispanics account for more than half of nation's growth in past decade Retrieved April 1, 2011, from http://pewhispanic.org/reports/report.php?ReportID=140

Ramos, H. A. J. (1999). Latino philanthropy: Expanding U.S. models of giving and civic participation. In Council on Foundations (Ed.), *Cultures of caring* (pp. 147–187). Washington, DC: Council on Foundations.

Rivas-Vásquez, A. G. (1999). New pools of Latino wealth: A case study of donors and potential donors in U.S. Hispanic/Latino communities. In D. Campoamor, W. A. Diaz, & H. A. J. Ramos (Eds.), *Nuevos senderos: Reflections on Hispanics and philanthropy* (pp. 115–138). Houston, TX: Arte Público Press.

Scully, M. K. (2008). Untangling diversity. Retrieved April 10, 2010, from http://www.case.org/Publications_and_Products/CURRENTS/CURRENTS_Archive/2008/November-December_2008/Untangling_Diversity.html

Seidman, I. (2006). *Interviewing as qualitative research: A guide for researchers in education and the social sciences* (3rd ed.). New York, NY: Teachers College Press.

U.S. Census. (2008). Hispanics in the United States. Retrieved February 27, 2008, from http://www.census.gov/population/www/socdemo/hispanic/hispanic.html

University of Michigan. (2008). Hispanic alumni council. Retrieved March 20, 2010, from http://hac.umclubs.com/index.php?page=hac---purpose

Yosso, T. J. (2005). Whose culture has capital? A critical race theory discussion of community cultural wealth. *Race Ethnicity and Education, 8*(1), 69–91.

Yosso, T. J. (2006). *Critical race counterstories along the Chicana/Chicano pipeline.* New York, NY: Routledge.

4

CHINESE AMERICAN PHILANTHROPY

Cultural Contexts Behind Major Gifts in Higher Education

Kozue Tsunoda

Introduction

As higher education continues to experience racial and ethnic diversification of student populations, one of the challenges of development offices becomes to understand and incorporate unique cultural perspectives into their fundraising practices. This chapter highlights charitable giving by Chinese American donors, an unquestionably influential donor population within higher education that has not yet garnered sufficient scholarly attention. Today, Chinese Americans constitute the largest ethnic group among Asian Americans, and as more Chinese students and scholars study in the United States each year, universities can no longer afford to ignore the philanthropic behaviors and motivations of this growing population.

In order to provide practical implications for expanding an ethnic minority donor base in higher education, this chapter highlights Chinese American donor behaviors, particularly how cultural factors affect their decisions to give to U.S. higher education. The chapter begins by reviewing earlier research on diversity in university fundraising and then uses 14 in-depth interviews of Chinese American major-gift donors in U.S. higher education to explore their giving patterns and donor motivations. These are individual perceptions shared by the Chinese American donors who have given major gifts between $50,000 and $90 million dollars to U.S. higher education. By integrating existing research on philanthropy and fundraising in higher education as well as interview data of donors, this chapter reveals holistic views of Chinese American educational giving and suggests ways in which development offices can better foster and harness philanthropic contributions by Chinese Americans.

Growing Needs to Diversify University Fundraising Strategies

Earlier research on diversity in fundraising highlights the significance of incorporating cultural traditions and beliefs behind charitable giving into the actual fundraising efforts (Bowman, 2010; Newman, 2002; Wagner & Ryan, 2004; Scanlan & Abrahams, 2002). Sanford Cloud Jr., the president and CEO of the National Conference for Community and Justice, stated that diversification is "desirable not only because it is the right thing to do, but also because doing so will increase the effectiveness of fundraising and charitable organizations" (cited in Wagner & Ryan, 2004, p. 66). Scanlan and Abrahams's (2002) study of minority giving in the United States documents that understanding traditional perceptions of different minority giving is a vital step in reaching out to diverse communities and fulfilling future fundraising endeavors. Other research further addresses ways of incorporating cultural traditions into fundraising practices. Primary importance lies in recognizing and serving diverse cultures by learning and experiencing the fundraising practices of these local communities (Newman, 2002). More recent research documents the importance of diversifying fundraising strategies, particularly by understanding cultural giving behaviors and also recruiting fundraising professionals from minority groups (Bowman, 2010). These earlier studies document the importance of diversifying fundraising strategies, particularly by understanding cultural giving behaviors and also recruiting fundraising professionals from minority groups. Nevertheless, the findings from previous studies rely heavily on descriptive data of minority giving and overlook the meaning of diversity from donors' perspectives. The voices and perspectives of actual actors involved in philanthropy and fundraising practices remain largely unconsidered.

Early studies that have examined Asian American giving categorized Asian American donors as a homogeneous group (Chao, 1999; Ho, 2004; Pettey, 2002; Shao, 1995). While these studies have provided significant knowledge and information to understand ethnic minority giving, they have failed to adequately describe the diversity present among various sub-ethnic groups. Further research on philanthropic actions and attitudes of Chinese American students, alumni, and donors can contribute to developing a better understanding of these key similarities and differences among groups which can then be utilized in the development of ethnicity-specific university fundraising strategies.

Today, Chinese Americans comprise one of the largest sub-ethnic groups among Asian Americans, and China continues to be the number-one country of origin of international students in U.S. higher education (Institute of International Education, 2012). Despite a demonstrated history of philanthropy by Chinese Americans and tremendous possibilities for additional contributions from Chinese and Chinese American communities, there has not been a study that has explored Chinese and Chinese American donor behaviors, particularly in U.S. higher education. Examining the actual voices of Chinese American donors in U.S. higher education, this chapter explores more specific way to employ diversity within university fundraising practices.

Methodology

The study on which this chapter is based employed in-depth interviews with 14 Chinese American major gift donors in order to investigate how and why Chinese Americans have supported U.S. higher education. The original criteria of data collection included: (a) if the individual represented post-1949 Chinese immigrants from Hong Kong and Taiwan or second generation and beyond Chinese Americans; (b) if the individual donated more than $500,000 to American higher education; and (c) if the individual resided in the United States. To obtain the most information-rich sample, this study revised the criteria and expanded the sample by including smaller gift donors, those who gave less than $ 500,000. These donors supported more than a dozen private and public universities and colleges across the nation, mostly located on the East and West coasts. The study collected samples until it reached a saturation point.

The theoretical framework developed for this study comprised a meta-analysis of previous literature on the history of philanthropy and fundraising in U.S. higher education, including "traditional" and "non-traditional" donor motivation theories. This framework linked two dimensions: (a) History of philanthropy in U.S. higher education and research perspectives on "traditional" donor motivation; and (b) A macro-oriented level that takes into account the influence of socio-historical and socio-cultural factors related to "non-traditional" Chinese American giving. By synthesizing these two dimensions, this study advanced the previous studies of donor motivation theory and Chinese American giving. This framework categorizes philanthropic motivations into seven themes: donor altruism, personal benefits, psychological benefits, reciprocity, attachment, giving capacity, and culture.

Demographic Characteristics

Donor profiles demonstrated several notable characteristics of the donors interviewed for this study. Donors were more often male than female, and most were married and had children. The majority of donors were in their fifties or above, and some already had approached their retirement age. Many of the donors interviewed for this study owned venture capital firms, while several others were senior officers of international corporations, a physician, and a federal employee. The immigration history of each of these donors presented complex narratives; at different times in life, donors moved back and forth from the United States and China for educational and familial reasons.

Generally speaking, donors were highly educated individuals. All of the participants earned bachelor degrees or higher; several earned MBAs or Ph.Ds.

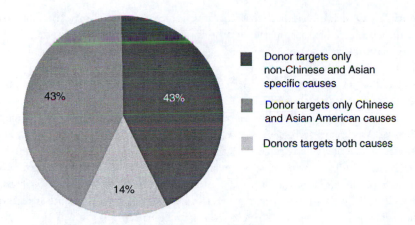

FIGURE 4.1 Chinese American donors by gift destinations.

Donors majored predominantly in the fields of science, engineering, and business and were less likely to major in the humanities or social science. During college, several donors received scholarships or fellowships, while others self-financed their education. Volunteer activities during college were less common among many of the donors. For most of them, voluntary commitments started at a later age. All donors interviewed for this study served on boards of university and nonprofit organizations. Some donors helped form alumni associations at their alma maters while others were currently serving on advisory boards, university foundations, and boards of trustees in order to better provide strategic advice. One donor served on a board of regents to oversee policy decisions of local universities and colleges. Recipient institutions recognized these donors' voluntary contributions with prestigious awards and medals.

While their amounts of donations ranged from thousands to millions, the 14 donors interviewed for this research supported a wide range of causes within U.S. higher education. Interestingly, as shown in Figure 4.1, more than half of the donors interviewed funded programs or scholarships related to Chinese and Chinese American causes. The proceeding section will discuss this trend further, but these causes include financial supports for Chinese and Chinese American students, fellowships for Chinese visiting scholars, and funds for Chinese American university leadership. Still, 86 percent of all participants supported causes not specific to any ethnicity; these donations often targeted individual departments, particularly in the fields of business, science, technology, engineering, and medicine.

Cultural Explanations of Chinese American Donor Behaviors

First and foremost, this chapter is not intended to state that cultural factors are the only reason why Chinese Americans support higher education. In fact, this multiple case study revealed that Chinese American major gift contributors embrace both traditional and non-traditional giving behaviors (Tsunoda, 2011). While cultural motivations remained one of the significant factors behind their charitable giving, donors similarly expressed a sense of obligation, self-satisfaction, and reciprocal incentives from college experiences, all of which are sentiments shared among non-Chinese American donors.

Still, additional findings reassert that cultural factors greatly influenced Chinese American donors interviewed. Using findings from this study, this chapter describes five key incentives that motivated Chinese American donors: (a) advancing Chinese and Asian American communities, (b) improving U.S.-China relations, (c) teaching Chinese culture and history to fellow Americans, (d) celebrating Asian American university leadership, and (e) demonstrating philanthropic leadership in Chinese American communities.

Advancing Chinese and Asian American Communities

Chinese American donors gave to advance Chinese communities in the United States. Some gifts solely targeted sub-set Chinese American communities, reflecting donor motivations to help Chinese people because of shared Chinese ethnicity. In the case of one donor, his discovery of Chinese American identity initiated his gift for Chinese students studying in American higher education. This donor was born in the 1930s and experienced intense segregation against minorities in his neighborhood. Growing up, he did not have any firsthand experiences of Chinese tradition. In fact, he and his brothers revoked their Chinese heritage. He said:

> Unfortunately, my father passed away when I was eight years old. My mother had to raise five of us. Essentially, I didn't grow up with any Chinese culture. I observed a little bit of what others in the Chinese community did, but I didn't experience it firsthand. My two brothers and I pretty much rebelled and quit speaking Chinese as a matter of fact. Just decided it didn't pay to be a Chinese person in Mississippi at that time, so we tried to blend in as much as we could. In our so-called wisdom at that time we wouldn't speak Chinese at that time. Consequently, not only I did not experience the culture, I sort of lost it.
>
> *(Personal Communication, June 9, 2010)*

The turning point came when he reached his retirement age. After separation from his wife, he started revisiting his identity. Right around the same time, he decided to volunteer as an English teacher at a middle school in an impoverished area of China. This was his first trip to China. He recalled, "My first trip to China ever because, like I said, I had ever had any idea that I will ever go back to China because I felt like I wasn't Chinese. But this trip, it was a great experience, and it really taught me that, 'Hey [donor name], you are Chinese'" (Personal Communication, June 9, 2010).

After he came back to the United States, he filed his retirement paperwork and spent two years in China teaching English at the university level. Today, he gives individual gifts directly to his former Chinese students studying in U.S. universities. Additionally, he serves on the boards of Chinese American-related nonprofit organizations and gives anonymous gifts to support internship programs for Asian American college students. When asked about his motivation to support Asian and American students, he said, "I just try to find people in the Chinese American and Asian American community who are pursuing their education when they need some help. That's what I have been doing" (Personal Communication, June 9, 2010). He continued:

> I just basically help young people. Since I had that great experience with university students in China, I can relate to them and feel like I can help them with the program in the APA nonprofit that I support, the internship program that specifically targets college students to help them grow much stronger and really to enlighten them about the experiences of being Asian American. To me, that is a very good target. Young people unlike me, who have an interest in helping the community. Unlike me when I was at their age, they realize I have connections with Chinese and wanted to help.
>
> *(Personal Communication, June 9, 2010)*

For another participant, his gifts benefitted the larger Asian American community. Both of his parents have passed away, and this participant considers the Asian American community as his family. Giving for the benefit of the Asian American community, from his perspective, is a Chinese tradition of supporting "family" (Personal Communication, June 24, 2010). He currently serves on boards of universities and Asian American nonprofit organizations, supporting and operating scholarships for Asian American college students. In response to the question of how Chinese heritage influenced his charitable decisions, he said:

> One of the things that is very important in Chinese culture is family. I actually think because I'm here in the U.S. that my extended family is actually fairly large. So, that family to me is a broader Asian American community in the U.S. that is still underrepresented but not as successful as we would like to see. As a result, because I'm successful, I've been one of the few to make it through all these things, then it's sort of my obligation to basically reach back and help some of the people who are not as well-off.
>
> *(Personal Communication, June 24, 2010)*

Despite differing degrees of attachment to Chinese and Chinese American communities, donors interviewed for this research identified themselves as

Chinese American. Donors considered themselves as American but with strong influences from their Chinese heritage. Either from their family upbringing, education, or volunteer activities, donors consistently expressed awareness of their Chinese heritage. They celebrated the richness of Chinese culture, hoping to share its value with other members of American society.

Improving U.S.-China Relations

Chinese American donors gave to strengthen bilateral U.S.-China relationships. Many donors interviewed for this research head companies that operate across the United States and Asia. Other donors spent time in mainland China, Taiwan, and Hong Kong either as adolescents or as volunteers. Within their professional and personal capacities, donors interacted with people and became increasingly aware of needs to develop their home country/regions. They believed that building a stronger China would improve U.S.-China relationships and ultimately advance the status of Chinese Americans in the United States.

This is the reason why one donor, for example, funded scholarly exchange programs targeting Chinese academic and business leaders. She was a long-time generous supporter of her alma mater, but, in addition to her gifts to campus infrastructure, she and her family supported scholarly exchange programs, including visiting scholarships for Chinese journalists and doctoral scholarships in the sciences for Chinese graduate students. When asked about her motivation to support Chinese American causes specifically, she referenced Chinese history around the late 1990s. She said:

> In 1997, they were starting to send more students from China to the United States, but a lot of them were not going back. So, we were trying to figure out, well what we can do to help China, but that means whoever we educate has to have a chance of going back. There's nothing we can do to stop that. So that's why we targeted young professors who were five to ten years into their careers, had labs, had students who were judged to be rising stars, to come and enhance their experiences at the [university]. And then they would go back and utilize not only what they've learned but also now they have sort of connections and networks to go back, and that would propel them. And we were hoping that that would really propel China.
>
> *(Personal Communication, May 13, 2010)*

As an entrepreneur and a philanthropist, another participant's philanthropic activities aimed to advance U.S.-China relationships. In addition to her contributions to Asian American nonprofit organizations, this donor funded a visiting Chinese scholar program at a business school, bringing Chinese senior academic and/or business leaders to the United States. When asked about her motivations, she said:

> Obviously my work with [Asia Pacific American nonprofit] was really to foster better relationships between the U.S. and Asia. My work with [university] gave me access to great scholarly resources. If I set up this scholarship at [university], I can help bring over very bright individuals and further their career and expose them to all the resources I had at [university] and [Asia Pacific American nonprofit]. At the same time, I wanted to make sure that the fellowship was another building block on that bridge between the U.S. and Asia.
>
> *(Personal Communication, July 14, 2010)*

Using philanthropy, Chinese American donors interviewed for this study served as ambassadors of U.S.-China relations. As renowned members of their Chinese and Chinese American communities—most of them having achieved senior positions at international corporations and venture capital firms that operate globally—these donors used the many resources and networks at their disposal to help support their home country/region as well as foster and further bilateral bridges between the United States and China.

Teaching Chinese Culture and History to Fellow Americans

Additionally, Chinese Americans gave to advocate Chinese heritage to fellow Americans. An entrepreneur and third-generation philanthropist, one participant said, "I want to share the heritage and what China has to offer with my adopted country" (Personal Communication, June 17, 2010). His giving to U.S. higher education focused primarily on two areas: Chinese culture and education. When asked why these two areas, he said:

> Education, because that's a very strong commitment, and Chinese culture, because when I first came here as a child, I was a lone Chinese in a sea of Caucasians. There were few Asians. Unlike now, there were very few Asians. Contemporary China, at that point, had nothing to be proud of. In 1949, it was basically almost a failed society… China was stuck in backwardness. But Chinese history and culture was something that I could look to, to find some pride in my roots. So this is really the reason that I support people learning Chinese, learning about Chinese culture, history, etc.
>
> *(Personal Communication, June 17, 2010)*

Because Chinese Americans focus their efforts on Americans, they gave to universities and colleges in the United States. As people of Chinese descent living in the United States, giving to Chinese causes was a legitimate way to acknowledge American affinity and to share Chinese culture with fellow Americans. Within the American context, donors strongly promoted, celebrated, and shared the richness of Chinese culture. One participant elaborated on this point:

> My point of view is that I am an American with Chinese heritage. So, part of the motivation is that I want Americans who know so little about Asia to learn more about Asia generally and China specifically. That impulse on my part probably started with a personal need to share something that I could be proud of with my fellow Americans. Now, it's really driven by, I think, the sense that this country needs very much to know more, for its own good, a lot more about Asia.
>
> *(Personal Communication, June 17, 2010)*

While Chinese American donors interviewed for this study expressed complex immigration history and cultural identities, they all considered themselves to be Chinese Americans—Americans of Chinese heritage. Donors embraced and celebrated the richness of Chinese culture and history, and they wanted to share this culture and history with fellow Americans. Such motivations also help to explain why donors gave to U.S. universities and colleges instead of schools in mainland China, Hong Kong, Taiwan, or other parts of the world. For them, building awareness and appreciation of Chinese history and culture at American higher education institutions was a crucial step to further advance Chinese American communities and bilateral U.S.-China relationships.

Celebrating Asian American University Leadership

Chinese Americans gave to recognize Asian American leadership in U.S. universities and colleges. In the late 1990s, one public university attracted a large number of Chinese American donations after the university hired a high-ranking Chinese American official. Chinese Americans contributed their wealth to the university to celebrate the official's accomplishment and to support his future endeavors. One participant and her family established a relationship with the official on the first day of the official's appointment and left a $1 million gift on his desk. She said:

> The day that [Chinese American leader] took office, there was a million dollar check on his desk from us. And, it was to do with however he pleased. Our message was, you know, congratulations for being the first of many. We want to support you, so we are going to give this money to do it. You can spend it the way you need to spend it. And, so of course, we got to know him. I got to know him really well, and I miss him because he was really a great man. He did a lot not only for [university] but for Chinese Americans. I think that may have been the best gift that

we have ever made because it really led the way for Chinese American leadership in the universities.

(Personal Communication, May 13, 2010)

The family allocated the gift to a fund specifically for the leader. This was an unrestricted gift, and the official directed funds until his resignation. After the official left the university, the participant's family managed the gift for the benefit of Chinese visiting scholars and journalism programs. The family's close relationship with the official eventually produced another gift: when the official sought external funding to support the health center, the participant's family contributed an additional $1 million.

Even more recently, Chinese Americans continue to honor the official's accomplishments. In 2008, Chinese American donations supported the renovation of the East Asian library at this university. At the entrance of the library there stands a tall plaque of contributing donors, many of whom gave in memory of the official. An alumnus interviewed, stated:

> Would another [leader] have been successful? No, because before and after, no one has given that amount of money. It was a success because he had a Chinese face? No, not exactly. It was a success because people wanted to support him as the first Chinese [leadership role]. They wanted to show he could raise money better.
>
> (Personal Communication, June 30, 2010)

As described by this donor, appointment of the first Chinese American chancellor provoked significant philanthropic interest among the members of Chinese and Chinese American communities. For them, this chancellor signified a very public success of Chinese and Chinese American accomplishments in U.S. higher education. That is the reason why this university attracted not only those who had existing relationships with the university but even those who had very few affiliations. As self-identifying members of Chinese and Chinese American communities, people gave to help ensure that this chancellor could demonstrate the capability to raise funds for the university and that his successes would be celebrated widely.

Demonstrating Philanthropic Leadership in Chinese American Communities

Chinese American major donors gave to demonstrate philanthropic leadership within the Chinese American community. Donors interacted with recipients to empower their philanthropic impetus, while they publicized their contributions to encourage fellow Chinese Americans.

The family of one participant is one of the most influential Chinese American donor entities in U.S. higher education. To date, the family has distributed millions of dollars to U.S. universities all across the nation. While the purpose of giving varied across different causes, one focus remained consistent: the importance of teaching philanthropic behaviors to the next generation. With regard to her million-dollar gift to a scholarship program for Chinese Ph.D. students, this participant said:

> What we've done now is we try to have an annual dinner with these graduate students to get to know them a bit, and they also get to know us. The idea is that when they're in a position after they graduated, you want them to also contribute.
>
> *(Personal Communication, May 13, 2010)*

To another participant, giving demonstrated philanthropic leadership within the Asian American community. As a successful corporate senior officer and vice president of an Asia Pacific American nonprofit organization, this participant acknowledged his philanthropic roles. He said:

> I can't save the world. I can't save everyone in poverty, and I can't feed the world. I can do a reasonable part to help other people in the Asian American community, make sure that as a role model, I give some guidance and do the things that I'm capable of doing. I am not going to be a protester and carry a sign and do that. What I can do is from within the limits of my position, providing those scholarship programs for military veterans or Asian Americans or things like that. Therefore I can be much more effective in doing that than other things. And so the [university] and [Asian Pacific American nonprofit] are better off because I'm in a senior position and backing them.
>
> *(Personal Communication, June 24, 2010)*

Notably, a strong desire to promote philanthropy drove one participant and her husband to "come out of the closet" and announce their contributions for the first time to the public. Previously, this participant and her husband remained anonymous about their major gifts. When they gave a mega-gift to her alma mater, however, they decided to do so publicly. She said:

> In [university]'s case, they said, "this is such an incredible gift. It's record breaking. It will really put [university] on the map. It would inspire other people to do so. We're working on other friends to do another generous thing. Can we possibly use your name?"
>
> *(Personal Communication, July 14, 2010)*

She continued:

> In the past, we have given large gifts but anonymously. [university] was really the first instance in which we came out of the closet, and this was because the institution asked us to. We felt that it could serve a purpose.

> We never asked to have publicity because frankly, my husband and I don't care about the fanfare and the credits. It's really doing the right thing for the institution. But when the institution asked if they could use our name to inspire other people to give, then we allowed our names to be used. Many times we will give anonymously, but where there's something that is notable and the institution has asked, we will say yes.
>
> *(Personal Communication, July 14, 2010)*

Beyond recipients and Asian American communities, Chinese American donors showcased Chinese Americans giving to mainstream U.S. society. Donors believed that giving not only encourages Chinese Americans to give but also announces in public that Chinese Americans do give for the collective good. One participant said:

> Though in recent years, it's been changing as more and more Chinese have been willing to be public about their gifts. I think they realize that they are setting examples for other Chinese. If they give, then maybe other Chinese will be more generous and show the American community that Chinese Americans are also grateful to be in this country. I think there are many ways to set an example for your fellow Chinese, to tell your fellow Americans that Chinese Americans are grateful and give back to the community because we truly value education.
>
> *(Personal Communication, July 14, 2010)*

Chinese American donors gave to advance the status of Chinese Americans in the States. Their gifts strengthened U.S.–China relationships and furthered public awareness of Chinese history and culture. They also give to celebrate Chinese American university leadership, as demonstrated in the case of first Chinese American leader at a public university. These Chinese American donors became philanthropic role models among students, Chinese American communities, and American society as a whole.

Implications for Practice

The findings of this research reassert the value of diversity in fundraising strategies, especially developing alternative strategies that target specific donor groups. For Chinese American donors, emotional attachments to Chinese and Chinese American communities remained a significant impetus to give. Philanthropic giving paralleled with their desire to advance Chinese American communities, both by improving bilateral U.S.–China relations and promoting Chinese culture and heritage education for U.S. society. Within the higher education system, Chinese American donors celebrated the recognition of their heritage, supporting Chinese and Chinese American leadership and promoting philanthropic spirit amongst fellow members of the community. All of these incentives relate closely to their cultural background, further demonstrating the strong ties between their philanthropic contributions and their obligations as Chinese descendants.

Universities and colleges need to explore and evaluate solicitation strategies that best appeal to historical and cultural contexts undergirding each Chinese American donor's belief in philanthropy. This chapter concludes by providing five specific fundraising efforts that could be employed when engaging donors of Chinese and Asian American backgrounds. As documented in earlier studies on Latino and African American giving in U.S. higher education, these suggestions have many similar implications when engaging donors of different ethnic minority groups (Drezner, 2008, 2009, 2010; O'Connor, 2007; Reaves, 2006). As diversity and internationalization continue to grow in every aspect of university and college settings, development offices cannot survive without exploring alternative strategies to diversify their fundraising practices. The following suggestions present fundamental steps for universities and colleges to develop and strengthen more effective and long-lasting relationships with donors of ethnic minority groups, particularly Chinese and Chinese American donors.

Organizing Alumni Events Specific to Chinese American Interests

It is no coincidence that more than half of donors interviewed for this research supported Chinese and Asian American-related causes. Communal ties are the primary channel of Chinese American giving. Universities and colleges should develop alumni events or activities specific to Chinese American alumni's interests.

For instance, universities and colleges should organize a collaborative Lunar Chinese New Year event. Currently, many different community organizations, student associations, and university entities host their Lunar New Year events at different locations. There could be an effort to combine these events into one holistic activity, where students, faculty, community leaders, university leaders, and other members of the community get together and celebrate. Universities and colleges could facilitate additional incentives, such as inviting Chinese American celebrities to speak and offering authentic Chinese food. Events like this will bring communities and universities together, and, at the same time, help build communal attachments among students and faculty and nurturing, trustworthy, community-university relationships.

These events and activities could be coordinated by the efforts of the local Chinese or Chinese American Alumni Club. Appointing core members of the community to serve on the board of these clubs will promote organizational spirit to raise funds for shared ethnic-specific causes. Additionally, these community members function as gateways by which fundraising professionals can reach out to other prospects who share ethnic backgrounds. Overall, universities' "giving" efforts must appeal to Chinese American alumni and their individual interests.

Recruiting Chinese American Leaders in University Administration

Another strategy to solicit Chinese American major gifts is visibly employing Chinese American leadership in university administrations. This study showed that the first Chinese American in a major leadership role at a public university solicited tremendous gifts from Chinese Americans. Many Chinese Americans were willing to share their wealth because he was the first Chinese American leader in U.S. higher education history. Donors who had stronger communal involvements praised his remarkable achievements and supported his initiatives. At the same time, the fact that this official worked at one of America's top universities further strengthened donor incentives. The official was nominated and selected by the U.S. mainstream, which further resonates with Chinese American donors' incentives to support within the U.S. context. Learning from these actual examples, universities should recruit Chinese Americans in leadership positions, individuals who are professionally capable and are willing to serve for the Chinese American community.

What is important here, however, is that recruiting a Chinese American leader could be a springboard for a variety of supporting efforts and activities. One donor interviewed for this study mentioned the importance of continuous personal relationships with the university leadership. This continuous relationship contributed significantly toward motivations to donate repeatedly to the institution, and in greater quantities. In order to generate and support these relationships, universities and colleges must ensure their Chinese American leadership develops and fosters relationships with individual donors and Chinese American communities specifically. These existing donors and other community members need to know how the Chinese American leadership can help realize donors' philanthropic endeavors. Without leaders' continuous contributions, recruiting Chinese American leadership alone does not maximize impacts on institutional fundraising efforts targeting Chinese American donor populations.

Tracking and Promoting Alumni and Donor Ethnicity

In order for advancement offices to enact these recommendations, institutions must know the race and ethnicity of their alumni. While most institutions have fairly good records of the ethnicity of more recent graduates, such data for older graduates may be missing; beyond race, institutions do not typically record ethnicities. Universities and colleges must strive to implement more comprehensive methods for tracking donor ethnicity. By doing so, institutions can build quantitative datasets to aid them in completing results-based analysis. Proper quantitative data would expand the understanding of Chinese American giving and provide broader understanding of current trends and patterns of philanthropic giving by different ethnic groups. From this analysis, development officers would be able to identify the overall characteristics of giving destinations and areas of interests among Chinese American (and other ethnic group) donors.

Specializing Development Officers in Chinese American Philanthropy

Developing trustworthy relationships between donors and development offices is essential to cultivating successful fundraising strategies. To that end, development offices need to encourage development officers to, instead of working with donating populations generally, specialize in Chinese American philanthropy in higher education. Specialization of staff could be further supported by recruiting more Chinese and Asian American development officers as well as development offices offering workshops or training regarding cultural sensitivity and donor behaviors that are particularly unique to Chinese American donors. As mentioned in the previous chapters when applied to other donor groups, sophisticated Chinese American donors do not necessarily perceive ethnic/racial background of development officers as their primary credential, but rather it is his or her understanding of cultural nuances and whether the person is capable of integrating cultural sensitivity with existing professional fundraising skills that is important. In order to do so, development offices may be able to utilize institutional support to employ graduate assistants who could help collect and further knowledge about Chinese and Asian American giving to higher education.

Additionally, universities and colleges should invite Chinese development officers who are working in mainland China, Taiwan, and Hong Kong to attend their professional development workshops. Philanthropy is still a growing field in Chinese university development, and thus development officers will benefit tremendously from such professional experiences. In contrast, American development officers, by sharing their experiences, will develop professional relationships that help them understand Chinese culture and traditions. Such personal interactions are by far the best way to understand sensitive cultural nuances persistent within Chinese American donor relations.

These are only selective pathways to building a professional bridge to promote cultural understandings among practitioners. By supporting the professional development of graduate students and international fundraisers within the practice-based contexts of development offices, fundraisers working at U.S. universities and colleges would benefit, exchanging knowledge of fundraising practices while gaining valuable data regarding cultural sensitivities.

Recruiting Chinese American Leaders in "Asking" for Donations

The findings from this research supported the impact of involving Chinese American leaders in solicitation processes. Universities and colleges should identify prominent Chinese American leaders in the community, business, and politics who have knowledge, cultural understanding, and, more importantly, personal ties with high-profile individuals. These are individuals who know who to ask, how to ask, and what to ask. Recruiting these individuals in fundraising will increase effectiveness and efficiency when approaching Chinese American donors. A single visit by these individuals is far more effective than multiple visits by individuals who have no affiliation with prospects' professional or communal ties. As one donor mentioned, these individuals know how to "wine, dine, and then when to ask" (Personal Communication, May 13, 2010). Especially since asking directly is often considered disrespectful and there is no right time to ask, universities should depend on these "experts" to ask in the most sensitive way possible.

In order to involve Chinese American community leaders, universities and colleges must facilitate on-campus events that appeal to these leaders' interests. In addition to Lunar New Year events and other social gatherings suggested above, institutions must develop additional efforts to maintain personal relationships with these community leaders. Inviting them to campus-organized events is only the start of their relationship; institutional "giving" processes need to persist until these leaders feel obligated to give back. At these events institutions can promote the details of other Chinese and Chinese American alumni. After all, developing reliable relationships with community leaders and engaging them into fundraising strategies is one of the most effective ways to promote Chinese American donations, especially among those who have stronger communal obligations. Table 4.1 reviews these implications for practice.

Conclusion

In today's fragile fiscal environment, soliciting donations from the private sector is vital for universities and colleges to survive. The findings from this chapter indicate that while current developmental practices at universities and colleges, most commonly all-inclusive and Westernized, attract Chinese American constituents, employing more culturally-specific strategies will provide opportunities to broaden the Chinese American prospect base, especially with those who share greater interests in supporting Chinese and Asian American-related causes. Additionally, we cannot ignore diversity within the Chinese American population. Depending on their identity orientations and backgrounds, Chinese American prospects will represent distinctly different giving patterns. Diversifying university fundraising strategies by highlighting cultural elements not only allows for the continued engagement of existing prospects but also attracts donors who have not responded to traditional solicitation efforts. In this

regard, Chinese and Chinese American communities present a unique potential for institutions to explore alternative giving channels.

As Americans of Chinese descent, donors espoused differing desires to
give for the benefit of Chinese and Asian American communities. This sense
of communal attachment appeared in multiple aspects of Chinese American
giving, including donors' motivations to advance the community, to teach

TABLE 4.1 Recommendations for Enhancing Chinese American Giving and Strategies for Implementation

Recommendation	Strategies for Implementation
Organizing Alumni Events Specific to Chinese American Interests	• Organize a collaborative Lunar Chinese New Year event among community organizations, student associations, and universities entities. • Appoint core members of the Chinese American community to serve on the boards of Chinese and Chinese American Alumni Clubs.
Recruiting Chinese American Leaders in University Administration	• Visibly employ Chinese American leadership in university administrations. • Develop and foster relationships among Chinese American administrative leadership, individual donors, and Chinese American communities.
Tracking and Publicizing Alumni and Donor Ethnicity	• Build quantitative data sets and results-based analysis on donor ethnicity. • Recognize major contributions of Chinese American donors by encouraging prominent Chinese American donors to share their experiences with other prospects. • Publicize philanthropic contributions by Chinese American ethnic groups utilizing publications and social media.
Specializing Development Officers in Chinese American Philanthropy	• Encourage development officers to specialize in Chinese American philanthropy in higher education. • Recruit more Chinese and Asian American development officers. • Offer workshops or trainings regarding cultural sensitivity and donor behaviors that are particularly unique to Chinese American donors. • Collaborate and share resources with Chinese development officers working in mainland China, Taiwan, and Hong Kong.
Recruiting Chinese American Leaders in "Asking" for Donations	• Involve prominent Chinese American leaders in the community, business corporations, and politics who have knowledge, cultural understanding, and personal ties with high-profile individuals associated with fundraising efforts. • Facilitate campus-organized events that appeal to Chinese American philanthropic leaders.

Chinese heritage to fellow American citizens, to improve U.S.-China relationships, to demonstrate philanthropic leadership, and to celebrate Chinese American university leaderships. In order to successfully embrace diversity in fundraising practices, universities and colleges need to utilize available financial and human resources wisely. Only from collaborative efforts among students, faculty, alumni, staff, and community members of various culture and backgrounds can development offices effectively diversify.

References

Bowman, N. (2010). Cultivating future fundraisers of color at Historically Black Colleges and Universities. *International Journal of Educational Advancement, 10*(3), 230–234.

Chao, J. (1999). Asian American philanthropy: Expanding circles of participation. *Cultures of Caring* (Council on Foundations), 189–254.

Drezner, N. (2008). *Cultivating a culture of giving: An exploration of institutional strategies to enhance African American young alumni giving* (Doctoral dissertation). Retrieved from ProQuest Dissertations and Theses. (Accession Order No. AAT 3328548).

Drezner, N. D. (2009). Why give?: Exploring social exchange and organizational identification theories in the promotion of philanthropic behaviors of African American millennials at private-HBCUs. *International Journal of Educational Advancement, 9*(3), 147–165.

Drezner, N. D. (2010). Private Black colleges' encouragement of student giving and volunteerism: An examination of prosocial behavior development. *International Journal of Educational Advancement, 10*(3), 126–147.

Institute of International Education. (2012). "Top 25 Places of Origin of International Students, 2010/11–2011/12." Open Doors Report on International Educational Exchange. Retrieved from http://www.iie.org/opendoors

Ho, A. (2004). *Asian-American philanthropy: Expanding knowledge, increasing possibilities.* Paper presented at the 2004 Annual Conference of Association for Research on Nonprofit Organization and Voluntary Action (ARNOVA), Indianapolis, IN.

Newman, D. S. (2002). Incorporating diverse traditions into the fundraising practices of nonprofit organizations. *New Directions for Philanthropic Fundraising, 37*, 11–21.

O'Connor, W. J. (2007). *Factors that motivate Hispanic donors to philanthropically support higher education* (Doctoral dissertation). Retrieved from ProQuest Dissertations and Theses. (Accession Order No. AAT 3262004).

Pettey, J. G. (2002). *Cultivating diversity in fundraising.* New York, NY: Wiley.

Reaves, N. (2006). *African-American alumni perceptions regarding giving to historically Black college and universities* (Doctoral dissertation). Retrieved from ProQuest Dissertations and Theses. (Accession Order No. AAT 3223196).

Scanlan, J. B., & Abrahams, J. (2002). Giving traditions of minority communities. In M. L. Worth (Ed.), *New Strategies for educational fund raising* (pp. 197–205). Westport, CT: ACE/Praeger.

Shao, S. (1995). Asian American giving: Issues and challenges (a practitioner's perspective). *Culture of giving II: How Heritage, Gender, Wealth and Values Influence Philanthropy, 8*(Summer), 53–64.

Tsunoda, K. (2011). *Unraveling the myths of Chinese American giving: Exploring donor motivations and effective fundraising strategies for U.S. higher education* (Doctoral dissertation). Retrieved from ProQuest Dissertations and Theses. (Accession Order No. AAT 3461597).

Wagner, L., & Ryan, J. P. (2004). *Achieving diversity among fundraising professionals. New Directions for Philanthropic Fundraising, 43*, 63–70.

SECTION 2

Other Alumni Constituencies

5

WOMEN AS A DONOR GROUP TO HIGHER EDUCATION

Sara Kaiser and Amy Wells Dolan

Women in Higher Education

Welcomed later than men to most American college campuses, women found increased opportunity for higher education when institutions like Oberlin College began to admit females for collegiate-level instruction and women's colleges such as Mount Holyoke Female Seminary (1837) and Georgia Female College (1836) became established (McCandless, 1999; Thelin, 2011). When admitted to coeducation, women often encountered hostile environments where their participation was constrained and their behavior monitored (Bashaw, 1999; Gordon, 1987). Philanthropists like Josephine Louise Newcomb, who founded H. Sophie Newcomb Memorial College, and Grace Hoadley Dodge, who donated part of her estate to Teachers College, changed the landscape of higher education when they directed gifts specifically for the education of women.

Opportunity for women to attend college expanded as philanthropists appealed to other women and to the public for support of women's education, advocating for its social benefits. Women philanthropists, such as Mary Lyon, solicited contributions from other women in parts of New England to establish Mount Holyoke. Lyon made educating women a "matter of public concern" (Porterfield, 1997, p. 11). Sophia Smith left most of her estate to establish Smith College, a women's college in Massachusetts. Smith wrote in her will:

> It is my opinion that by the education of women, what are called their "wrongs" will be redressed, their wages adjusted, their weight of influence in reforming the evils of society will be greatly increased, as teachers, as writers, as mothers, as members of society, their power for good will be incalculably enlarged ...
>
> *1870, p. 10)*

Yet many women's institutions, especially those in the South, often lacked financial resources. As McCandless (1999) explained, most southern women's colleges were formed in the early 1900s to educate teachers, and only one southern college for women, H. Sophie Newcomb Memorial College for women in New Orleans, had an endowment in 1900. As turn of the 20th century higher education advanced from a historic era of university-building fueled by well-known philanthropists that included John D. Rockefeller, Leland and Jane Stanford, and Cornelius Vanderbilt, who founded the University of Chicago, Stanford in California, and Vanderbilt University in Tennessee, respectively (Thelin, 2011), the 21st-century philanthropic landscape is less dedicated to the founding of colleges and universities. Rather, upgrading facilities, supporting the student experience, and improving access to higher education captures the ingenuity of contemporary philanthropists. Although women contribute meaningfully to each of these endeavors, they are often overlooked by colleges and universities as potential donors.

Women are participating in higher education to a greater extent than ever before. Today, 57 percent of college students are women, compared to only 41 percent in 1970 (U.S. Department of Education, National Center for Education Statistics, 2011). Although women are attending college in higher numbers, women faculty are still outnumbered by their male colleagues. According to the *Almanac of Higher Education* (2011) women comprised 43 percent of full-time faculty in the fall of 2009. The percentage included faculty rank of professor, associate professor, assistant professor, instructor, lecturer, and other. At the professor level, women made up only 28 percent of the group. Still, women are making large contributions to college campuses through their enrollment as students and through their teaching, research, and service as faculty and administrators.

Not only do women comprise a large percentage of the total number of students enrolled in higher education, more women participate in today's labor force compared to four decades ago. According to the U.S. Bureau of Labor Statistics (2011) in 2009, 60 percent of women were in the labor force, up from 43 percent 40 years ago. As more women share in the nation's labor force, opportunities for women to participate in charitable giving activities expand. In this way, women have unique giving philosophies, interests, and more choices in how to give and what to support than ever before. This chapter will explore the niche of women in giving to the higher education sector, the importance of relationship building with potential women donors, the differences between married and single women donors, and the involvement of alumnae as potential donors.

Women as Givers

For decades women have given their time and talents to charitable causes from serving as leaders for their daughter's Girl Scout troop or son's Cub Scout Den, making a casserole for the funeral guild at church, or volunteering for the PTA board at their local elementary school. Today, women still donate their time and talents to causes they support, but women's philanthropy expands beyond volunteerism and small, nominal donations. For women, having the opportunity to make a difference motivates them to give when choosing to make a donation to a particular organization over another. For example, Openshaw (2002) found women to be more interested in improving life for future generations. Therefore, it is important for women to know how their gift will bring about lasting impact. Weerts and Ronco (2007) revealed that some alumni donate because of the difference the gift (or volunteer service) may have on the organization. Weerts and Ronco described this as expectancy theory and defined it as the impact that women donors perceive their gift will make on the organization. Institutions can influence those expectations by the way they campaign and market the needs of the institution.

According to the *2011 Study of High Net Worth Women's Philanthropy* (The Center on Philanthropy at Indiana University, 2011), 86 percent of high net worth women volunteered. Volunteerism can lead to a connection between a potential donor and an organization. Fostering that relationship in higher education can be a unique challenge for a university development office, but a worthwhile endeavor. According to Walton and Gasman (2008), the importance of volunteerism "is too often overshadowed in our public discourse and scholarship about philanthropy" (p. 363) as the emphasis tends to focus on financial successes rather than overall improvement of society. In this way, volunteering for special events or for service on an alumni advisory board may be a necessary entrée for women that better informs them about the organization generally and establishes a firm foundation for a long-term relationship characterized by future donations.

Relationship-building cannot be overlooked; it is an important element to women philanthropists. For example, human services organizations were more likely to receive a donation from women who had previously volunteered with the organization than those women who had not volunteered (Marx, 2000). Relative to higher education, Weerts and Ronco (2007) found that alumni who volunteer at their alma maters believe that the institution "needs their support" (p. 30), and this notion contributes to their commitment to give of their time. Additionally, Marx (2000) discovered "those who had been asked to give ... were about twice as likely to give to human services as those who had not been asked" (p. 33). Marx argued that women valued the opportunity to "improve the welfare of others" (p. 34) more so than men in the study and responded when asked to do so.

Women as potential donors have different needs and wants than their male counterparts, and it is important to meet the needs of both men and women donors. Often this means approaching women in a different way than male donors. According to Webber-Thrush (2008), fundraising professionals in education need to focus on women as givers. Many women who were first generation law and business school students are now in a position where they are able to give to education and they tend to give in large numbers. In fact, for many women education is their preferred cause to give. The good news is that today, women have more power to give as their professional opportunities are expanded from previous generations (Webber-Thrush, 2008).

Relationship Building with Women Donors

Relationship building stands out as a key component for building constituencies and for fostering future donations at any institution of higher learning or charitable organization. Rosso (2003) explained that an important mix of three measures—namely linkage, interest, and ability characterize "likely donors," motivating them to support organizations at higher levels over time (p. 44). With the increase of women attending college and the increase of women in the U.S. labor force, the opportunity to create linkages to institutions, interests in specific causes, fostered with the understanding of financial ability, there is an increased opportunity for women to become major donors. For fundraising professionals it is important to recognize and acknowledge the moment a women becomes a participant in the organization whether through attendance, volunteer opportunity, family connection, or employment, as they are potential donors.

Many avenues exist for building relationships between women and institutions. Once a relationship is established, the opportunity exists to further cultivate that relationship into a charitable gift. Networking or "friend-raising," as Salopek (2008) described, further cultivates the relationship between a potential donor and an institution. Women want to know all of the pieces of the puzzle before they decide how or where to give (Openshaw, 2002). Mesch, Brown, Moore, and Hayat (2011) found that women respond more positively to the emotional appeal to give than do men. For fundraisers, understanding and making a connection to that emotion is important when asking women for donations.

Relationship building varies by institution type and by each individual woman. One of the most recognizable relationships institutions can form with individuals is through their governing board. Historically, women have been underrepresented on college boards. According to Chamberlain (2008), male members dominated the boards of even the elite women's colleges in their early history. Increased relationship-building can occur by asking women to serve on college governing boards, alumni councils, or professional panels. Once women are selected to serve on an institutional board, it is valuable to utilize their strengths. Chamberlain cautioned that while women's memberships on boards have increased, they are still underrepresented and underutilized. Strong relationships between potential donors and institutions can help match needs of the institutions with the vision of the donor. Developing relationships and getting women to commit to a gift may take time. Hall (2005) advised fund-raisers often acknowledge, "most women take a long time to decide whether to give" (p. 7). Weerts and Ronco (2007) found that those alumni who are asked to serve on boards are typically older and more established in their careers; so this will manifest differently for women than men.

Regardless of how long it takes for a woman to decide to give, the relationship with that individual made the gift possible. According to the *2011 Study of High Net Worth Women's Philanthropy,* (The Center on Philanthropy, 2011), the top reason woman gave was due to their personal experience with that organization. Furthermore, James (2009) learned that donors who gave to charitable organizations and volunteered were more likely to leave a charitable estate gift.

Besides board members, one of the strongest relationships an institution can facilitate is through alumni donors. According to the U.S. Bureau of Labor Statistics (2011), 23.4 percent of women between the ages of 18 and 23 hold bachelor's degrees compared to only 14.3 percent of men in the same age group. Reaching out to alumni is a critical component for higher education development offices, especially among younger alumni. Developing a strong relationship with early career alumni can translate into a long-established giving relationship and may lead to an increased level of giving as the donor's career becomes established. This also comes with nuance for gender, as Matthews (1991) found that women give more nominal gifts ($10–$250 range) to their alma maters while men contribute more major gifts. At a time when state support is decreasing for public institutions, alumnae can use their connections and personal relationships to influence support in other areas including foundations, and even legislative connections (Weerts & Ronco, 2007) and this too contributes to the institution.

For women, one of the most influential factors on whether to give to an organization or not is determined by the connection the organization has on an individual level, or through a connection with family or friends (The Center on Philanthropy, 2011). For development offices, there is an opportunity to build relationships with non-alumni givers including parents of students—a situation not lost on many universities as evidenced by the increased number of parent programs and services.

College development offices often see an improved relationship with alumnae when the development officer approaching them is a woman (Matthews, 1991). Unfortunately, according to Joslyn (2010), women are less likely to hold the top fund-raising job in charitable organizations. Gasman, Drezner, Epstein, Freeman, and Avery (2011) found that those women who are in nonprofit leadership roles were exposed to philanthropic giving and volunteerism throughout their life up through taking their leadership role. As Baby Boomers begin to retire, there is an opportunity to increase diversity in fundraising offices and on institutional governing boards. New opportunities may also exist to hire women fundraisers to cultivate alumnae over time, starting with outreach to young alumni.

The Power of the Bequest

Bequests are becoming a popular giving option for many women. A report by Schervish and Havens (2001a) that examined some of the wealthiest households in the United States, found that 89 percent of participants had a written estate plan. According to a year-end report conducted by the *Chronicle of Philanthropy* (2012), the most generous donor in 2011 was heiress Margaret A. Cargill. Cargill gave a bequest of $6 billion to two separate foundations supporting the arts, environment, and various disaster relief efforts (Di Mento & Preston, 2012). Cargill's example shows that higher education fundraisers may see long-term results from renewed attention to the area of planned giving with women donors.

There are other generational differences development offers should consider when working with potential women donors. Bequests continue to be a popular way for women to give. Salopek (2008) suggested that women who were born during the Great Depression may still be frugal with their finances and, if they do give, are more likely to support causes their husbands valued. As a result, Kaminski (2003) found that some institutions are receiving more bequests from women living through the Great Depression when the institution was important to their husband. According to Shaw-Hardy and Taylor (2010), the women from this "traditionalist" generation may not be comfortable with public acknowledgement of their gift "unless it is in the family or spouse's name" (p. 71). To help this generation of women feel comfortable making a gift, Shaw-Hardy and Taylor recommend encouraging bequests. After husbands die, many widows are left with an estate and the ability to decide to where the money will be donated. Often, those widows leave the money to causes or programs the husband supported, not the programs closest to them (Matthews, 1991). Women of this generation may also limit their giving to scholarships and not to meet operational costs.

Baby Boomer women, born between 1946 and 1964, are the "largest and best educated generation in U.S. history" (Shaw-Hardy & Taylor, 2010, p. 76). Shaw-Hardy and Taylor described the Baby Boomer women as a group who want to ensure that their gifts make an impact and that the recipient organization demand accountability for how the money is spent. Moreover, many Baby Boomers have established their own wealth and tend to be "very socially conscious and empowered by philanthropy" (Salopek, 2008, n.p).

Generation X women, born between 1965 and 1979, tend to be cautious with their monetary funds as they are quite aware of the volatility of the economy. Women of this generation are tech savvy. Shaw-Hardy and Taylor (2010) stated that to engage Generation X women, utilizing social media to keep women involved can be a useful tool in making connections with them as potential donors.

The issues of intergenerational wealth transfer will be an important topic for development officers to watch. Webber-Thrush (2008) projected that women will control more of the wealth as it is passed between generations in the next 50 years. Havens and Schervish (1999) estimated a wealth transfer of $41 trillion by the year 2052, possibly more. Furthermore, Schervish and Havens (2001c) found 22 percent of those among the highest wealth categories in the United States unconfident about the financial security of their heirs—and different vehicles for planned giving, like charitable lead trusts, could be a way to gain participation without sacrificing the well-being of heirs.

As discussed earlier, women tend to donate to causes where they can see the impact of their donation. However, as Openshaw (2002) described, it is important that women remain financially stable, thus bequests are a unique giving option that is popular with women donors. Communicating with women donors about the various giving opportunities available is important to build a strong and trusting relationship to further cultivate a charitable gift through a bequest or an estate gift.

For campus fundraisers and those who assist women with planning their charitable estate giving, it is important to understand the intergenerational transfer of wealth that will be happing in the United States. According to Webber-Thrush (2008), "women are expected to control a disproportionate share of the projected $41 trillion that will pass from one generation to the next over the next 50 years in the United States" (n.p.). For fundraising offices, providing women with information and resources on how their gift can support and change experiences for students can be a valuable tool in growing potential estate gifts.

When families, and especially women, are concerned about their own economic stability, bequests and estate gifts are a more secure way for donors to still ensure their financial stability, yet support an important cause. Schervish and Havens (2001b) explained that the more wealth and income increase, planned giving becomes the preferred method of giving to charitable organizations. Perhaps the volatile economy of the last few years has created a level of uncertainty for women to donate. According to *Giving USA* (2012) bequeathed gifts rose 12.2 percent in 2011. Of all gifts by individuals, charitable bequests accounted for 8 percent of all total gifts in 2011, approximately the same level from 2010. Havens and Schervish (1999) found that in estate giving the more valuable the estate the higher the percentage goes to charity.

Charitable organizations are also dependent upon the economic times and the ability of others to give. Marx (2000) found women listed affordability as a "reason for not contributing more money to charitable causes" (p. 31). The economic challenges facing the United States have affected colleges and universities in their fundraising endeavors, budget allocations, and spending habits. For public colleges and universities, philanthropic donations have become an important funding source especially as funding from state allocations decreased. Some institutions have been counting on private donors for decades to fill the gap in college budgets, and those donors are no longer only male givers (Matthews, 1991). As Elliott (2006) called the newest millionaires in the United States the "new breed of givers" (p.15), assuredly women comprise the ranks of this new breed.

Men versus Women

The overall college experience can impact a donor's decision to give back to his or her alma mater. Academic and major choices and campus engagement can be factors in determining a gift to the institution. Overall, more women than men are attending college, but there are gender gaps in certain academic disciplines. Women are significantly more likely to pursue a degree in education compared to men (Sax & Arms, 2008). Men are more likely to major in engineering and business. Furthermore, Sax and Arms found that women are more likely to come "from families with lower socioeconomic status and parental education" (p. 42) than are male students when entering college, therefore, women reported they are more worried about financing their tuition.

Women are making a financial impact in the workforce and in their homes. In 1970, only 4 percent of women earned an income that exceeded their husband's, but by 2007 that number rose to 22 percent. Coincidently, the percentage of women who had a higher education level than their husband's rose from 20 percent in 1970 to 28 percent in 2007 (Fry & Cohn, 2010). With more financial means than ever before, women cannot be ignored in campaigns to promote giving opportunities at colleges and universities. The "ask" needs to help women understand the impact their gift has on the organization—both in the short and long term.

Although there has been discussion on the motivational factors that influence women to give, Levine (2007) argued it does not matter if women want to be more creative with the use of their funds or address social change. What is important is that women are included in the conversation in major giving campaigns and are educated about the opportunities to give. Most importantly, Levine found women must be asked to give. Shaw-Hardy and Taylor (2001) recommended that when soliciting married couples, it is important to ask both the husband and the wife about their wishes to give. Women valued the opportunity to see their financial contribution make a difference in the lives of others rather than support operating costs of an organization (Marx, 2000).

Regardless of the reasons women choose to support a cause, knowing what kind of recognition, if any, a donor wishes to receive is important. According to Levine (2007), the need for public recognition varies among women. It may seem that men are celebrated for their monetary donations more than women, but studies have indicated that women are more generous in their giving as anonymous donors than men (Eckel & Grossman, 1998; Kamas, Preston, & Baum, 2008). However, according to Kamas et al. (2008), "an individual who cares about social image may increase giving once another person knows the amount of the gift" (p. 27). Communicating the recognition options available to the donor will provide the donor the opportunity to decide how she best wants to be acknowledged for her gift.

Married? Who Decides?

The definition of "family" has changed over time. The dynamics of giving decisions are different for each family, and each individual person. For colleges and institutions, it is important to know how women make their giving decisions within their own family. One could expect that married women tend to give more than single women, partly because they are more likely to have dual-incomes with their partner. Their social and philanthropic circle may also be enhanced from networking opportunities with their partner. However, the trend over the last two decades has seen women getting married later in life, if at all. According to a study by the Pew Research Center (2010), marriage rates have fallen from 72 percent in 1960 to 52 percent in 2008. In 2008, 64 percent of the population who had a college degree or higher were married compared to 48 percent who had a high school diploma or less. As a fundraiser, it is important to reach married and single women in meaningful ways at all levels of the giving spectrum. In a study by The Center on Philanthropy at Indiana University, Mesch (2010) found "female-headed households are more likely to give to charity than male-headed households" (p. 4). Reaching out and focusing energies on female-headed households can expand the donor base and generate gifts from a population of women willing and able to give.

A study by *Giving USA* (2012) found that gifts to the education sector have risen slightly over 10 percent in the last two years (2009 to 2011). In married households where women are the main decision maker in determining whether or not to give to education, that household is "much more likely to give to education" (Rooney, Brown, & Mesch, 2007, p. 238). In the same study, Rooney et al. found that level of education by both the husband and the wife "positively associated with the amounts donated to education" (p. 238). Moreover, couples with a higher level of educational attainment are "more likely to make joint decisions" (Andreoni, Brown, & Rischall, 2003, p. 127) on giving. Here especially, women's influence within the family may result in increased attention to giving to higher education.

Conclusion and Recommendations

The commitment and value of women in higher education is immeasurable. The philanthropic giving from women comes in many forms including advocacy, volunteerism, and financial gifts. Including women in all solicitation efforts strengthens the relationship between the institution and women by showing the value women bring to the organization. The manner in which women are addressed is a vital component in soliciting donations (Shaw-Hardy & Taylor, 2010). For example, women want to be addressed by their own name. Materials that are mailed to the family home should include the woman's name on the envelope. It is important that women see themselves in the materials through photographs, in the stories of giving, by generation, and in giving level. Furthermore, women need to be included on the institutional side of fundraising. Women must be more than figure heads on alumni and fundraising boards, and women must be on alumni and development office staffs.

Moreover, women want to know how their gifts will impact the organization. Providing a clear picture of that usage can enable women donors to have a vision for their gifts. Additionally, allowing women to understand the needs of the institution, the demographics of the students, and the opportunities for change brought by their gift can help establish a connection between the needs of the institution and the emotion and wishes of the donor. Developing a strong understanding and relationship to meet the common goals of both parties is essential to a positive donor relationship.

Finally, as discussed, it is important for women to feel financially secure. Bequests are a rising option for women to give to causes that matter to them the most without sacrificing their financial security during their lifetime. Providing opportunities for women to plan their estate gifts is a useful tool for institutional fundraisers. Providing outlets for women to gather information on important causes, to understand the legal and tax implications of their gift, and, most importantly, to know how their gifts will have a lasting impact are important to strengthen bequest giving by women. Table 5.1 summarizes suggested strategies for engaging women in philanthropic activities.

Determining how a woman donor's relationship with a higher education institution will unfold begins when women first establish a relationship with the institution characterized by many linkages—often as a student, then graduate turned alumni, but also as an employee, a non-alumni spouse or partner, or even a non-alumni parent or member of the community. Her personal response and relationship to the institution will deepen as she feels a growing sense of personal involvement and respect as a future "major donor" of time, talent, and treasure. President Bill Clinton wrote in his book *Giving* (2007), "the example of how much money we could give also applies to gifts of time, skills, things, reconciliation, and new beginnings. If we just all gave according to our ability, the positive impact would be staggering" (p. 206). Women can have a powerful and meaningful impact on college and universities through various gifts. Approaching women consistently with sincerity and a sense of personal relationship and respect will strengthen rapport so that a long-term relationship becomes established and nurtured over time. For women, this is a necessary condition that unlocks the power of a multitude of their unique gifts.

TABLE 5.1 Strategies for Engagement of Women in Philanthropic Activities

Recommendation	Strategies for Implementation
Include women in all fundraising materials and activities.	• Marketing pieces should include photographs and stories of women donors and women as recipients. • Generational differences should be addressed. • Seek to promote a stronger emotional response and involvement for women in collateral materials and at events. • Work to include women faculty, staff, non-alumni spouses or partners and parents as vital contributors to the institution.
Demonstrate and provide a clear picture of how the gift has an impact on the organization.	• Clearly articulate the needs of the institution to help potential donors understand how their gift may address those needs. • Include various gift levels that allow smaller gifts and constancy in giving to be recognized as important to the institution. • Provide accurate information on current student demographics including financial need of students. • Provide information about strategic plans and goals to keep donors informed over time.
Provide meaningful opportunities for women to be involved in the institution.	• Consider the gender make-up of the institutional governing board, alumni board, or other councils on campus. Increase diversity and responsibility levels as necessary. • Review annual giving lists to generate prospects for increased attention from key personnel. • Ask parents and other non-alumni prospects to participate and deepen involvement. • Increase the number of women working with alumni and in development.
Women are potential donors, but only if they are asked to give.	• Create educational opportunities for women to understand and benefit from planned giving; include discussion of family and responsibilities so as to hear their concerns. • Create opportunities for women to leave bequests. • Talk to women about their history and experience with the institution; find out more about their interests and what is important to them. Ask them to directly support their interests in meaningful ways over time. • Cultivate women's networks and networking skills to enhance contacts and learn more about the community. • Treat all women as future major donors, giving care and respect over time.

References

Almanac of Higher Education. (2011). Chronicle of Higher Education (2011). *Percentage of full-time faculty members by sex, rank, and racial and ethnic group, fall 2009.* Washington, DC: Author.

Andreoni, J., Brown, E., & Rischall, I. (2003). Charitable giving by married couples: Who decides and why does it matter? *Journal of Human Resources, 38*(1), 111–133.

Bashaw, C. T. (1999). *Stalwart women: A historical analysis of deans of women in the South.* New York, NY: Teachers College Press.

Center on Philanthropy at Indiana University, The. (2011). *The 2011 study of high net worth women's philanthropy and the impact of women's giving networks.* Retrieved from http://philanthropy.iupui.edu/Research/docs/2011BAC_HighNetWorthWomensPhilanthropy.pdf

Chamberlain, M. K. (2008). Women as trustees. In A. Walton & M. Gasman (Eds.), *Philanthropy, volunteerism & fundraising in higher education* (pp. 528–541). ASHE Reader Series. Boston, MA: Pearson.

Chronicle of Philanthropy. (2012). Philanthropy 50. Retrieved from http://philanthropy.com/article/A-Look-at-the-50-Most-Generous/130498/

Clinton, W. (2007). *Giving: How each of us can change the world.* New York, NY: Random House.

Di Mento, M., & Preston, C. (2012, February 6). College benefactors lead 'Philanthropy 50' rankings of 2011's top donors. *Chronicle of Higher Education.* Retrieved from http://www.chronicle.com

Eckel, C. C., & Grossman, P. J. (1998). Are women less selfish than men?: Evidence from dictator experiments. *The Economic Journal, 108*(448), 726-735.

Elliott, D. (2006). *The kindness of strangers: Philanthropy and higher education.* Lanham, MD: Rowman & Littlefield.

Fry, R., & Cohn, D. (2010). New economics of marriage: The rise of wives. Retrieved from Pew Research Center Publications website: http://pewresearch.org/pubs/1466/economics-marriage-rise-of-wives

Gasman, M., Drezner, N. D., Epstein, E., Freeman, T. M., & Avery, V. L. (2011). *Race, gender, and leadership in nonprofit leadership.* New York, NY: Palgrave Macmillan.

Giving USA: The annual report on philanthropy for the year 2011. (2012). Chicago, I: Giving USA Foundation. Retrieved from http://www.givingUSAreports.org

Gordon, L. D. (1987). The Gibson girl goes to college: Popular culture and women's higher education in the progressive era, 1890–1920. *American Quarterly, 39*(2), 211–230.

Hall, H. (2005). Power of the purse. *Chronicle of Philanthropy, 17*(9), 7–10.

Havens, J. J., & Schervish, P. G. (1999). *Millionaires and the millennium: New estimates of the forthcoming wealth transfer and the prospects for a golden age of philanthropy.* Retrieved from Boston College, Social Welfare Research Institute website: http://www.bc.edu/content/dam/files/research_sites/cwp/pdf/m_m.pdf

James, R. N., III. (2009). Health, wealth, and charitable estate planning: A longitudinal examination of testamentary charitable giving plans. *Nonprofit and Voluntary Sector Quarterly, 38*(6), 1026-1043.

Joslyn, H. (2010). Women and minorities lag in getting top fund-raising jobs. *Chronicle of Philanthropy, 22*(17), 16.

Kamas, L., Preston, A., & Baum, S. (2008). Altruism in individual and joint-giving decisions: What's gender got to do with it? *Feminist Economics, 14*(3), 23-50.

Kaminski, A. R. (2003). Women as donors. In H. Rosso & E. R. Tempel (Eds.). *Hank Rosso's achieving excellence in fund raising* (2nd ed., pp. 200-214). San Francisco, CA: Josey-Bass.

Levine, N. (2007, September). Closing remarks: He gave, she gave. *Currents: Council for Advancement and Support of Education.* Retrieved from http://www.case.org/Publications_and_Products/2007/September_2007/Closing_Remarks_He_Gave_She_Gave.html

Marx, J. D. (2000). Women and human services giving. *Social Work, 45*(1), 27–38.

Matthews, A. (1991, April 7). Alma maters court their daughters. *New York Times Magazine,* pp. 40, 73, 77-78.

McCandless, A. T. (1999). *The past in the present: Women's higher education in the twentieth-century American South*. Tuscaloosa: The University of Alabama Press.

Mesch, D. J. (2010). *Women give 2010*. Center on Philanthropy: Indianapolis, IN. Retrieved from http://www.philanthropy.iupui.edu/womengive/docs/womengive2010report.pdf

Mesch, D. J., Brown, M. S., Moore, Z. I., & Hayat, A. D. (2011). Gender differences in charitable giving. *International Journal of Nonprofit and Voluntary Sector Marketing, 16,* 342–355.

Openshaw, J. (2002, March). Pulling their own purse strings: Advancement officers can better court women by understanding their attitudes and knowledge about wealth. *Currents: Council for Advancement and Support of Education*. Retrieved from http://www.case.org/Publications_and_Products/2002/March_2002/Pulling_Their_Own_Purse_Strings.html

Pew Research Center. (2010). The decline of marriage and rise of new families. Retrieved from http://pewresearch.org/pubs/1802/decline-marriage-rise-new-families

Porterfield, A. (1997). *Mary Lyon and the Mount Holyoke Missionaries*. New York, NY: Oxford University Press.

Rooney, P., Brown, E., & Mesch, D. (2007). Who decides in giving to education? A study of charitable giving by married couples. *International Journal of Educational Advancement, 7*(3), 229–242.

Rosso, H. E. (Ed.). (2003). *Hank Rosso's achieving excellence in fund raising* (2nd ed.). San Francisco, CA: Jossey-Bass.

Salopek, J. J. (2008, October). Raising her sights: Which development strategies work best with women? Savvy institutions take up the challenge. *Currents: Council for Advancement and Support of Education*. Retrieved from http://www.case.org/Publications_and_Products/2008/October_2008/Raising_Her_Sights.html

Sax, L. J., & Arms, E. (2008). Gender differences over the span of college: Challenges to achieving equity. *Journal About Women in Higher Education, 1*(1), 23–48.

Schervish P. G., & Havens, J. J. (2001a). *Extended report on the wealth with responsibility study/2000*. Retrieved from Boston College Center on Wealth and Philanthropy website: http://www.bc.edu/content/dam/files/research_sites/cwp/pdf/wwr1.pdf

Schervish, P. G., & Havens, J. J. (2001b). Wealth and the commonwealth: New findings on wherewithal and philanthropy. *Nonprofit and Voluntary Sector Quarterly, 30*(1), 5–25.

Schervish, P. G., & Havens, J. J. (2001c). The mind of the millionaire: Findings from a national survey on wealth with responsibility. *New Directions for Philanthropic Fundraising, 12,* 75–107.

Shaw-Hardy, S., & Taylor, M. A. (2010). *Women and philanthropy: Bolding shaping a better world*. San Francisco, CA: Jossey-Bass.

Smith, S. (1870). *Last will and testament of Sophia Smith*. Smith College Archives. Retrieved from http://clio.fivecolleges.edu/smith/sophia/found/found.htm

Thelin, J. R. (2011). *A history of American higher education* (2nd ed.). Baltimore, MD: The Johns Hopkins University Press.

U.S. Bureau of Labor Statistics. (2011). *BLS spotlight on statistics: Women at work*. Retrieved from http://www.bls.gov/spotlight/2011/women/pdf/women_bls_spotlight.pdf

U.S. Department of Education, National Center for Education Statistics. (2011). *Fast facts: Enrollment*. Retrieved from website: http://nces.ed.gov/fastfacts/display.asp?id=98

Walton, A., & Gasman, M. (2008). Volunteerism: Service to campus and society. In A. Walton & M. Gasman (Eds.), *Philanthropy, volunteerism & fundraising in higher education* (pp. 363–369). ASHE Reader Series. Boston, MA: Pearson.

Webber-Thrush, D. (2008, October). A gift of her own: Women wield more financial power than ever-and their strength is growing. What does it mean for educational philanthropy? *Currents: Council for Advancement and Support of Education*. Retrieved from http://www.case.org/Publications_and_Products/2008/October_2008/A_Gift_of_Her_Own.html

Weerts, D. J., & Ronco, J. M. (2007). Profiles of supportive alumni: Donors, volunteers, and those who "do it all." *International Journal of Educational Advancement, 7*(1), 20–34.

6

ALUMNI GIVING IN THE LGBTQ COMMUNITIES

Queering Philanthropy

Jason C. Garvey and Noah D. Drezner

Introduction

Philanthropy scholars and practitioners have traditionally understood higher education alumni giving through the experiences of people with majority identities (e.g., White, middle-class, heterosexual, and male; Drezner, 2011). With declining financial support from donors, coupled with decreasing federal and state resources for college and universities, advancement officers must begin recruiting and retaining diverse alumni that they have previously not engaged. Unfortunately, though, there exist barriers for advancement officers to create meaningful relationships with alumni from marginalized communities.

People with minority identities may feel disenfranchised and shunned from mainstream nonprofit organizations because of prior experiences. This barrier rings especially true for alumni and their relationships with their alma maters (Gasman, 2002; Gasman & Anderson-Thompkins, 2003; Gasman, Drezner, Epstein, Freeman, Avery, 2011; Sanlo, 2002; Smith, Shue, Vest, & Villarreal, 1999). Minority alumni have unique histories with their colleges and universities, sometimes making it difficult for them to look past negative and marginalizing experiences to create meaningful connections and mutually beneficial relationships with their alma maters. Further, advancement staff often evoke discomfort and fear within minority communities because of their limited knowledge of marginalized identities and cultural differences (Drezner & Garvey, 2012a; Newman, 2002).

Regardless, though, if higher education institutions are to continue garnering increased alumni support, advancement officers must build their capacity to attract and serve donors from more diverse backgrounds. Institutions that diversify their practices and internal structures will better position themselves to serve a more diverse constituency and increase both alumni engagement and philanthropic support. The success and effectiveness of advancement officers' outreach depends on a willingness and ability to create philanthropic strategies that attract new and diverse populations (Gasman & Bowman, 2012; Newman, 2002). Recently, philanthropy scholars have begun examining differences in perceptions and patters of giving in marginalized communities to create effective and empirically sound practices.

People in underrepresented communities understand giving differently than do individuals with dominant identities. As such, advancement staff must recognize the unique motivations and reasons for giving among diverse donors, as they are likely different than those of majority donors. For example, marginalized individuals often give to non-profit organizations that provide uplift and support within their communities and for their interests (Scanlan & Abrahams, 2002). Diverse donors express an importance in seeing organization leadership that is inclusive of people with similar identities and beliefs to their own.

There is a strong case to increase multicultural competency and practices to improve donor relationships and maximize giving among marginalized donors. While scholars have begun examining the unique experiences of diverse donors, most research has concentrated on giving among racial and ethnic minority communities (e.g., Gasman, 2002; Gasman & Anderson-Thompkins, 2003; Smith et al., 1999). Advancement officers have yet to consider groups with other marginalized identities as vibrant communities of prospective donors. One such group that has received limited attention from both researchers and advancement staff is lesbian, gay, bisexual, transgender, and queer (LGBTQ) alumni.

Similar to racial and ethnic minority communities, giving and volunteering has played an essential role in serving LGBTQ people. However, virtually no research exists to understand motivations and patters of giving among LGBTQ donors, making it difficult for organizations to develop effective fundraising practices (Institute for Gay & Lesbian Strategic Studies, 1998). "Research on LGBT issues in education and higher education must be supported and valued by institutions and committees, primarily because, in the big picture of research, there is so little on LGBT issues in education and especially in higher education" (Sanlo, 2002, p. 176). Colleges and universities should embrace and seek to understand the philanthropic attitudes of LGBTQ alumni in order to broaden their donor base.

LBGTQ Philanthropy

The LGBTQ community is a growing but often overlooked segment of the population in terms of philanthropy. Historically, LGBTQ people have given funds and donated time to help create and sustain organizations that directly serve their community. In both theory and practice, though, there is little literature to guide fundraisers when working with this specific population. Despite a level of commitment and support to their community, there is a dearth of empirical research on the giving patters and motivational factors of LGBTQ people.

To address the scarcity of research, we conducted an extensive research project examining philanthropy and giving among LGBTQ higher education alumni. As there is little scholarship examining LGBTQ alumni experiences, throughout our project we relied heavily on philanthropy scholarship within diverse communities. Specifically, much of our question construction and theoretical framing was adapted from literature examining fundraising and philanthropic giving in historically underrepresented and underserved communities. For the research study, we employed a constructivist epistemology. A constructivist worldview relies on participants' perspectives within bounded systems, understanding the context and experiences of both the institutions and individuals involved (Creswell, 2007). We employed a multi-institutional case study methodology (five institutions; three private and two public), enabling us to reveal the intricacies behind the effectiveness of the diverse practices, policies, and materials at each institution and commonalities and differences across cases. Data collection involved a two-tier approach, interviewing both advancement officers (71 participants) and LGBTQ alumni (30 participants). We employed team-based analysis (MacQueen, McLellan, Kay, & Milstein, 1998), conferring trustworthiness through data triangulation (Stake, 2000) and member checking.

The following sections introduce philanthropy among and towards LGBTQ people broadly, utilizing findings from our study on LGBTQ alumni giving and insight from additional scholarship. Specifically, we highlight motivations for giving among LGBTQ people, as well as benefits and barriers with engaging LGBTQ alumni. The chapter closes with recommendations for advancement staff in addressing these barriers for working with LGBTQ alumni.

Motivations for LGBTQ People to Give

As previously stated, prior philanthropy scholarship largely understood motivations for giving through White, wealthy, and heterosexual men (Drezner, 2011). For the most part, this literature did not account for cultural and identity-specific philanthropic motivations, therefore ignoring other identities, namely marginalized and oppressed individuals. A growing, yet narrow, body of literature has begun exploring motivations to give philanthropically among LGBTQ individuals and other marginalized communities. Broadly, these studies approach motivations in two general categories: community uplift and salient aspect of identity (Drezner & Garvey, 2102a; Horizon Foundation, 2008). The following section will adopt these broad categories of giving to discuss motivations among LGBTQ people, incorporating and integrating scholarship across several bodies of work.

Community Uplift

For many marginalized communities, members often engage in philanthropic giving as a form of social uplift and obligation through providing services and opportunities (Carson, 2008; Gasman, 2002; Gasman et al., 2011; Smith et al., 1999). People from disenfranchised and marginalized communities prefer to support organizations that uplift their communities and/or support interests that are centrally important to them (Scanlan & Abrahams, 2002). Cultivation and engagement grows within marginalized communities when advancement staff highlight advocacy work that enacts social change, illustrating the short- and long-term goals and impact of the college and university's worth on the marginalized group (Gasman & Anderson-Thompkins, 2003; Smith et al., 1999).

In recent decades, LGBTQ communities have become more visible and accepted in mainstream American society, developing a socially cohesive shared identity through similar lived experiences (Vaid, 1995). In the 1960s and 1970s small, community-based alternative foundations emerged as a direct result to LGBTQ communities' public commitment to social justice and change (Gallo, 2001; Vaid, 1995). Consequently, there has been a rapid growth of LGBTQ financial support for public service organizations over the past few decades to respond to community needs and demands. Outside of LGBTQ communities, however, there are relatively few external funding sources for LGBTQ-focused services. As such, individuals find it important to uplift their communities through charitable contributions (Kendell & Herring, 2001). For example, women within one lesbian giving community donated 87 percent of their general funds to organizations that sponsored lesbian projects (Magnus, 2001). A Horizons Foundation (2008) study found similar patterns among San Francisco donors towards LGBTQ-related causes and non-profits. However, scholars know little about motivations for LGBTQ giving outside of LGBTQ-related organizations, including to higher education.

Anecdotally, some LGBTQ alumni are interested in giving money directly to benefit LGBTQ individuals at their alma maters, with many gifts taking the form of large donations and endowments. University of Pennsylvania alumnus David R. Goodhand and his partner Vincent J. Griski gave $2 million to the LGBT Center. In discussing the motivation behind their giving, Goodhand commented that "When I think about influencing change in society, there are a number of mainstream organizations that have their hearts in the right place—that have a sense of mission and I want to help them" ("Couple Gives," 2000, p. A34). Many LGBTQ alumni give to their alma mater to provide social uplift by making their institutions more welcoming and affirming for LGBTQ students, faculty, and staff (Drezner & Garvey, 2102a). Accordingly, colleges and universities are likely to increase engagement among these alumni when they communicate the institution's commitment to act in a socially responsible manner (Waters, 2009). Indeed, "organizations must demonstrate through their actions that they are worthy of supportive attitudes and behaviors" (Kelly, 2001, p. 285). In our study on LGBTQ higher education alumni philanthropy, we interviewed LGBTQ alumni from varying institutions. Many of the donors in our study gave to support LGBTQ students and uplift on campus, with alumni creating endowed and current-use scholarships to support openly LGBTQ students on at their alma mater (Drezner & Garvey, 2012a).

Salient Aspect of Identity

LGBTQ identities are largely invisible in philanthropic scholarship and practice. Few studies have examined LGBTQ alumni and the salience of their identities on their philanthropic giving. In our focus groups with both advancement staff and LGBTQ alumni at various colleges and universities, we discovered unique and often unconscious aspects of LGBTQ identities that influence alumni giving to one's alma mater (Drezner & Garvey, 2012a).

Throughout our interviews, when directly asked if their sexual or gender minority identity affected their philanthropic giving towards their alma mater or non-profits more generally, most participants simply said, "no." However, when delving into their philanthropic priorities and reasons for supporting or not supporting their alma mater, many of their philanthropic priorities involved supporting LGBTQ communities (Drezner & Garvey, 2012a).

One gay male alumnus proclaimed his philanthropic giving was not connected to his sexual identity, saying "I'm single. I have no children. My siblings do not need money. My estate is going to charities … That's more of the reasoning rather than being gay, or lesbian, or whatever" (Drezner & Garvey, 2012a, p. 19). However, when speaking about his giving to his alma mater, he mentioned that he created a scholarship within the university's athletic program to support an openly LGBTQ athlete. This alumnus did not feel that his sexual identity affected his motivations to give, yet his giving was clearly for the purpose to support and uplift a student within the LGBTQ community.

For some alumni, their LGBTQ identities were a factor in their giving because they wanted to promote a welcoming and affirming community for current LGBTQ students. Similarly, though, these alumni did not consciously believe their LGBTQ identities impacted their motivations to donate to their alma maters. One alumnus stated, "I know I would definitely not give to [my alma mater] if there was ever some type of press release or something that was negative or anti-gay … I would be more militant not to give if I knew it was a non-affirming school" (Drezner & Garvey, 2012a, p. 19). Another study participant said that "If my university isn't being supportive of me for who I am, then I'm not gonna support my university … I believe strongly in not sitting at the back of the bus" (Drezner & Garvey, 2012a, pp. 19-20).

Alumni in our study also discussed that they withheld gifts to their alma mater based on campus climate and level of affirmation of their LGBTQ identities. One gay male alumnus, who also served as the alumni relations staff member for LGBTQ alumni outreach, said that "I think if there have been some really negative experience relating to my sexual identity, that would probably factor in [to my giving to my alma mater], but as it is not at all" (Drezner & Garvey, 2012a, p. 20). Similarly, another participant discussed that he chose not to donate to his alma mater after experiencing isolating and chilly campus experiences as an openly gay business student. Both of these alumni determined their philanthropic giving to their alma mater based on their perceptions of campus equity.

Benefits and Barriers in Engaging LGBTQ Alumni

There are inherent benefits and barriers when considering philanthropy and charitable giving within LGBTQ communities. The following section will discuss why LGBTQ alumni would be desirable donors to solicit, as well as possible challenges for working with LGBTQ alumni.

Benefits

As previously discussed, members of marginalized communities often engage in philanthropic giving as a form of social uplift and obligation through providing services and opportunities (Carson, 2008; Gasman, 2002; Gasman et al., 2011; Smith et al., 1999). This holds true within the LGBTQ communities as well. In her study on lesbian philanthropists, Gallo (2001) discussed that "our struggles for liberation are part of a broader social change agenda ... So we also give to coalitions that challenge racism, sexism, and homophobia, poverty, and the growing economic divide" (p. 67). A recently retired professor gave $2,000 to provide financial support for the GLBT Research Center at the University of Colorado at Boulder. Many LGBTQ alumni give to their alma mater to make their institutions more welcoming and affirming for LGBTQ students, faculty, and staff. Donations provide more access to services and resources unique and greatly needed among LGBTQ individuals. In celebration of their twenty-fifth anniversary as a couple, Bruce Fisher and his partner, both graduates of Macalester University, donated $25,000 to their alma mater to support speakers on gay and lesbian topics and provide financial support for LGBTQ students to attend academic conferences (Strosnider, 1997). More and more colleges and universities are establishing—through alumni, faculty, and staff support—emergency scholarship funds for LGBTQ students who in the coming out process are rejected and no longer financially supported by their parents (Drezner & Garvey, 2012a; Point Foundation, 2010).

LGBTQ people often have unique financial circumstances, making them attractive candidates for giving financially. In their research, DeLozier and Rodrigue (1996) showed that LGBTQ individuals are strong prospects for substantial philanthropic giving due to their high discretionary income levels and a common difficulty to easily bequeath large portions of their estates to their loved ones due to current laws not recognizing their relationships. As indicated, development and alumni relations officers should view LGBTQ alumni as favorable candidates for donating to their alma maters.

Barriers

Scholars have documented the prevalence of discrimination on college campuses for LGBTQ students (Bieschke, Eberz, & Wilson, 2000; Brown, Clarke, Gortmaker, & Robinson-Keilig, 2004; Reason & Rankin, 2006). Recently, Campus Pride released the 2010 State of Higher Education for LGBT People (Rankin, Blumenfeld, Weber, & Frazer, 2010). Surveying 5,149 LGBTQ students, staff, faculty, and administrators across all 50 states and all Carnegie Basic Classifications of Institutions of Higher Education, this comprehensive examination gave voice to individuals marginalized on college campuses due to their sexual orientation, gender expression, and gender identity. Their findings illuminated negative experiences for LGBTQ individuals, from subtle to extreme forms of discrimination at higher education institutions. Among their discoveries, the report indicated that LGBTQ respondents experienced significantly more amounts of harassment and discrimination than their heterosexual and majority gender peers. These results indicate that LGBTQ students are at a higher risk than their peers for experiencing conduct that interferes with their ability to thrive on campus. Results also demonstrate that access to resources (e.g., LGBTQ centers, inclusive curriculum, student organizations) can improve students' sense of belonging on campus.

Becoming an active LGBTQ alumnus or alumna is an exciting and encouraging way for many individuals to (re)connect with their alma maters. Finding a positive avenue for becoming involved in the university helps alleviate resentment created from experiences of discrimination and marginalization. In our study examining LGBTQ alumni philanthropy, numerous participants discussed the importance of LGBTQ alumni affinity groups on their engagement and giving behaviors. Several participants in our study acknowledged that their overall giving to the university was higher because of their involvement and inclusion in the LGBTQ alumni group (Garvey & Drezner, 2012).

However, current students and alumni who identify as LGBTQ often express frustration for their institutions not recognizing or celebrating their sexual and gender identity with alumni engagements. Few campuses make thoughtful efforts to reach out to the LGBTQ communities to gain insights into their philanthropic giving. This gives the message to alumni that their alma mater is not interested with investing in and giving back to the LGBTQ communities (Scanlan & Abrahams, 2002).

Visibility among LGBTQ communities is difficult because it is not realistic to determine a person's sexual orientation and gender identity based on his or her appearance or performance. People who identify as LGBTQ may regulate their visibility through nonverbal strategies, such as the use of the body, gay cultural symbols, props, and even silence (Lasser & Wicker, 2008). Thus, institutions have difficulty in identifying members of the LGBTQ communities without self-identification. Universities rarely gather information from alumni that classify their sexual and gender identity. Recruitment and outreach efforts therefore cannot use records to concentrate on specific people within the LGBTQ communities.

In examining data collection techniques for LGBTQ alumni, we found that institutions struggle with whether and how to collect LGBTQ demographic information (Drezner & Garvey, 2012b). Most advancement offices use donor-centricity as a guiding principle, understanding the importance of discovering the personal stories of alumni and donors. Yet, advancement staff in our study exhibited confusion and unwillingness to collect identity-based data. One staff member said, "I would never put something in there about—it would never even come up about like someone's sexual orientation." To further compound the issue, staff members expressed frustration with campus partnership limitations in sharing databases, particularly among student affairs staff. As such, staff could not rely on student involvement data (e.g., LGBTQ student organizations, safe space training) to identify LGBTQ alumni. Many staff in our study therefore relied on self-identification, shadow databases, and limited efforts because there was no systemic LGBTQ university data collection. Regarding the data limitations, one staff commented that "We probably should be thinking about this differently, and are there things that we're doing that are creating barriers unnecessarily ... From a business standpoint, I realize that we might be shortsighted."

Recommendations for Practice

As previously stated, there is a significant lack of research that evaluates experiences and perceptions of LGBTQ alumni. Thankfully, practical applications have surfaced in our study and can be inferred from other marginalized communities to provide insight to recruiting and retaining LGBTQ alumni. The following section outlines practical approaches, paying particular attention to the strong connections within their respective communities, experiences of discrimination based on their social identity, and social uplift. Table 6.1 provides a brief outline of our recommended practices to engage LGBTQ alumni.

Community Connections

When working with LGBTQ alumni, it is important to foster trust and reliability. One way of effectively creating trust is to begin by involving those people who already have a positive, pre-existing relationship with the college or university. By asking people who are already engaged in alumni relations and are donors to take on a leadership role within the alumni community, staff can begin to widen the circle of trust and relatedness through networking and intentional outreach. For example, two alumni in our study served on their university's alumni advisory board. By engaging LGBTQ representatives in committees and boards, institutions demonstrate a commitment to diverse communities by increasing their visibility within influential circles and allow the LGBTQ communities to have a vocal advocate during institutional decisions.

Another way to foster trust is to increase visibility of LGBTQ individuals in print materials. Alumni communications staff can demonstrate a commitment to LGBTQ people by highlighting same-sex marriages, civil unions, and commitment ceremonies alongside other celebrations in the alumni magazines. Promotional materials, particularly for family and alumni reunions, should celebrate the diversity of family structures, including LGBTQ family images and stories.

Because many alumni staff may be unfamiliar with diverse communities, it is important to become more knowledgeable about specific cultures and values. Development officers and alumni staff must make thoughtful efforts to reach out to LGBTQ communities to learn from them, and to emphasize that their college or university is determined to give back and support the vitality of the donor's community (Kendell & Herring, 2001; Scanlan & Abrahams, 2002). Further, effective fundraisers in diverse communities must be aware of cultural sensitivities and varying meanings and values (Newman, 2002). Advancement offices may consider partnering with LGBTQ resource centers on campuses when staff are unfamiliar with LGBTQ language and cultures. Through safe zone training and inclusive language programs, advancement officers can become more comfortable and confident with LGBTQ community engagement.

When engaging perspective donors for personal solicitations, it is important to maintain an involved and reciprocal relationship. Like with all prospect engagements, staff should ask donors what organizations they are involved in, support, and why, so that further understand the donor. Many advancement officers in our study mentioned that they hesitate to record in their notes, prospect's and donor's involvement in LGBTQ organizations. These community involvements should be recorded as they are aspects of the alumnus/na's persona that they are sharing with the advancement officer and can be used in building the best engagement strategy and strongest solicitation in the future.

Inclusion Strategies

Becoming an active LGBTQ alumnus has been an exciting and encouraging way for many individuals to (re)connect with their alma mater. Many LGBTQ people experienced perceptions of discrimination and marginalization, and finding a positive way to become involved in the university could help alleviate resentment from past experiences of discrimination. Advancement offices should include alumni of diverse identities in all significant events so that they become a more active presence within the alumni community. Through inclusive outreach, offices will build trust and mutual respect (Scanlan & Abrahams, 2002). Participating in alumni events will give LGBTQ alumni a sense of ownership and identity in the university. One potential way to engage LGBTQ alumni is through events at homecoming, reunion, and family weekends that highlight the different LGBTQ student groups on campus. Should an institution's alumni weekends feature symposia or receptions, staff may consider having a panel that addresses any faculty research on queer-related topics followed by a reception so that alumni can network with each other and current students can meet alumni who also identify as LGBTQ.

Development officers and alumni staff should feel comfortable interacting in diverse settings with an array of people (Scanlan & Abrahams, 2002). An appreciation and understanding of LGBTQ cultures can help foster trusting relationships. Staff may want to attend festivals and celebrations within LGBTQ communities, both locally and within regions with high concentrations of alumni. Additionally, institutions may consider co-sponsoring joint programs with community organizations that directly benefit LGBTQ individuals.

Regarding data collection, advancement staff will likely receive the most information through community engagement, particularly during LGBTQ festivals and celebrations. Advancement staff might consider staffing a booth at local pride parades and celebrations to garner alumni and donor interests, and to collection important and relevant data. These data may be used to code LGBTQ identities and/or create listservs for future events and targeted solicitations.

Uplift Strategies

LGBTQ communities place emphasis on uplifting people within their community through social justice and mutual aid. To partner with these communities, development and alumni offices should integrate values of diversity, inclusion, and equity into their central mission (Gasman & Bowman, 2012, 2013; Newman, 2002). To do so requires sustained action and intentional strategies when addressing systemic issues within the office. Such endeavors will call for a commitment from the university, specific offices, and individuals in order to be successful. Resources of people, time, and money must be allocated to uplift and diversify the mission of development and alumni offices. Once this has been demonstrated to LGBTQ communities, then collaboration will likely be successful.

Conclusion

Neither empirical nor practitioner literature has extensively examined LGBTQ alumni philanthropy. This dearth of scholarship examining this unique population leaves advancement practitioners vulnerable to ineffective and culturally insensitive practices. While there are inherent barriers to cultivating and soliciting LGBTQ higher education alumni, the benefits far outweigh the concerns. LGBTQ alumni have unique motivations to give in relation to their desire for community uplift and recognizing their sexual and gender minority identities.

TABLE 6.1 Recommendations to Overcome Barriers and Engage LGBTQ Alumni

Barrier	Recommendation
Past or present experiences of discrimination distance LGBTQ alumni.	• Highlight ways in which alumni gifts can make their alma mater more welcoming and affirming for LGBTQ individuals. • Demonstrate how alumni can reconnect to alma mater in positive way and alleviate resentment from past experiences through volunteering and/or donating. • Create LGBTQ affinity group to increase participation and sense of belonging. • Create a panel during alumni weekend that addresses faculty research on LGBTQ-related topics followed by a networking reception.
Lack of data collection for LGBTQ identities.	• Partner with other campus units (e.g., multicultural office, LGBTQ student services, admissions) to share student and alumni databases. • Create systemic LGBTQ university data collection across varying departments, particularly in student affairs and admissions. • Staff a booth at local pride parades and celebrations to garner alumni and donor interests, and collect important and relevant data.
Difficulty in gaining trust among LGBTQ alumni.	• Involve people who have a positive, pre-existing relationship with institution. • Include LGBTQ representatives in committees and boards. • Increase visibility of LGBTQ individuals in print materials. • Co-sponsor joint programs with community organizations that directly benefit LGBTQ individuals.
Staff are unfamiliar with LGBTQ community cultures and traditions.	• Partner with LGBTQ resource centers to offer advancement staff safe zone training and inclusive language programs. • Record LGBTQ community involvements and share information with advancement staff to build the best engagement strategies and strongest solicitations. • Attend festivals and celebrations within LGBTQ communities, both locally and within regions with high concentrations of alumni.

References

Dieschke, K. J., Eberz, A. B., & Wilson, D. (2000). Empirical investigations of the gay, lesbian, and bisexual college student. In V. A. Wall & N. J. Evans (Eds.), *Towards acceptance: Sexual orientation issues on campus* (pp. 31–58). Washington, DC: ACPA

Brown, R. D., Clarke, B., Gortmaker, V., & Robinson-Keilig, R. (2004). Assessing the campus climate for gay, lesbian, bisexual, and transgender (LGBT) students using a multiple perspective approach. *Journal of College Student Development, 45*, 8–26.

Carson, E. D. (2008). Black philanthropy's past, present, and future. In A. Walton, M. Gasman, (Eds.), *Philanthropy, volunteerism & fundraising in higher education* (pp. 774–777). Upper Saddle River, NJ: Pearson.

Couple gives U. of Pennsylvania $2-million for gay center. (2000). *The Chronicle of Higher Education*, p. A34.

Creswell, J. W. (2007). *Qualitative inquiry & research design* (2nd ed.). Thousand Oaks, CA: Sage.

DeLozier, M., & Rodrigue, J. (1996). Marketing to the homosexual (gay) market: A profile and strategy implications. *Journal of Homosexuality, 31*, 203–212.

Drezner, N. D. (2011). *Philanthropy and Fundraising in American Higher Education.* San Francisco, CA: Jossey-Bass.

Drezner, N. D., & Garvey, J. C. (2012a, April). *(Un)Conscious queer identity and influence on philanthropy towards higher education.* Presented at the Annual Meeting of the American Educational Research Association, Vancouver, B.C., Canada

Drezner, N. D., & Garvey, J. C. (2012b, April). *When best practice and discomfort collide: The discord between donor centricity and data collection with LGBTQ alumni.* Paper presented at the American Educational Research Association, Vancouver, B.C., Canada.

Gallo, M. M. (2001). Lesbian giving — and getting: Tending radical roots in an era of venture philanthropy. *Journal of Lesbian Studies, 5*, 63–70.

Garvey, J., & Drezner, N. D. (2012, April). *Advancement staff and alumni advocates: Leaders in engaging LGBTQ alumni.* Presented at the Annual Meeting of the American Educational Research Association, Vancouver, B.C., Canada

Gasman, M. (2002). An untapped resource: Bringing African Americans into the college and university giving process. *CASE International Journal of Educational Advancement, 2*(3), 280–292.

Gasman, M., & Anderson-Thompkins, S. (2003). *Fund raising from Black college alumni: Successful strategies for supporting alma mater.* Washington, DC: Council for the Advancement and Support of Education.

Gasman, M., & Bowman, N. (2012). *A guide to fundraising at historically Black colleges and universities an all campus approach.* New York, NY: Routledge.

Gasman, M., & Bowman, N. (2013). *Engaging Diverse College Alumni: The Essential Guide to Fundraising.* New York, NY: Routledge.

Gasman, M., Drezner, N. D., Epstein, E., Freeman, T. M., & Avery, V. L. (2011). *Race, Gender, and Leadership in Nonprofit Organizations.* New York, NY: Palgrave Macmillan.

Horizons Foundation. (2008). *Building a new tradition of LGBT philanthropy.* San Francisco, CA: Author.

Institute for Gay & Lesbian Strategic Studies. (199)8. *Creating communities: Giving and volunteering by gay, lesbian, bisexual, and transgender people.* Amherst, MA: Author.

Kelly, K. S. (2001). Stewardship: The fifth step in the public relations process. In R. L. Heath (Ed.), *Handbook of public relations* (pp. 279–289). Thousand Oaks, CA: Sage.

Kendell, K., & Herring, R. (2001). Funding the National Center for Lesbian Rights. *Journal of Lesbian Studies, 5*, 95–103.

Lasser, J., & Wicker, N. (2008). Visibility management and the body: How gay, lesbian, and bisexual youth regulate visibility nonverbally. *Journal of LGBT Youth, 5*(1), 103–117.

MacQueen, K. M., McLellan, E., Kay, K., & Milstein, B. (1998). Codebook development for team-based qualitative analysis. *Cultural Anthropology Methods Journal, 10*(12), 31–36.

Magnus, S. A. (2001). Barriers to foundation funding of gay organizations: Evidence from Massachusetts. *Journal of Homosexuality, 42*, 125–145.

Newman, D. S. (2002). Incorporating diverse traditions into the fundraising practices of non-profit organizations. *New Directions for Philanthropic Fundraising, 37*, 11–21.

Point Foundation. (2010). *Point Foundation annual report 2009–2010*. Los Angeles, CA: Author.

Rankin, S., Blumenfeld, W. J., Weber, G. N., & Frazer, S. (2010). *State of higher education for LGBT people*. Charlotte, NC: Campus Pride.

Reason, R. D., & Rankin, S. R. (2006). College students' experiences and perceptions of harassment on campus: An exploration of gender differences. *College Student Affairs Journal, 26*, 7–29.

Sanlo, R. (2002). Scholarship in student affairs: Thinking outside the triangle, or Tabasco on cantaloupe. *NASPA Journal, 39*, 166–180.

Scanlan, J. B., & Abrahams, J. (2002). Giving traditions of minority communities. In M. L. Worth (Ed.), *New strategies for educational fund raising* (pp. 197–205). Westport, CT: ACE.

Smith, B., Shue, S., Vest, J. L., & Villarreal, J. (1999). *Philanthropy in communities of color*. Bloomington: Indiana University Press.

Stake, R. E. (2000). Case studies. In N. K. Denzin & Y. S. Lincoln (Eds.), *Handbook of qualitative research* (2nd ed., pp. 435–454). Thousand Oaks, CA: Sage.

Strosnider, K. (1997). Gay and lesbian alumni groups seek bigger roles at their alma maters; Some colleges welcome the involvement and gifts, but other institutions are wary. *The Chronicle of Higher Education, 44*(2), A59-A60.

Vaid, U. (1995). *Virtual equality: The mainstreaming of gay and lesbian liberation*. New York, NY: Anchor Books.

Waters, R. D. (2009). The importance of understanding donor preference and relationship cultivation strategies. *Journal of Nonprofit & Public Sector Marketing, 21*(4), 327–346.

7

FUNDRAISING FROM DOCTORAL ALUMNI

Going Beyond the Bachelor's

Anita Mastroieni

The vast majority of institutions of higher learning in the United States produce most of their alumni at the associate's or bachelor's degree level. However, for the more than 400 U.S. institutions that grant doctoral degrees, there is a potential source of alumni giving that is growing. According to the National Science Foundation's *Doctorate Recipients from U.S. Universities: 2010* (2011), over 49,000 individuals received research doctorates in 2010–11. Further, this report demonstrates a relatively consistent growth in the number of new research doctorates awarded annually for the past 50 years.

Unfortunately for most doctoral-granting institutions, doctoral[1] alumni giving does not match that of undergraduate alumni giving. The *2009 Voluntary Support of Education* report (Kaplan, 2010) showed that individuals are more likely to support the institution that granted them an undergraduate degree than they are to support the institutions from which they received graduate degrees.

Lagging Ph.D. alumni giving represents a loss of potential voluntary support for doctoral-granting institutions. The question with which most fundraisers grapple is why doctoral alumni do not give at similar rates as undergraduate alumni. Most Ph.D. students are enrolled in their doctoral programs as long as or longer than undergraduate students are enrolled in their bachelor's programs. Simple logic would follow that the institutional loyalty and commitment demonstrated through alumni giving should be the same or stronger among Ph.D. alumni as among undergraduate alumni, due to time on campus as a Ph.D. student relative to time a undergraduate student. Clearly, however, this is not the case.

Duronio and Loessin (1991) tell us that "one of the few general rules to be gleaned from our research is that fund raising must capitalize on the ...

untapped potential of institutions" (p. 224). Ph.D. alumni giving represents "untapped potential" for doctoral-granting institutions. In this study, I examined the motivations of existing doctoral alumni donors, demonstrating how alumni and fundraising activities can be specifically structured to promote this giving.

Literature Review

In order to better conceptualize issues around motivations for doctoral alumni giving, I reviewed literature related specifically to graduate alumni giving and more generally to donor motivations.

Graduate Alumni Giving

Most of the existing research referenced on alumni philanthropy looks only at undergraduate alumni giving, or does not differentiate between undergraduate and graduate alumni giving. However, Poock and Siegel (2005) surveyed graduate school fundraising practices and found that "graduate schools are in a relatively nascent stage of development activity" (p. 16). The difficulties facing graduate school fundraising are many. Graduate deans—generally the schools' chief fundraisers—do not represent any single discipline and therefore have no "clear constituency" (p. 12). Furthermore, few graduate school respondents to the survey had full-time dedicated development officers; without advancement professionals, fundraising programs are likely to be nonexistent, or organized by those with little knowledge of effective fundraising practices.

Okunade's 1996 study looked at determinants of graduate alumni philanthropy at the University of Memphis. His findings include that doctoral degree alumni have the highest giving profile among graduate school alumni; however, he includes J.D.s with Ph.D.s and Ed.D.s in this doctoral degree category. The J.D. is usually categorized as a professional degree. Since the law school experience is vastly different from doctoral education, and the earnings profiles of lawyers differ from that of Ph.D. holders, the inclusion of the J.D. in this study may be skewing this result significantly.

Pearson's (1999) work, providing market research for Stanford University, carefully separates undergraduate from graduate and professional alumni, and provides interesting comparison data on alumni giving. His surveys found that Stanford graduate alumni were twice as likely to identify with their department as with their school; therefore he recommends that fundraising appeals for graduate alumni should be department-based. When Stanford's School of Engineering adopted this strategy, there was a 44 percent increase in participation and a 28 percent increase in money raised. Additionally, Pearson recommends that communications to graduate alumni use a "two-tiered" approach, providing both school-wide messages for all alumni as well as more focused departmental news (p. 12). Pearson also found if offered online services, both undergraduate and graduate alumni primarily wanted to connect with classmates and their school or department.

Donor Motivations for Giving

Much of the research on philanthropy relies on rational choice models to explain motivations for donating. Rational choice theory asserts that individuals choose what they believe to be the best and most efficient means to achieve their goals. Under rational choice theory, donors are believed to gain something tangible, such as benefits to the community, or intangible, such as a measure of satisfaction, by giving to charity. Sun, Hoffman, and Grady (2007) believe that alumni donors "derive utility from the services provided by the recipients" (p. 311).

Related to rational choice theory is social exchange theory, which is also used frequently to explain donor motivations. George Homans (1958) developed social exchange theory in the late 1950s:

> Social behavior is an exchange of goods ... Persons that give much to others try to get much from them, and persons that get much from others are under pressure to give much to them. This process of influence tends to work out at equilibrium to a balance in the exchanges.
>
> *(p. 606)*

Cook and Lasher (1996) found that fundraising is based on "social exchange processes" (p. 38), which assumes interdependence between individual donors and institutions. Therefore, alumni can be motivated to give if they attribute their success to their education, or if they garner prestige by being associated with the university's campaign.

Other researchers found that donor motivations can be both selfish and altruistic (Frank, 1996; Kelly, 2002). According to Kelly, "The mixed motive model of giving describes two levels of donor motivation: (1) raising the amount of common good ... and (2) receiving some private good in return ..." (p. 46). Mixed motives are evident when generous donors support a worthy cause and also want their name attached to the target of their philanthropy.

Specifically looking at alumni philanthropy, several studies show that satisfying educational experiences can positively impact alumni attachment, which impacts motivation to give (Gallo & Hubschman, 2003; Monks, 2003; Pearson, 1999; Sun et al., 2007). Researchers have identified several specific attributes of a satisfying educational experience that seem to predict higher levels of giving. These include having a mentor and/or interactions with faculty outside of class (Clotfelter, 2003; Monks, 2003), earning one or more degrees from an institution (Pezzullo & Brittingham, 1993), and receiving financial aid (as opposed to loans) (Monks, 2003; Pezzullo & Brittingham, 2001).

Methodology

Relying on the few studies about graduate philanthropy and the theories about donor motivations, I structured a study to uncover the distinct motivations behind doctoral alumni giving and to demonstrate that a unique fundraising approach is required to appeal to these nontraditional donors. According to Kelly (2002), "Seeking simplistic answers to who will give and who will not denies the complexity of the problem and is unrealistic" (p. 49). Therefore, I conducted in-depth qualitative interviews with doctoral alumni donors from the University of Pennsylvania and reviewed institutional development data, which included information on lifetime giving by each donor, funds to which they directed donations, fundraising officers assigned to donors (if any), etc.

My goal was to give voice to the donors so they could articulate their distinct, complex motivations for giving to their doctoral alma mater. I chose the University of Pennsylvania as the site of my study because Penn is a large research university that produces, on average, 410 doctorates each year, thus providing a rich sample of Ph.D. alumni from which to choose. Nine different schools at Penn offer Ph.D. programs, and each has a separate development and alumni relations infrastructure, making comparisons of Ph.D. alumni giving across schools difficult. I therefore chose to focus on only one school: Arts & Sciences, which confers the largest number of Ph.D.s each year.

I used purposeful sampling—deliberately selecting particular subjects to achieve variation in the sample (Marshall & Rossman, 1999; Maxwell, 1996)—and identified doctoral alumni givers from a variety of disciplines, age groups, geographic areas, occupations, and giving profiles.

I began with the list of School of Arts & Sciences doctoral donors and removed alumni who received more than one degree from Penn, as well as alumni who worked at Penn, in order to minimize the impact of non-doctoral Penn experiences on the data. Next, I isolated donors who had a pattern of giving over time, making donations annually or semiannually for at least 10 donations. My goal was to highlight donors who had ongoing commitments to the university, as these were obviously more valuable to the institution. This effectively excluded any alumni who graduated recently, as they did not have time to establish a pattern of giving.

In 2008–09, I contacted more than 80 donors, requesting their participation in the study. Over time, 24 individuals agreed to be interviewed (see Table 7.1). An additional donor declined to be interviewed but instead sent me a detailed e-mail outlining his reasons for giving—then discontinuing his giving—to Penn. Fifteen interviews were conducted in person and nine were conducted over the phone.

The number of discrete gifts per donor ranged from 10 to 67, made annually or semiannually. Their individual donations ranged from $10 to $100,000. The majority, however, were giving $50 to $100 per donation. Total lifetime giving among the participants ranged from $700 to $600,000.

TABLE 7.1 Mix of Discipline/Career/Gender Characteristics among 24 Participants

		Social Sciences/Humanities	Natural Sciences
Female donors	**work in academia or research**	Jennifer Manley (Sociology)[1] Rosemarie Moyer (History) Leslie Trainor (Sociology)	Christine Titterton (Chemistry) Sarah Prince (Biology) Denise Waters (Math)
Male donors	**work in academia or research**	Robert Finter (Sociology) Harry Jones (American Civilization) Frank Idamarco (Archeology) Walter Dunbar (English)	Joseph Andrews (Geology) John Lambino (Physics) Christopher Meehan (Biochem) Edward Klein (Physics)
	work in industry	Richard Johnson (American Civilization) Marc Simmons (Economics)	Adam Ludwig (Geology) Sam Baker (Physics) Aaron Carroll (Chemistry) Ben Dillon (Chemistry)
	work in both	David Fenton (Economics) Robert Kramer (Economics)	James McMaster (Chemistry) Daniel Cheung (Math)

1 Pseudonyms are used to protect the identity of participants. In addition, other identifying information—such as undergraduate institution, employers, etc.—has been masked.

I crafted interview questions relying on Sun et al.'s (2007) work that found multiple variables predict alumni giving: satisfactory student experiences, satisfactory alumni experiences, donor motivations, as well as specific demographic variables. Accordingly, my interview questions included the participant's experience as a student, as an alumnus/a, and as a donor. Student experience questions included topics such as time to degree, faculty mentoring, stipend support, adequacy of doctoral training, career preparation, and involvement in campus life. Alumni experience questions included topics such as attending alumni activities, volunteering for the university, reading alumni publications, and visiting campus. Finally, questions about the donor's motivations delved into why the donor makes gifts, how the gifts are designated, the effectiveness of fundraising materials, and the donor's other giving habits.

Findings Related to Doctoral Donor Motivations

When asked why they give to Penn, three themes emerged. By far, most doctoral alumni demonstrated the social exchange theory of donor motivation, citing gratitude and indebtedness for the support they received as grad students as their primary motivation. Second, a few donors wanted to see themselves as making an impact with their giving, thereby demonstrating rational choice theory. Finally, many donors showed mixed motives, with several demonstrating an internalized expectation to give back in addition to social exchange or rational choice motivations, citing it as the "right thing to do."

Social exchange motivations for giving stem exclusively from the donors' experiences as students, and not from their experiences as alumni. Donors— even those who graduated decades ago—vividly recalled classmates, faculty, campus eateries, lab work, library research, and socializing at local bars and restaurants. Most of these same donors have little or no connection with the university currently. All but one donor in my study received full tuition and stipend from Penn, and the desire to "give back" in recognition for the financial support was the overriding motivation for their current donations. Since these donors have few existing associations with university, the desire to help current students, or to further the university's agenda, did not provide strong motivations for their giving.

Robert Finter (Sociology 1990) is among the majority of donors who demonstrated social exchange theory as motivation. He told me, "I've always felt in some ways I owe Penn more than I owe (my undergraduate school) ... I feel indebted to the school for the way it supported me." Walter Dunbar (English 1966) told me, "Part of my motivation for contributing is that I always kind of thought I wanted to give that money back. I think I have by now, but the habit is there." Many donors used the word "scholarship," a word that is largely absent in current doctoral education terminology. Marc Simmons (Economics 1978) said, "It was the first time I ever received a scholarship ... It was a luxury in a sense to be able to attend a school like Penn and have it paid for." The findings of Pezzullo and Brittingham (1993) and Monks (2003)—that receiving financial aid contributes to greater student satisfaction and later alumni giving —are demonstrated in these statements.

Several donors also cited faculty mentoring as the factor for which they are most indebted. For these donors, good advisors and mentors created a positive student experience and helped to establish a successful career. Daniel Cheung (Mathematics 1978) told me, "Dr. Valluri was my thesis advisor and my mentor and I'm grateful to him for his mentoring and his way of doing research. Part of the success that I have comes from his input in mentoring me." These donor sentiments reflect the findings of Clotfelter, Ehrenberg, Getz, and Siegfried (1991) and Monks (2003) that faculty interaction and mentoring contributes to greater student satisfaction and alumni giving.

There were alumni in my study who had less than optimal student experiences due to poor faculty mentoring, and yet were still donating regularly, but they ascribed their giving behavior to gratitude for the stipend alone. However, there is an impact of unsatisfactory student experiences: The donors in the study who have the ability to give significantly more but do not are, without exception, those with negative student experiences. Leslie Trainor (Sociology 1977), whose advisor sexually harassed her, explained that she has the capacity to give much more, but does not. "I feel so bad but I just don't want to give them more money. So it's like a token. I give significant sums to (other charities)." Likewise Robert Kramer (Economics 1989) has the ability to give more, but his dissatisfaction with the lack of mentoring and encouragement he received as a student is also expressed with small donations compared to this ability. On the other hand, there were other donors in the study who had very satisfactory experiences and who were giving small amounts, but those amounts reflected their ability. All of the major donors in my study—those giving discrete gifts of $5,000 or more—had three things in common: capacity, gratitude for receiving financial support, and positive doctoral experiences.

Donors motivated by social exchange theory often also demonstrated an internalized expectation to give. This internalized expectation was able to override negative experiences in graduate school for certain donors. When I asked Robert Kramer (Economics 1989) why he donated at all, he told me, "There's a social responsibility to give back."

The rational choice theory of charitable motivation applied to those donors who are primarily interested in making an impact with their giving. These donors derive satisfaction in believing that their donations are making a difference to the institution receiving them. Aaron Carroll (Chemistry 1961) told me, "Not that I'm really close to the university, but it's one of the outstanding universities in the country, if not the world, and everybody likes to support a winner." Interestingly, most of the donors motivated by rational choice theory used it as a reason to give less to Penn (believing their giving had little impact at a large institution) or to discontinue giving to Penn (believing their suspended donations would make an impact). The donors giving less were designating the bulk of their giving to their smaller undergraduate institutions. However, they were giving some amount to Penn because of the internalized expectation to give back. Jennifer Manley (Sociology 1980) said, "The amount of money that we're able to give makes a big difference to (my undergraduate school). It does not or would not make a big difference to Penn … Penn was great but it's huge and very wealthy." Nevertheless, she does give a small amount Penn "because we just believe we should give something back."

Findings Related to Alumni Relations and Fundraising Practices

My interviews also uncovered several interesting findings about fundraising and alumni relations conventions that should prove useful to practitioners looking to engage doctoral alumni. Most alumni reported that while they were students, they were not instilled with an expectation to give or to be involved after graduation. Sarah Prince (Biology 1975) said, "I don't think there was any discussion when I was at Penn about our responsibility as alumni."

There was no consistency among study participants' giving patterns to undergraduate institutions. Some donors gave more to their undergraduate alma maters than to Penn, some gave less, some gave the same, and some gave nothing to their undergraduate schools. Nevertheless, it is commonly accepted that alumni will always donate more to their undergraduate institutions. Marc

Simmons (Economics 1978) told me that he was advised by university offi-
cials to designate his donations to undergraduate scholarships partly because
"undergrads were the only reliable future donors." This belief is so persistent
that Dr. Simmons followed this advice, despite the fact that he gives less to his
undergraduate school than to Penn. Certainly, the aggregate data from Penn
show that undergraduate alumni give more (measured both by participation
and amount) than graduate alumni, but there are enough exceptions to question this logic when approaching individual alumni.

Half of the donors in my study began donating to Penn more than five years
after their graduation. Most participants cited economic reasons—wanting to
"get back on their feet" financially—for this lag. There is an opportunity cost
to attending a doctoral program in the form of foregone income for four or
more years, as well as potential accumulation of student loans, which likely
contributes to the delay in contributions (Okunade, 1996).

The donors overwhelmingly felt that alumni activities, particularly regional
alumni events, were geared to undergraduate alumni, and therefore they did
not attend. Edward Klein (Physics 1966) said, "You know, I'm on the list and
I get these invitations for Penn alumni events here … but I just, I kind of feel
that it's largely for the people who have undergraduate degrees." John Lambino
(Physics 1989) told me, "They are setting up a (local) alumni group … but
I realize I'm an outlier in that group in that I was a graduate student." This
widely held perception creates a self-fulfilling situation: If graduate alumni
don't attend because they feel the events are for undergraduate alumni, then in
reality they become strictly undergraduate alumni events.

In addition, doctoral alumni identify not with the students with whom they
graduate, but with their entering cohort within the department. However, the
graduation year identification is almost uniformly applied to all alumni at most
institutions. Since doctoral students move through their programs at individual
paces, members of the same entering cohort may graduate over a span of three,
four, or more years. Therefore, it is somewhat meaningless to identify doctoral alumni as members of the Class of 1990, for example, when those graduates probably entered in—and therefore identify with—different years. Sarah
Prince (Biology 1975), whose husband graduated from the Penn Dental School,
told me "I don't go to my reunion ever because I don't feel like I was part of a
class. We go to his because he felt very much part of his class." Marc Simmons
(Economics 1978) said, "I haven't shown up to alumni events … because at
Penn I wasn't a member of a class. It's a different kind of feeling there."

Most donors acknowledged that their real connection is with their department. Christine Titterton (Chemistry 1993) told me,

> If my experience is typical, most of the time you spent at Penn was depart-
> ment specific … I come back and I have interactions with people in the
> Chemistry department. I visit every few years and give a seminar. I have

good ties to the department. I can't think what else would attract me back there or encourage me to socialize with Penn alumni closer to home.

Many of the donors echoed this sentiment. When asked if she could envision alumni activities that she would attend, Rosemarie Moyer (History 1991) replied, "The way I'd want to be involved is seeing former classmates." John Lambino (Physics 1989) told me, "If they just created Facebook groups for the physics classes … maybe a bigger Penn graduate alumni group like that." Pearson (1999) also found that alumni would like institutional online offerings to help them connect with classmates and departments.

On the other hand, several donors expressed frustration that there was no outreach from their departments. Leslie Trainor (Sociology 1977) told me, "There's no attempt to get me involved, to get me engaged in some intellectual way that I could give back." Alumni who are engaged by the institution are more likely to donate than those not engaged (Sun et al., 2007; Webb, 2002); therefore this lack of outreach can have negative ramifications for the institution.

Three donors in my study had stopped giving over a disagreement with an administrative action, such as closing an academic department. Each of these former donors held a rather myopic view about the specific action, its effect on the overall operation of the university, and the effect of their discontinued donations. Each believed that he was sending a message with his absent donations. In reality the administrative action in each case likely reaped more economic benefit for the university than lost donations. On the other hand, there were discontented donors who maintained a more global perspective and continued giving despite disagreements with the institution. For example, Harry Jones (American Civilization 1973) was unhappy when the university closed his department: "That's when my support fell. But then I hooked up with some people in the History department and began to send them some checks …"

Recommendations for Practice

In this study, doctoral donors' motivation fit within our understanding of social exchange theory and, in fewer cases, by rational choice theory. However, most donors were using rational choice theory as a justification for giving less to the University of Pennsylvania. Therefore, fundraisers would be wise to appeal to the social exchange motivations behind doctoral giving. Because the social exchange motivations for doctoral alumni giving are particularly specific—gratitude and indebtedness for Ph.D. funding and positive student experiences (mostly centered on faculty mentoring)—a distinct fundraising approach is required for doctoral alumni. Approaches that traditionally work for undergraduate alumni fundraising will not be as effective. Instead, appeals to doctoral alumni should focus on reminding donors of the support they received as doctoral students and how that support enabled their ability to attend graduate school and contributed to their careers. Also, including tailored information about departments and faculty will likely garner additional attention from recipients.

In addition to receiving funding, several donors cited indebtedness for positive faculty mentoring as a motivator for donating. Therefore, engaging faculty in doctoral alumni fundraising efforts will likely produce results for fundraising officers. Determining which faculty have good reputations as mentors with many advisees, and establishing funds in their honor, may well be a productive initiative. Faculty milestones could provide a rationale for creating these funds. When a faculty member wins an award or retires, for example, a fund could be established and solicitations sent to the faculty member's advisees. In addition, when a doctoral alumnus/a with high giving potential is identified, the fundraising officer should attempt to bring the prospect's mentor, or a current departmental faculty member, on the visit with the prospect. The idea of meeting with a former mentor or current faculty member may be enticing enough for the prospect to agree to a visit.

Fundraisers would do well to take a "crash course" in doctoral education at their institutions, spending time with the graduate dean, departmental chairs, graduate faculty, and current doctoral students to learn about the broad idiosyncrasies of Ph.D. education. Each time a Ph.D. prospect is identified, fundraisers need to do additional "homework," not just researching the prospect's current capacity, but also seeking to understand the prospect's time as a student: what was the departmental culture like when the prospect was enrolled, who was his/her mentor, was he/she fully-funded. The fundraiser should learn about contemporary departmental developments that may be of interest to the prospect; for example, updates on the faculty mentor or improvements to the department's facilities. In addition, fundraisers should also be well versed in any university-wide improvements to the doctoral experience (for example, increased stipends and services, family-friendly policies, etc.), so they can enthusiastically communicate improvements to potential doctoral donors.

In addition, fundraisers should approach individual doctoral alumni with the recognition that they may be willing to give as much or more to Penn than to their undergraduate alma mater. My study shows that this giving pattern is probable. A less optimistic approach may lead the donor to feel that his/her support is not valued.

Some of the doctoral alumni in my study showed delayed giving patterns, so it is important to stay in contact with doctoral alumni in the years after they graduate, even if they are not donating right away. It is not unusual for recent doctoral alumni to carry large student loans. Combined with their foregone income, these alumni may not have an immediate capacity to donate. Fundraising and alumni relations offices should strive to maintain current postal and e-mail addresses and professional information for doctoral graduates, and should use this information to stay in touch with frequent communications, publications and appeals; requests to volunteer; and invitations to appropriate doctoral alumni activities.

The donors in my study all stated that they perceived alumni activities to be for undergraduate alumni and therefore the activities were not appealing. In order to be successful, activities should be purposefully organized for doctoral alumni. Clustering doctoral alumni by entering cohorts, departments, or occupation, and organizing activities for these clusters will work much better for doctoral alumni than general offerings that are viewed as being for undergraduate alumni only. Simply hosting events specifically marketed for doctoral alumni will likely generate good will and attendance. More specific examples could include a networking event for doctoral alumni in psychology that is organized in the same city at the same time as the annual meeting of the American Psychological Association.

Departmental outreach is important to doctoral alumni, who largely associate more with their department than the university at large. Many alumni in my study genuinely wanted to be connected to their departments and faculty, and complained that there was no such outreach. Doctoral alumni could be engaged to mentor current doctoral students, give departmental colloquia, advise dissertating students, etc. These types of alumni involvements can also contribute to better experiences for current students.

Furthermore, several alumni indicated a desire for institutional online offerings to help them connect with classmates and departments. Such connections could be achieved through the creation of online communities or through the utilization of free social networking tools like Facebook. The key would be to ensure these sites are well populated with the intended audience and contain interesting and relevant content from the institution. Targeting certain alumni to join the site before heavily publicizing it to the intended audience, and identifying staff or volunteers to regularly add departmental news and information about alumni activities would ensure the success of such endeavors. Maintaining one site for every academic department may be unrealistic on a central level, but such upkeep could be relegated to each department.

Many donors demonstrated that their disposition to give to Penn was internalized when they stated that it was "the right thing to do." This idea of internalizing the expectation to be philanthropic is important not only because future donors will learn this behavior from social affiliations through family or friends, but also through institutional expectations. Donors in my study reported no recollection of anyone creating an expectation to give or be involved as an alumnus/a while they were students. This strategy is commonly employed with undergraduate students, in the form of senior gift drives, etc. Providing regular reports to current doctoral students highlighting how much money has been raised from doctoral alumni for stipends, for example, is one way to help students internalize the expectation to give. Furthermore, resurrecting the idea that doctoral students are receiving a "scholarship" and instilling an expectation to someday pay it back may help increase doctoral alumni giving since these factors are greatly influencing current donors. Finally, involving current doctoral students in alumni activities and departmental online communities will also help them to understand their roles and responsibilities as alumni.

These recommendations for departmental initiatives are not without problems. If institutions rely solely on departments to fulfill graduate alumni relations, the initiatives will become decentralized and inconsistent. Furthermore, leadership in the academic departments changes frequently, making it likely that inconsistencies will exist even within one department over time. Furthermore, most individual academic departments do not have the staff expertise to operate an effective alumni relations program, nor are they likely to make that kind of human resource investment. However, an institution could employ one staff person to handle a collection of departments—for example, all of the sciences—in order to manage these initiatives efficiently. Working through these obstacles and organizing activities that work for graduate alumni—events that are discipline-specific and draw students from a range of cohorts—and engaging them in departmental volunteer activities, would greatly increase attachment and engagement of graduate alumni.

Another strategy is to engage doctoral alumni on a central level through university-wide volunteer activities. A small number of donors in my study were engaged in interviewing prospective Penn undergrads. Most others reported they had never been asked to do this for Penn, although several were admissions volunteers for their undergraduate institutions. Doctoral alumni could be tapped more frequently to perform these types of volunteer functions especially in regions where alumni representation is scarce.

Finally, frequent communications can help to mitigate the perceptions around negative actions on the institution's part. University decisions that might cause donors to cease giving—in the examples from my study, selling the off-campus observatory or closing an academic department—could be better explained, or at least put in context of other more positive actions that might offset the one negative. If alumni are better educated about, and supportive of, the larger goals and vision of the institution, they are less likely to react badly to a single initiative. This could be achieved with quality communications about both the department and the larger institution.

Limitations

This study was limited to doctoral alumni at one elite private institution. Although the results are not generalizable to other institutions, there may be findings and recommendations that are transferable to similar institutions and should be considered by alumni relations professionals and fundraising officers as they seek ways to engage doctoral students and alumni, while simultaneously increasing income for the institution (see Table 7.2).

TABLE 7.2 Recommendations for Alumni Relations and Fundraising Practices Aimed at Better Engaging Doctoral Alumni

Recommendations	Strategies for Implementation
Appeal to social exchange motivations.	• Tailor fundraising appeals to focus on doctoral support that donors received as students and how that support enabled their ability to attend graduate school. • Tailor fundraising appeals to focus on how faculty mentoring contributed to donors' careers and successes. • Establish funds in honor of well-loved faculty members.
When approaching potential donors, be well versed in the culture of doctoral education at the university and within specific departments.	• Understand both the history and current culture of doctoral education at the institution. Communicate broad improvements to doctoral student life. • Understand the history and current culture of doctoral education within the donor's academic department. Be knowledgeable about departmental news, awards, and honors. • Be knowledgeable about current activities of the potential donor's advisor/mentor. • Involve faculty from the potential donor's academic department in visits and solicitations.
Engage doctoral alumni with targeted activities.	• Cluster doctoral alumni by entering cohorts, departments, or occupation, and organize alumni activities for these clusters. • Market activities as specific for doctoral alumni. • Create departmental volunteer opportunities for doctoral alumni, such as mentoring current doctoral students, giving departmental colloquia, advising dissertating students, etc. • Create online communities for doctoral alumni from individual academic departments. Regularly add departmental news and information about alumni activities. • Engage doctoral alumni through university-wide volunteer activities.
Engage doctoral alumni with targeted communications.	• Maintain current postal and e-mail addresses and professional information for doctoral alumni. • Provide regular publications and appeals, requests to volunteer, and invitations to appropriate doctoral alumni activities. • Communicate frequently about both departmental news as well as university-wide vision and goals.
Establish an expectation to give among current doctoral students.	• Provide regular reports to current doctoral students highlighting how much money has been raised from doctoral alumni for stipends. • Use the term "scholarship" to describe doctoral funding. • Provide annual "scholarship" reports to current doctoral students, outlining the total worth of their funding package (as applicable): stipend, tuition, health insurance, etc. • Invite current doctoral students to doctoral alumni activities and online communities.

Conclusions

Findings from this research indicate that social exchange theory can be used to motivate doctoral alumni giving. Donors in my study all cited gratitude and indebtedness for the doctoral student funding they received as their motivations for donating. However, those with both full-funding and positive doctoral experiences are likely to give more relative to their capacity. While a few donors exhibited rational choice theory by expressing a desire to make an impact with their giving, these donors often used this motivation as a rationalization to give less to the University of Pennsylvania, believing they cannot make an impact at an institution of Penn's size and wealth.

In addition, this study shows that Ph.D. alumni are eager to be involved with their doctoral institutions in appropriate ways. These findings highlight that a distinct fundraising and alumni relations approach is required for doctoral alumni. Approaches that traditionally work for undergraduate alumni will not be as effective. The idiosyncrasies of doctoral education lead to different kinds of relationships between alumni and their doctoral institutions, and universities should dedicate staff and resources to doctoral alumni fundraising in order to best serve this unique population and tap into their philanthropic motivations.

Note

1. I use the term "doctoral" to refer to Ph.D. programs only. Other types of doctorates, for example Ed.D.s, are not included in this study.

References

Clotfelter, C. T. (2003). Alumni giving to elite private colleges and universities. *Economics of Education Review, 22*(2), 109–120.

Clotfelter, C. T., Ehrenberg, R., Getz, M., & Siegfried, J. (1991). *Economic challenges in higher education*. Chicago, IL: University of Chicago Press.

Cook, W. B., & Lasher, W. F. (1996). Toward a theory of fund raising in higher education. *The Review of Higher Education, 20*(1), 33–51.

Duronio, M. A., & Loessin, B. A. (1991). *Effective fund raising in higher education: Ten success stories*. San Francisco, CA: Jossey-Bass.

Frank, R. (1996). Motivation, cognition, and charitable giving. In J. B. Schneewind (Ed.), *Giving: Western ideas of philanthropy* (pp. 130–152). Bloomington: Indiana University Press.

Gallo, P. J., & Hubschman, B. (2003 April). *The relationship between alumni participation and motivation on financial giving*. Paper presented at the Annual Meeting of the American Educational Research Association, Chicago, IL.

Homans, G. C. (1958). Social behavior as exchange. *American Journal of Sociology, 63*(6), 597–606.

Kaplan, A. E. (2010). *2009 Voluntary support of education*. New York, NY; Council for Aid to Education.

Kelly, K. S. (2002). The state of fund-raising theory and research. In M. J. Worth (Ed.), *New strategies for educational fund raising* (pp. 39–55). Westport, CT: American Council on Education and Praeger.

Marshall, C., & Rossman, G. B. (1999). *Designing qualitative research*. Thousand Oaks, CA: Sage.

Maxwell, J. A. (1996). *Qualitative research design: An interactive approach* (Vol. 41). Thousand Oaks, CA: Sage.

Monks, J. (2003). Patterns of giving to one's alma mater among young graduates from selective institutions. *Economics of Education Review, 22,* 121–130.

National Science Foundation, National Center for Science and Engineering Statistics. (2011). *Doctorate Recipients from U.S. Universities: 2010.* Special Report NSF 12-305. Arlington, VA. Retrieved from http://www.nsf.gov/statistics/sed/start.cfm

Okunade, A. A. (1996). Graduate school alumni donations to academic funds: Micro-data evidence. *American Journal of Economics and Sociology, 55*(2), 213–229.

Pearson J. (1999). Comprehensive research on alumni relationships: Four years of market research at Stanford University. In J. Pettit & L. H. Litten (Eds.), *A new era of alumni research: Improving institutional performance and better serving alumni* (pp. 5–21). San Francisco, CA: Jossey-Bass.

Pezzullo, T. R., & Brittingham, B. E. (1993). Characteristics of donors. In M. J. Worth (Ed.), *Educational fund raising: Principles and practice* (pp. 31–38). Phoenix, AZ: Oryx Press.

Poock, M. C., & Siegel, D. J. (2005). Benchmarking graduate school development practices. *International Journal of Educational Advancement, 6*(1), 11–19.

Sun, X., Hoffman, S. C., & Grady, M. L. (2007). A multivariate causal model of alumni giving: Implications for alumni fundraisers. *International Journal of Educational Advancement, 7*(4), 307–332.

Webb, C. H. (2002). The role of alumni relations in fund raising. In M. J. Worth (Ed.), *New strategies for educational fund raising* (pp. 332–338). Westport, CT: American Council on Education and Praeger.

8

EXAMINING YOUNG ALUMNI GIVING BEHAVIOR

Every Dollar Matters

Meredith S. Billings

In the current economic climate, colleges and universities are relying more heavily on support from their alumni to maintain the financial health of their institutions and to reduce costs for their current students. According to a recent survey by the Council for Aid to Education, alumni donated $7.13 billion in 2009, which comprised of 25.6 percent of the voluntary support to education. In fact, alumni are the second largest voluntary contributors followed by foundations, which donated a total of $8.24 billion in 2009 (Kaplan, 2010). Therefore, it is essential for colleges and universities to retain this financial base, to grow this source of income by targeting new alumni donors, and to strategize how to cultivate philanthropic graduates to maintain this trend of individual giving to higher education.

For many colleges and universities, young alumni represent an untapped or underutilized source of potential donors. Since young alumni typically have lower participation rates and lower giving capacity than their older counterparts, they are often overlooked in fundraising strategies. However, young alumni at many institutions of higher education represent too large of a population to be ignored. In addition, previous studies have found that current and future giving is significantly correlated with past giving behavior (Lindahl & Winship, 1992; Okunade & Justice, 1991). Monks (2003) argued, "Identifying young alumni who are more likely to give and encouraging them to do so, even in modest dollar amounts, may have significant lifetime giving effects" (p. 123). Therefore, alumni and development offices need to create effective strategies to target these potential donors and begin building lasting relationships with these individuals.

In this chapter, I examine young alumni giving behavior and describe Green Hills University's[1] approach to target this group by developing a donor prediction model. In addition to the donor model, young alumni's demographic, academic, and attitudinal characteristics are examined to explore the differences between donors and non-donors as well as the differences among different types of donors. Lastly, I study the current motivators and priorities of young alumni by focusing on their preferred solicitation methods, the likelihood of donating to particular areas within the university, and their preferred acknowledgment of their donations. Drawing from the findings of the research, I suggest several strategies to administrators and practitioners looking to target, identify, and manage young alumni donors for their campuses.

Literature Review

Typically research examining alumni giving is focused on two main areas of inquiry: institutional characteristics of colleges and universities and personal characteristics of alumni donors (Baade & Sundberg, 1996). The research on institutional characteristics focuses on academic quality (Baade & Sundberg, 1996; Leslie & Ramey, 1988), institutional prestige (Holmes, 2009; Liu, 2006), fundraising expenditures (Leslie, 1979), retention and graduation rates (Gunsalus, 2005), and financial characteristics (Gunsalus, 2005; Liu, 2006). The research on alumni examines financial capacity (Clotfelter, 2003; Dugan, Mullin, & Siegfried, 2000; Monks, 2003; Volkwein & Parmley, 1999), motivational factors (O'Malley, 1992; Volkwein & Parmley, 1999), and collegiate experiences (Clotfelter, 2003; McDearmon & Shirley, 2009; Monks, 2003; Volkwein & Parmley, 1999). This review of the literature explores the characteristics and experiences of alumni that influence their decision to donate as it directly relates to the young alumni giving behavior research at Green Hills University.

In 1999, Volkwein and Parmley developed a theoretical model of alumni giving that relied on individuals' motivation and their capacity to give. Motivation was characterized by physical proximity to the institution, alumni involvement, perceived need for support, and multiple degrees received from the college whereas capacity to give was represented by occupational status, income, education in progress, and highest degree earned. Volkwein and Parmley also stressed the importance of the individual's demographic background along with the individual's college experiences as factors for alumni giving. The background characteristics in their conceptual model included age and graduation year, race/ethnicity, gender, socioeconomic status, intergenerational attendance, and whether alumni were "native" freshman, i.e., they started as freshmen at that institution instead of transferring into the school. The college experiences variables were represented by academic characteristics such as GPA, major, native freshman status, and faculty relations as well as other social and campus connectedness variables such as involvement in co-curricular activities, their level of personal and intellectual growth, and strength of their peer relationships.

Monks (2003) found that undergraduate experience was a critical factor in alumni's decision to give to their institution. In his research, alumni who reported that they were "very satisfied" with their collegiate years gave over 2.6 times as much compared to alumni who were dissatisfied or neutral about their undergraduate experience. Similarly, Clotfelter's (2003) research on giving behavior at elite private colleges and universities stressed the importance of alumni's undergraduate experience. Alumni who attended colleges or universities that were their first choice, connected with mentors during college, and were satisfied with life in general reported a higher level of satisfaction during their undergraduate years. This undergraduate satisfaction variable was highly correlated with the level of donations to the institution.

Other research on alumni giving focused on whether the alumni had received financial aid from the university. Dugan et al. (2000) found that alumni who received need-based loans were 13 percent less likely to give to Vanderbilt University whereas alumni who received need based grants were 12 percent more likely to give to the university. Monks (2003) had similar findings and reported that undergraduate loans and, to a lesser extent, graduate loans decreased the likelihood that alumni would give to their alma mater. In fact, alumni who graduated with at least $10,000 in undergraduate debt gave 10 percent less than alumni who graduated without any debt. In Clotfelter's (2003) research study, alumni who received need-based financial aid gave 23 percent less than other alumni.

More recently, McDearmon (2010) took a different approach in exploring young alumni donation behavior by analyzing the comments of non-donors from a free response question on an institutional survey. Non-donors suggested offering incentives to young alumni to give such as rewarding donors with university gear in exchange for particular levels of financial support. Drezner (2009, 2010) in his study on student and young alumni giving at private historically Black colleges and universities (HBCUs) cautioned against the use of too many rewards. He found that those who received gifts in exchange for a small donation did not see their contribution as philanthropy; thereby, lessening the effects and benefits of continuous annual giving on the possibility of building a sustained culture of giving. Other suggestions focused on providing donors with access to university services such as library resources, online databases, and permanent e-mail accounts (McDearmon, 2010).

Further, McDearmon (2010) found that young alumni prefer to take an active role on how their donations are spent and who benefits from their generosity. Most young alumni who are non-donors reported that they would only give if their donations were guaranteed to improve the student experience. They also expressed concern that alumni donations, in general, do not impact students directly. Other young alumni mentioned that they would give if their donations benefited specific academic departments or student organizations instead of the university as a whole. They indicated that giving to the entire university was not worthwhile or the best use of their funds.

Young Alumni Giving Initiative at Green Hills University

Green Hills University (GHU) is a private research institution that attracts an academically talented, traditional college-age population. The campus is near a large city in the Northeast and the students are typically from middle-class to upper middle-class backgrounds. The undergraduate students are educated either in the School of Arts and Science or the School of Engineering. There are approximately 5,000 undergraduate students and 4,700 graduate or professional students. The six-year undergraduate graduation rate is high at 90 percent.

In 2006 GHU publicly announced a university-wide fundraising initiative to raise over $1 billion. As the largest of the eight schools, the School of Arts and Sciences' fundraising goal is $425 million and the School of Engineering's goal is $125 million. As undergraduate students are educated in both schools, the GHU Fund was created to target undergraduate alumni, parents, and friends. In an effort to meet the fundraising goals, the university conducted a research study to gain a better understanding of the priorities and motivators of young alumni. Young alumni are classified as individuals who have graduated from GHU within the last 10 years and represent approximately 23 percent of GHU's alumni population. The main objectives of the study are to help inform the GHU Fund's young alumni fundraising strategy for the remaining two years of the campaign, to create a positive experience for respondents, and to identify opportunities for future research.

During the fall of 2008, the university sent the last 10 graduating classes (1999–2008) an alumni survey. The survey was designed to assess recent graduates' perceptions of their undergraduate and alumni experiences, to gauge their level of interest in alumni events and activities, and to understand where GHU fits into their philanthropic priorities. Several questions were designed to assess the complex behavior of alumni giving by addressing alumni's motivations and their capacity to give. The purpose of these attitudinal questions was not only to compare how donors and non-donors responded, but also to assess whether there are differences in giving behavior among different types of donors.

In designing the survey, we limited the survey to a maximum of 20 questions in order to reduce completion times and increase response rates. Each alumnus/na was assigned a unique identification number making it unnecessary for participants to answer demographic information, which also decreased completion time of the survey. This unique identifier links the survey data to giving information maintained by the Office of University Advancement and institutional data from the GHU Data Warehouse. Therefore, alumni did not need to answer questions on their race/ethnicity, gender, age, graduation year, undergraduate GPA, major, and current location. Alumni are tracked by the National Student Clearinghouse to determine their enrollment history after they graduated from GHU. As the National Student Clearinghouse typically does not provide program-level enrollment data while students are in school, I could not determine whether alumni were enrolled in graduate or professional programs or whether they were non-degree seeking students. Therefore, I had to change my original variable of interest (enrollment in graduate or professional school) to enrollment in higher education at the time of the survey.

A total of 1,405 alumni completed the survey with a response rate of 16.3 percent. The typical respondent of the survey was a 21-25 year old, White female currently living in the same city as GHU and working in the government/public policy/non-profit sector.[2] In addition, 60 percent of the respondents had donated to GHU in the last six years (as verified by Advancement's donor records).

Methodology

Donor Predictor Model

To create a donor predictor model, the author used binary logistic regression to predict whether young alumni were donors (coded as 1 for "yes" and 0 for "no") based on a set of survey, academic, and biographical information. The general purpose of logistic regression is to predict group membership of an individual by calculating the probability that the individual will belong in the event (Meyers, Gamst, &Guarino, 2006). In this study, the event is whether an alumnus was a donor of Green Hills University. For the donor predictor model, a donor is classified as any alumnus/na who donated to the annual fund within the last six years.

In light of the research literature on young alumni donating behavior, I collected the following biographical data: race/ethnicity, gender, year of graduation, GPA, major, residency, double alumni status,[3] total and type of financial aid awards, current distance from the university, current enrollment in higher education, and whether the alumnus is in a reunion year. Although age is a significant predictor in past research studies, age and year of graduation had a high correlation, and therefore, age was removed from the analysis. In addition, survey responses that evaluated respondents' experience as undergraduates, level of involvement in alumni activities, and philanthropic aptitude were also tested as predictors of donor status.

To further explore the differences between donors and non-donors, chi-square tests analyze participants' responses to the likelihood of donating to particular areas or funds and whether receiving gifts or services would make an impact on young alumni's future giving behavior. Donors and non-donors also were compared on preferred solicitation methods as well as the average amount of financial aid received from the university. Lastly, I examined the free response questions on the survey to determine whether there were qualitative differences between how donors and non-donors responded to questions about their motivations to donate or not to donate to GHU.

Donor Comparison Profiles

Donors were classified into five categories (Current Year,[4] LYBUNTs,[5] SYB-UNTs,[6] Annual,[7] and Major[8]) based on the amount, frequency, and how recently the alumnus/na has donated. It is important to note that Current Year, LYBUNT, SYBUNT, and Annual donors were mutually exclusive categories. All Major donors except one individual were also Current Year, LYBUNT, or SYBUNT donors.

ANOVAs and independent sample t-tests were conducted to compare different types of donors on age, gender, distance from the university in miles, college affiliation (Engineering or Arts and Sciences), GPA, undergraduate financial aid received, and average donation to GHU. In addition, chi-square tests analyze the likelihood of donors giving to particular areas or funds within the university. Lastly, the different types of young alumni donors were compared based on which solicitation methods they prefer, how they would like to be thanked after they donate to the university, and what influences their decision to donate.

Results

Donor Predictor Model

Logistic regression was used to predict whether young alumni were donors based on a set of survey and biographical information. Initially, 19 predictors were simultaneously entered into the model, but the author found that 10 predictors were not statistically significant. These non-significant variables (distance from GHU, double-alumni status, undergraduate financial aid, being an "active" alumnus/na,[9] undergraduate major,[10] current enrollment in higher education, ever attending Homecoming, considering oneself "philanthropic,"[11] and volunteering at GHU[12]) were removed from the model. The final nine-variable model correctly predicts whether an alumnus/na would be a donor 82 percent of the time and whether an alumnus/na will be a non-donor 56 percent of the time. In addition, the final model had a high overall predictive success rate of 72 percent and accounted for 27 percent of the variance in the outcome variable, donor status. The practical implications of the logistic regression model is that University Advancement now has a specific set of characteristics that they can use to target potential new donors.

The nine significant predictors are based on young alumni's demographic information, undergraduate experience, and current alumni engagement. Table 8.1 summarizes pertinent information for each predictor in the final model. Race/ethnicity is classified into four categories: White, Asian, underrepresented minority, and unknown.[13] As there was a small number of young alumni in the sample who identify as Hispanic (N = 86), Black (N = 43), American Indian or Alaskan Native (N = 5), Native Hawaiian or Other Pacific

TABLE 8.1 Final Nine Predictor Logistic Regression Model for Young Alumni Giving Behavior

	B	S.E.	Wald	Exp(B)	95.0% C.I. for Exp(B)	
					Lower	Upper
Female*	0.319	0.133	5.768	1.376	1.060	1.784
Underrepresented minority[a],*	−0.533	0.217	6.043	0.587	0.383	0.898
Asian[a]	−0.322	0.185	3.017	0.725	0.504	1.042
Unknown race/ ethnicity[a] *	−0.442	0.183	5.841	0.643	0.449	0.920
Living near GHU*	0.322	0.149	4.684	1.380	1.031	1.848
Years out***	0.299	0.029	106.08	1.349	1.274	1.428
Undergraduate experience**	0.274	0.097	8.018	1.315	1.088	1.589
GPA 3.49 – 3.0[b]	−0.122	0.140	0.764	0.885	0.672	1.164
GPA below 3.0[b] ***	−0.764	0.220	12.018	0.466	0.303	0.718
In reunion year**	0.661	0.223	8.806	1.937	1.252	2.998
Attended alumni event***	0.486	0.136	12.702	1.626	1.244	2.123
Rank of GHU for giving***	0.541	0.093	33.698	1.718	1.431	2.063
Constant***	−2.958	0.444	44.329	0.052		

*** $p \leq 0.001$; ** $p < 0.01$; * $p < 0.05$
[a] Relative to White alumni
[b] Relative to GPA 3.50 – 4.00

Islander (N = 3), and multiple races (N = 1), they were collapsed into one category (underrepresented minority) for the model to converge. Since there are enough alumni who identify as Asian (N =187) and White (N =7 92), these races were entered into the model separately. The comparison group, White alumni, was the largest race/ethnicity group in the sample.

Current location is a dichotomous variable and classifies alumni by whether they are currently living near the university. As GHU is near a major city in the Northeast, "near" means that alumni are living either in that major city or in the surrounding suburbs of that city. Undergraduate experience is measured on a 5-point Likert scale from "excellent" to "poor" and requires alumni to reflect on their overall experience with the university. Undergraduate GPA is classified into three categories: GPA between 4.0 and 3.50, GPA between 3.49 to 3.0, and GPA below 3.0. As the largest GPA group is alumni who earned GPAs between 4.0 and 3.50, this group serves as the comparison group. The ranking of GHU in their list of philanthrophic priorities was measured on a

4-point Likert scale from "top priority" to "low priority." There was also a "not applicable" category if GHU was not a philanthropic priority for particular individuals.

The three significant demographic predictors are gender, race/ethnicity, and current residency. Women were more likely to donate to the Green Hills University than men. This finding is similar to research by Eckel and Grossman (1998) who reported that women are more likely to make charitable donations in larger amounts. However, previous research in higher education show conflicting evidence on the influence of gender in giving behavior. Okunade (1996) found that male alumni, not females, are more likely to donate to the University of Memphis. In addition, several studies reported that there were no significant differences in the giving behavior of male and female graduates (Dugan et al., 2000; Monks, 2003).

For race/ethnicity, underrepresented minorities were 41 percent less likely to donate to GHU compared to White alumni. Clotfleter (2003) reported similar findings for race/ethnicity from the College and Beyond data. Alumni in the 1976 cohort who identify as non-White were less likely to give to their school in 1995. Monks (2003) found that young alumni who identify as Black, Hispanic, and multiracial give 39 percent, 23 percent, and 27 percent less to their undergraduate alma maters, respectively, compared to their White counterparts. There was no significant difference between the donation behavior of White young alumni and Asian young alumni on the likelihood of donating to GHU.

Young alumni listed as unknown for their race/ethnicity were 36 percent less likely to donate to GHU compared to White young alumni. It is difficult to interpret the findings for the unknown race category as it is unclear why these alumni have no race/ethnicity listed in the Data Warehouse. It is possible that being listed as unknown for race/ethnicity is a proxy for disengagement with GHU if these alumni failed to respond to inquiries to update their race/ethnicity with the university when they were students.

While the findings in this study were significant with regards to giving by race/ethnicity to GHU, Drezner (2011) cautioned about how to intereprate predicitive modeling results easpecially with regards to race. Drezner suggested that these results should not be read as a lack of intererest or lack of generosity towards ones's alma mater. Rather, Drezner advised, insitutions who see significant differences in giving by race should look at its engagement strategies and how more culturally sensitive fundrasing strategies might be employed.

The last demographic variable correlated with giving behavior for Green Hills University was the current location of young alumni. Alumni living near the university were more likely to donate than graduates who do not live near GHU. This is similar with what Gaier (2005) found, i.e., that alumni living in the same state as the university are more likely to give and to participate in university activities and events than alumni who live further away.

The three significant predictors from undergraduate experience were the number of years that have elapsed after graduation, the overall rating of their undergraduate experience, and undergraduate GPA. Each year that passes after alumni graduated increases the odds that they will donate to Green Hills University. In fact, young alumni who graduated six years ago are 2.45 times more likely to donate than young alumni who graduated three years ago. In addition, there was an increase in the odds for every one-unit increase in their satisfacation with their undergraduate experience. Therefore, young alumni who rated their undergraduate experience as "excellent" were 1.73 times more likely to donate than alumni who rated their undergraduate experience as "average." These findings are aligned with previous research that found that undergraduate satisfaction influences alumni's decision to donate to their alma mater (Clotfelter, 2003; McDearmon & Shirley, 2009; Monks, 2003).

Lastly, academic performance during their undergraduate years was shown to be related to their decision to donate. Young alumni with GPAs below 3.0 were less likely to donate than young alumni with GPAs between 3.50 to 4.00. It is possible that undergraduate students with lower GPAs than their classmaters' mean GPA were less engaged as students or less satisfied with their educational experience which lead them to be less engaged as alumni. At a state university in the Midwest, Gaier (2005) found a positive relationship between alumni's statisfaction with their academic experience and their engagment as alumni. In fact, experiences that emphasized academic work such as satistfication with coursework in major and quality of instruction in major were positive correlated with whether alumni chose to donate to their institution.

The three significant predictors that represent current alumni engagement are whether alumni are in a reunion year, whether alumni have attended at least one alumni event, and the rank of Green Hills University in their philanthropic priorities. In the year of their fifth or tenth reunion, young alumni were 1.94 times more likely to donate than alumni not in a reunion year. This finding was consistent with the research by Wunnava and Lauze (2001) who reported an increase in donating behavior for occasional and consistent donors during reunion years at a small private liberal arts college in Vermont. This outcome could highlight the sustained effort by University Advancement to target this group as they have specific fundraising goals and events for alumni in their reunion year. In addition, alumni who have attended at least one alumni event (excluding Homecoming) were 1.63 times more likely to donate than alumni who have not attended these events. Lastly, alumni who ranked GHU as a "high priority" are 2.95 times more likely to donate than alumni who ranked GHU as a "low-priority."

The final logistic regression model for donor behavior predicted that young alumni who are female, identify as White or Asian, graduated in the late 1990s/early 2000s, rated their undergraduate experience as positive, attended at least one alumni event excluding Homecoming, ranked GHU as a priority in their list of philanthropic priorities, were experiencing their fifth or tenth year reunion, and lived near GHU were a strong profile for potential donors. On the other hand, the logistic regression model predicts that non-donors tend to be males, identify as underrepresented minorities or have unknown race/ethnicity listed within the Data Warehouse, graduated in the last couple years, and earned GPAs below 3.0.

Donor Comparison Profiles

As I am interested in differences among donors, I created a donor comparison profile for examining differences in demographic characteristics, alumni engagement, undergraduate experience, and financial variables. The donor comparison profile is shown in Table 8.2. Current Year, LYBUNT, SYBUNT, and Annual donors are compared to each other while Major donors are

TABLE 8.2 Comparison Profile of Specific Type of Donors from a Sample of 750 GHU Young Alumni

	CY	LYBUNT	SYBUNT	Annual	Major
N	87	266	362	34	55
Male (%)	35.6%	37.2%	34.5%	38.2%	50.9%★
Underrepresented minority (%)	10.3%	9.0%	8.6%	11.8%	0%★
Age (in years)	26.5	25.7	25.9	26.0	27.7★★★
Distance from the institution	583	742	878	743	636
Active alumnus (% Yes)	50.6%	56.9%★★★	36.8%★★★	53.1%	58.5%
Volunteered for GHU (%Yes)	62.1%	58.9%	53.3%	79.4%★	67.3%
Arts & Sciences (%)	94.3%	86.1%	85.4%	85.3%	80.0%
GPA	3.43	3.47	3.43	3.45	3.36★
Undergraduate experience[1]	4.59	4.59★	4.45★	4.56	4.51
Total amount of grants[2]	$27,814	$17,165	$17,829	$15,414	$11,213
Total amount of loans[3]	$9,312	$7,517	$10,872	$4,328	$1,903★★
Total financial aid received	$38,316	$26,161	$30,175	$21,364	$13,398★★
Average donation last five years	$149	$720	$117	$588	$3,969★★★
Average lifetime donation	$162	$1,022	$165	$643	$5,733★★★

★★★ $p < 0.001$; ★★ $p < 0.01$; ★ $p < 0.05$

1 Undergraduate experience is a 5-point scale ranging from 5= excellent to 1=poor
2 Total amount of grants include all federal, state, and university grants
3 Total amount of loans include Stafford, Perkins, PLUS, and alternative loans

compared with the overall donor group. Due to space concerns, overall donors are not included in Table 8.2. For demographic characteristics, there is a significantly higher percentage of Major donors who are male (50.9%) compared to overall donors (34.7%) and Major donors are, on average, significantly older (27.7 years) than overall donors (25.7 years). This age difference still holds when controlling for alumni within their fifth or tenth year reunion. Another demographic difference between Major donors and overall donors is that no Major donors identified as underrepresented minorities compared to the 73 overall donors who identified as one of these racial/ethnic groups. Since three-quarters of underrepresented minority donors are female and the mean age of the group is 26.0 years, it is not a surprising result as the demographic characteristics of these donors are inconsistent with the profile of Major donors. Current Year, LYBUNT, SYBUNT, and Annual donors have no significant differences based on demographic characteristics.

Alumni engagement examined whether the graduates consider themselves "active" alumni, whether the alumni had volunteered for Green Hills University, and the average distance alumni are currently living from the university. The analysis displays how important constant contact and involvement are for young alumni as there is a larger percentage of LYBUNTs (56.9%) and a lower percentage of SYBUNTs (36.8%) that rate themselves as "active" alumni compared to the other donor types. In addition, Annual donors (79.4%) more frequently volunteered for Green Hills University compared to other donors. Alumni who donated more recently (in the case of LYBUNTs and Annual donors), reported stronger engagement behavior by either labeling themselves as "active" alumni or by volunteering for their alma mater. Therefore, it is important for development and alumni offices to maintain consistent communication with young alumni and try to involve them in campus affairs and activities. These offices may be less successful in retaining donors if they are only reaching out to young alumni for the purpose of soliciting donations. In addition, the analysis found no significant differences on the average miles young alumni are living from GHU for the different types of donors. The university should continue to reach out to young alumni who have already donated in the past regardless of how far away they are from the institution and offer them opportunities to feel involved.

The donors are fairly similar on the academic experience variables. A similar proportion of young alumni are affiliated with the School of Arts and Sciences for each type of donor. Major donors earned lower undergraduate GPAs by approximately a quarter of a standard deviation. In general, undergraduate GPAs are high for all donors (3.45) and there were no significant differences between Current donors, LYBUNTs, SYBUNTs, and Annual donors. SYBUNTs rated their undergraduate experience slightly lower than LYBUNTs by approximately 0.20 standard deviations. However, the mean undergraduate experience is high for all donors as each type of donor rated their undergraduate experience as better than "good." Therefore, it is possible that once the quality of alumni's undergraduate experience reaches a certain threshold, undergraduate experience does not play a significant role in determining the frequency, consistency, or size of alumni's donations.

Lastly, the donor comparison profiles examine the amount of financial aid the different types of donors received and the size of their contributions to GHU. Major donors, on average, received significantly less in undergraduate loans ($1,903 compared to $9,766) and significantly less in overall undergraduate financial aid from Green Hills University ($13,398 compared to $30,511). All donors received a similar amount in undergraduate grants. Major donors also donated more in the last five years ($3,696 compared to $69.62) and over their lifetime ($5,733 compared to $76.59) compared to all donors. This is to be expected since the definition of Major donors has them giving more to their alma maters than the other types of donors. Surprisingly, there were no statistically significant differences in the size of the donations among Current donors, SYBUNT, LYBUNT, or Annual donors.

Alumni Preferences: Solicitation, Acknowledgments, and Specific Funds

Young alumni were asked their preferences of how they wished to be solicited for donations, how they want to be thanked after their donation, and which areas within the university that they are more likely to contribute. In general, donors and non-donors preferred direct mail and e-mail. Neither donors nor non-donors preferred requests from social networking sites, telephone calls from students or staff members, or requests from classmates or friends. Several young alumni suggested for the advancement office to honor their solicitation preferences and to streamline how many times within a year that alumni are asked to donate either to the university as a whole or particular groups within GHU. In addition, non-donors explained how they did not have the financial capacity to give because they were unable to find employment, were currently in graduate school, and/or were paying back student loans from attending the university. It is important to note that non-donors' qualitative comments did not match the quantitative evidence that found no significant relationship between whether they were currently attending higher education and their likelihood to donate and whether they received financial aid from GHU and their likelihood to donate. It is possible that non-donors mention continued enrollment in higher education and repayment of education loans as excuses not to donate because these reasons are difficult to counteract by the university since they will not be solved through increased marketing or continued outreach. Instead, it requires the university to "wait it out"—so to speak—until these alumni graduate or pay off their loans, which may take years if not decades to achieve. In reality, their decision to not donate was probably more nuanced than they described as they may fear increased solicitation efforts if they provided reasons that the university deems easier to change.

Young alumni were asked whether receiving special gifts or activities would make an impact on their future giving behavior. A larger percentage of donors indicated that receiving information that explains the impact of their donation was "somewhat important" on their decision to make a future donation compared to non-donors. Also, a higher proportion of donors reported that knowing that alumni donations affected *U.S. News & World Report* rankings is "extremely important" on their decision to donate in the future. Several young alumni (donors and non-donors) expressed the opinion that they did not need to be thanked for their donation especially if it was going to cost GHU money or it would waste paper. Other young alumni suggested that they would appreciate receiving letters or e-mails from people or groups that their donation helped to support. In general, young alumni who wished to receive acknowledgments prefer to get thank you letters from either students or university leaders such as the president or provost.

Young alumni were also asked the likelihood of donating to particular funds or groups. They were presented with a list of 11 areas that ranged from student-focused areas such as student activities, financial aid and scholarships, Greek life, and student organizations to academic areas such as research, academic departments or majors, and faculty salaries. The list also included athletics, facilities, unrestricted funds, and endowment funds. The most popular areas selected were financial aid and scholarships (65.4%), specific academic departments or majors (64.7%), and research (45.0%). While most of the areas did not have significant differences between donor and non-donor responses, there were significant differences for the likelihood of donating to two areas: unrestricted funds and endowment funds. There was a higher percentage of donors willing to donate to unrestricted funds (30.7%) and endowment funds (37.8%) compared to non-donors (10.9% and 27.4%, respectively).

Different types of donors also have significant differences in the likelihood of donating to particular funds or areas. Annual donors were more willing to donate to unrestricted funds, faculty salaries, student activities, and endowment funds. Similarly, Major donors were more willing to donate to unrestricted funds and endowment funds compared to overall donors. SYBUNTs were less willing to donate to unrestricted funds and endowment funds whereas Major donors are less likely to donate to academic departments and facilities. Current Year and LYBUNT donors did not differ significantly on their likelihood to donate to particular areas within the university.

Limitations

One limitation of this study was not collecting income information from young alumni to use in the donor predictor model and donor comparison profiles. Monks (2003) found that an increase of $10,000 in personal income raises the expected donor contribution by 2 percent and an increase of $10,000 in household income raises the financial contribution by 9 percent. In addition, Melchiori (1988) identified that a higher proportion of major donors from the University of Michigan had annual incomes of $100,000 to $200,000 while the majority of other donors had personal incomes from $60,000 to $100,000.

In order to be sensitive to the privacy of alumni and to create a positive experience for respondents, income information was not asked on the survey. University Advancement rationalized that even if income information was a significant predictor of donating behavior, this information is not readily available for them to use to target specific young alumni as potential donors. In addition, alumni may choose not to respond to questions of this nature. Melchiori (1988) reported that only 84 percent of alumni responded to personal-income questions and 65 percent of alumni answered household-income questions as compared to an almost perfect response rate for the other demographic questions on the survey.

As financial capacity is a significant predictor of whether alumni donate and the amount of the donation in previous studies, it cannot be ignored. Therefore, I used other variables to assess alumni's financial profile such as undergraduate financial aid received as an indicator of debt and family's wealth, years after graduation as an indicator of earning potential, and whether the alumnus was currently enrolled in higher education as an indicator of reduced financial capacity to give. While undergraduate financial aid was not a significant predictor of donor status for young alumni, donors, on average, received $9,915 less in financial aid compared to their non–donor counterparts.[14]

Suggestions to Administrators and Fundraising Staff

The findings from the young alumni giving behavior study at Greens Hills University offer practical suggestions to staff members and administrators in alumni and development offices. Overall, young alumni are most influenced by their undergraduate experience and their current alumni engagement. Therefore, staff members need to capitalize on this information to help them plan effective strategies to target potential young alumni donors and retain their current donor base.

Alumni think about their undergraduate experience when deciding to donate, and it is important for colleges and universities to actively engage students during college and to facilitate initial connections with their classmates, faculty, and staff members. When reflecting on how they define their connection to GHU, young alumni report that friends and classmates (91.3%), field of study (84.7%), and graduating year (85.6%) are the most influential. Thus, alumni and development offices may want to play up these themes in their solicitation materials or organize events that bring together alumni of the same major or professional field to network and socialize. It is important to note, however, that young alumni prefer not to receive solicitation requests directly from their friends or classmates.

Current alumni engagement is a critical factor for young alumni especially for those who have donated to their alma mater in the recent past. Therefore, colleges and universities need to maintain open and consistent communication with their alumni and find alternative methods of engaging young alumni who do not live near the institution. One method that Greens Hills University uses and is successful is to involve young alumni in the admission and recruitment process for potential new undergraduate students. In this program, alumni interview applicants, represent GHU at campus fairs, and participate in out-of-state recruitment events. This allows alumni to actively engage with the university regardless of their location and provides opportunities to feel that they are helping to select the next group of students for the institution. Other methods to engage alumni and to be sensitive of young alumni's reduced capacity to give is to have young alumni mentor current students, participate in university-sponsored community service events, or solicit their feedback on the future direction or goals of the institution.

As many fundraising and alumni staff members are probably aware, building successful donor bases are about maintaining relationships and responding to the needs of their clients. In order to effectively achieve this, staff members need to understand the priorities, motivators, and concerns of young alumni. Therefore, advancement and development offices in conjunction with alumni relations need to conduct research on their alumni (if they are not already) by collecting data through surveys, focus groups, and interviews as well as linking these responses to institutional databases that contain demographic, academic, and giving information. If staff members carefully design surveys and protocols for interviews and focus groups, they will obtain a more nuanced understanding of young alumni's needs and be able to determine strategies that are not working as evidenced by the data. In addition, these offices may stumble upon new ideas or different approaches through analyzing young alumni's responses, giving information, and institutional data.

Table 8.3 summarizes recommendations to increase the proportion of young alumni who donate to their alma mater as well as offers several strategies to implement these suggestions.

Conclusions

This study found a set of observable characteristics that the GHU Fund staff can use to effectively identify and target young alumni who are strong candidates for potential donors. Staff members also can use this study to pinpoint alumni who are unlikely to donate and remove these individuals from solicitation lists. This will help save scarce office resources, which is extremely important in the current economic climate. In addition, the GHU Fund staff now have a better understanding of how young alumni would like to be contacted, how they would like to be thanked (after their donations), and to what areas they will most likely donate. This is extremely beneficial as the office begins to craft a more targeted strategy for their current campaign and for future endeavors.

Surprisingly, the study did not find many significant differences among different types of donors in regards to demographic, academic, or financial characteristics. The most interesting finding was the differences in alumni engagement between different types of donors. LYBUNTs and Annual donors typically reported stronger connections to the university than did the other types of donors. While this finding provided some insight, more research is needed to discover why some young alumni are consistent donors and why some young alumni are only occasional donors. If it is simply a matter of a more targeted outreach to turn occasional donors into consistent donors, that would be a very invaluable finding.

TABLE 8.3 Recommendations for Increasing Young Alumni Giving and Several Strategies for Implementation

Recommendation	Strategies for Implementation
Develop fundraising strategies based on data that targets young alumni	• Examine past giving data to create profiles of young alumni donors and non-donors at your institution. • Conduct surveys, interviews, and/or focus groups with young alumni to have a better understanding of their motivations and priorities. • Set realistic fundraising goals for young alumni given their reduced capacity to give. • Value the frequency of their donations over the monetary value of their gifts to encourage a pattern of giving.
Strengthen the connection between young alumni and their alma maters	• Work with multiple campus units to provide opportunities for young alumni to volunteer for your institution. • Cultivate and strengthen alumni chapters in areas where there are large proportions of young alumni. • Invite young alumni to campus at least once a year to reconnect with your institution and their classmates outside of Homecoming activities. • Reach out to young alumni to solicit their opinions on the future direction or goals of your institution.
Refine communication and solicitation strategies for young alumni	• Communicate with young alumni via their preferred method(s). • Ask young alumni to support specific campus units, events, and activities that are important to them. • Use cost effective methods to thank alumni for their donations. • Coordinate solicitation efforts across campus units to not overwhelm young alumni with requests.

Notes

1. Green Hills University is a fictitious name for a university in the Northeast.
2. Less than 40 percent of the data was available for survey respondents' occupational sectors.
3. A double alumnus is defined as one who has received a bachelor's degree and a graduate or professional degree from GHU.
4. Current year donors were individuals who have pledged or given during the current fiscal year (July 1, 2008–June 30, 2009) excluding Annual Donors.
5. LYBUNTs were alumni who gave the last fiscal year, but have not given during the current fiscal year.
6. SYBUNTs were individuals who gave in the last five years, but have not given in the last or current fiscal year.
7. Annual donors were individuals who have given consecutively since they have graduated to a maximum of six years.
8. Major donors were defined in a context of being young alumni, as those who have given $500 or more over the course of their lifetime.
9. Participants were asked on the survey whether they considered themselves "active alumnus/na" and they responded either "yes" or "no."
10. Undergraduate major was coded by academic discipline. The academic disciplines are Arts & Humanities, Social Science, Natural Science, Interdisciplinary, and Engineering.
11. Participants were asked on the survey whether they considered themselves "philanthropic" and they responded either "yes" or "no."
12. Participants were asked on the survey whether they had ever volunteered for GHU and they responded either "yes" or "no."
13. Race/ethnicity was taken from GHU Data Warehouse and based on the race/ethnicity categories from IPEDs.
14. Financial aid includes all loans, grants, and work study received for the alumnus's bachelor's degree.

References

Baade, R. A., & Sundberg, J. O. (1996). What determines alumni generosity? *Economics of Education Review, 15*(1), 75–81.

Coltfelter, C. (2003). Alumni giving to elite private colleges and universities. *Economics of Education Review, 22*(3), 109–120.

Drezner, N. D. (2009). Why give?: Exploring social exchange and organizational identification theories in the promotion of philanthropic behaviors of African American millennials at private-HBCUs. *International Journal of Educational Advancement, 9*(3), 147–165.

Drezner, N. D. (2010). Private Black colleges' encouragement of student giving and volunteerism: An examination of prosocial behavior development. *International Journal of Educational Advancement, 10*(3), 126–147.

Drezner, N. D. (2011). *Philanthropy and fundraising in American higher education.* San Francisco, CA: Jossey-Bass.

Dugan, K., Mullin, C., & Siegfried, J. (2000). Undergraduate financial aid and subsequent giving behavior. Williams Project on the Economics of Higher Education Discussion Papers. DP-57. Retrieved from http://www.eric.ed.gov/ERICWebPortal/search/detailmini.jsp?_nfpb=true&_&ERICExtSearch_SearchValue_0=ED475423&ERICExtSearch_SearchType_0=no&accno=ED475423

Eckel, C., & Grossman, P. (1998). Are women less selfish than men?: Evidence from dictator experiments. *The Economic Journal, 108*(448), 726–735.

Gaier, S. (2005). Alumni satisfaction with their undergraduate academic experience and the impact on alumni giving and participation. *International Journal of Educational Advancement, 5*(4), 279–288.

Gunsalus, R. (2005). The relationship of institutional characteristics and giving participation rates of alumni. *International Journal of Educational Advancement, 5*(2), 162–170.

Holmes, J. (2009). Prestige, charitable donations and other determinants of alumni giving: Evidence from a highly selective liberal arts college. *Economics of Education Review, 28*, 18–28.

Leslie, L. (1979). Variations in fund-raising potential among colleges and universities. In W. Heeman (Ed.), *Analyzing the cost-effectiveness of fundraising* (pp. 59–70). San Francisco, CA: Jossey-Bass.

Leslie, L., & Ramey, G. (1988). Donor behavior and voluntary support for higher education institutions. *Journal of Higher Education, 59*, 115–132.

Lindahl, W., & Winship, C. (1992). Predictive models for annual fundraising and major gift fundraising. *Nonprofit Management and Leadership, 3*, 43–64.

Liu, Y. (2006). Determinants of private giving to public college and universities. *International Journal of Educational Advancement, 6*(2), 119–140.

Kaplan, A. E. (2010, February 3). *Contributions to colleges and universities down 11.9 percent to $27.85 billion greatest decline ever recorded.* New York, NY: Council for Aid to Education.

McDearmon, J. T. (2010). What's in it for me: A qualitative look into the mindset of young alumni non-donors. *International Journal of Educational Advancement, 10*(1), 33–47.

McDearmon, J. T., & Shirley, K. (2009). Characteristics and institutional factors related to young alumni donors and non-donors. *International Journal of Education Advancement, 9*, 83–95.

Melchiori, G. S. (1988). Applying alumni research to fundraising. In G. S. Melchiori (Ed.), *Alumni research: Methods and applications* (pp. 51–65). San Francisco, CA: Jossey-Bass.

Meyers, L. S., Gamst, G., & Guarino, A. J. (2006). *Applied multivariate research.* Thousand Oaks, CA: Sage.

Monks, J. (2003). Patterns of giving to one's alma mater among young graduates from selective institutions. *Economics of Education Review, 22*, 121–130.

Okunade, A. (1996). Graduate school alumni donations to academic funds: micro-data evidence. *American Journal of Economics and Sociology, 55*(2), 213–229

Okunade, A., & Justice, S. (1991). Micropanel estimates of the life-cycle hypothesis with respect to alumni donations. In *Proceedings of the Business and Economics Statistical Section of the American Statistical Association* (pp. 298–305). Alexandria, VA: American Statistical Association.

O'Malley, M. (1992). *Another look at charitable giving: The importance of non-economic determinants of philanthropy.* Working paper. Cambridge, MA: Massachusetts Institute of Technology.

Volkwein, J. F., & Parmley, K. (1999). Testing why alumni give: A model of alumni gift-giving behavior. In D. Shoemaker (Ed.), *Research in alumni relations: Surveying alumni to improve your programs* (pp. 59–62). Washington, DC: CASE Books.

Wunnava, P. V., & Lauze, M. A. (2001). Alumni giving at a small liberal arts college: Evidence from consistent and occasional donors. *Economics of Education Review, 20*, 533–543.

SECTION 3

On-Campus Constituencies and Future Donors

9

FACULTY AND STAFF AS PROSPECTS AND DONORS

Giving on Campus

Genevieve G. Shaker

> *We're not just here doing a job. This is something we believe in so strongly that we're willing to, in a sense, forgo any money that we might leave to our children.*

> —Faculty major donor

In 2011, the State University of New York at Stony Brook (SUNY Stony Brook) announced the seventh largest gift ever to public higher education in the United States. The $150 million dollar gift came from a couple, the wife an alumna and the husband a former chair of SUNY Stony Brook's mathematics department, who left academia and became a billionaire hedge-fund manager. The donation was triple what the institution typically raised in any given year. The couple had already given $100 million to SUNY Stony Brook, bringing their grand total of support for that institution to more than $250 million (Eaton, 2011; Pérez-Pena, 2011).

Very few faculty or former faculty, of course, can afford to make gifts of such magnitude. Many colleges and universities, however, do have faculty, staff, and administrators who can afford to, and indeed do, make gifts and bequests in the thousands and millions of dollars (e.g., Penn State University, 2010; University of Florida Foundation, n.d.), and the SUNY Stony Brook story illustrates the strength of the bond that a faculty member can form with his or her institution. This kind of commitment is what led 11,000 faculty, staff, and retirees to contribute $67 million during the University of Minnesota's 1996-2003 comprehensive campaign and, during a comparable campaign, for Penn State's employees to give $41 million (Palmer, 2004; Penn State University, 2011). At my institution, Indiana University-Purdue University Indianapolis, an annual faculty and staff fundraising campaign held since the 1980s has amounted to millions of dollars over the decades; in 2011, for example, hundreds of retired and current faculty and staff together gave $2.4 million. Perhaps most strikingly, in 2012 the 70 faculty of New England College pledged $100,000 in the span of a few days in order to help prevent staff layoffs (Nadolny, 2012).

Neither faculty and staff campaigns nor giving in the workplace are anomalies. Indeed 25 percent of all Americans are invited to make donations at work and most colleges and universities are thought to have their own employee giving campaigns (National Committee for Responsive Philanthropy, 2003; March, 2005). Faculty and staff giving, however, has remained relatively unexplored in scholarly circles and only a few research-based recommendations are available to build or improve faculty and staff fundraising efforts. This chapter both introduces readers to what we know about faculty and staff giving and provides a series of recommendations for enhancing annual and major gift fundraising efforts "at home," on the campus where faculty and staff are personally as well as professionally invested. An overview of faculty and staff giving information from the Voluntary Support for Education (VSE) survey and the literature on faculty and staff giving, including exploratory research focused on faculty major donors (Shaker & Palmer, 2012), ground the discussion. The recommendations are also informed by professional experience honed over 12 years of raising money from university employees.

National Data about Faculty and Staff Giving

[Philanthropy] gives you the feeling that you're doing something longer lasting for the campus and the program. It's satisfying.

—Faculty major donor

In 2011, higher education received $30.30 billion in philanthropic support, with $13.45 billion (44%) given by individuals according to the Council for Aid to Education's (CAE) annual VSE survey of 2- and 4-year public and private colleges and universities (CAE, 2012a). Information about faculty and staff giving is collected as a part of the survey but institutions are not required to include these data in their responses, and they are not reported publically by the CAE. In 2011, only 682[1] of the 1,009 participating institutions (68%) provided faculty and staff giving data. With this in mind and recognizing that the VSE is self-reported, creating the potential for discretionary error, significant limitations exist in relation to these data. Nevertheless, the VSE provides the only national data about faculty and staff giving currently available and survey participants are able to use the data set to benchmark and make institutional level comparisons. Despite its shortcomings, the VSE data on faculty and staff giving are included in this chapter to provide fundraising practitioners with information about this practical tool, one that can be useful for self-assessment as well as for seeking best practices.

Using the VSE Data Miner utility (CAE, 2012b), available to all survey participants, Megan Palmer and I analyzed the information submitted about faculty and staff giving for 2001 to 2011.[2] Our experience with the data demonstrate its challenging nature. The analysis in this section required the removal of 18 institutions with significant data anomalies, the correction of data from one institution, and the removal of a piece of another institution's data. These adjustments were made in order to assure the analysis hewed most closely to the overall faculty and staff giving trends.

Over the past decade, higher education has benefitted from upward trends in both the average number of faculty and staff donors and total average giving among institutions (see Figures 9.1 and 9.2). The total dollars given by faculty and staff per institution spiked in 2007, and almost certainly due to economic fluctuations, donations dipped in 2009 before trending back up in the subsequent two years. The number of donors, on the other hand, has maintained a smoother trajectory suggesting that while faculty and staff may give less during difficult times, they do give and that new donors have continued to join the ranks. It is important to recognize that public institutions have substantially more faculty and staff on average than private institutions, leading at least in part to the higher average numbers of donors and dollars.

Of the $13.45 billion given by individuals in 2011, approximately $171.87 million (1.3%) can be counted as contributions from college and university employees (an increase of approximately $23 million or 13.4% from the prior year across all reporting institutions). An average of 289 people, or 24.2 percent of institutions' faculty and staff gave. Individual gifts across institutional types averaged $766 for a grand total of $252,385 per institution. Of that total, 84

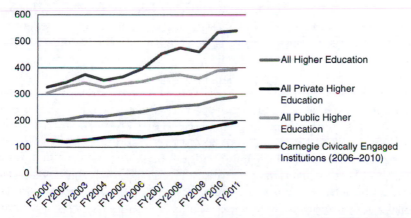

FIGURE 9.1 Average number of faculty and staff donors (2001–2011) for all reporting higher education institutions, public institutions, private institutions, and Carnegie Community Engaged Classified institutions. *Source*: CAE VSE Data Miner. The Carnegie Civically Engaged Classification was instituted in 2006; data from this selection of institutions is included prior to that time because the classification requires an existing commitment to civic engagement.

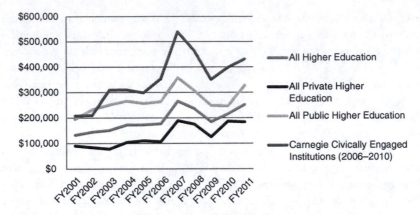

FIGURE 9.2 Average total dollars given by faculty and staff (2001-2011) for all reporting higher education institutions, public institutions, private institutions, and Carnegie Community Engaged Classified institutions. *Source:* CAE VSE Data Miner. The Carnegie Civically Engaged Classification was instituted in 2006; data from this selection of institutions is included prior to that time because the classification requires an existing commitment to civic engagement.

percent of the gifts and 63 percent of the dollars supported current operations, with the remainder directed toward areas including capital expenditures and endowments. The highest faculty and staff total given to a single institution was $21.4 million and the most donors reported was 7,870; the lowest faculty and staff total was $350 and the fewest donors reported was 3. Across all of higher education, the median number of faculty and staff donors was 142 and the median gift was $477.

Figure 9.1 examines institutions by public, private, and Carnegie Classification, providing a range of data about participation, gift size, and institutional averages. Naturally, some diversity of the numbers among institutional types relates to institutional size, but certain data are notable such as the high rate of participation at associate degree institutions (29.4%) and the comparatively low rate at research and doctoral institutions (19.4%). Despite the high rate of participation, at associate's institutions the average gifts were comparatively small; thus, the total cash value of the giving was less than elsewhere. In 2011, both the average and median gifts at research/doctoral institutions were noticeably higher than elsewhere, which aligns with the higher salaries at these institutions (American Association of University Professors, 2011), and suggests that these institutions received the largest faculty and staff gifts. Overall, instructional staff salaries are 9% higher at private institutions (Knapp, Kelly-Reid, & Ginder, 2011), and average giving per individual was higher at these schools than at public entities as was the rate of participation.

Throughout most of the tables, Megan Palmer and I have included figures for institutions that participate in the Carnegie Community Engagement Elective Classification as a method of exploring a cross section of institutional types and those colleges and universities with an expressed commitment to the philanthropic value of civic engagement. Intuitively, institutions that have voluntarily sought the Community Engagement Classification might be expected to have a higher degree of interest in the overall well-being of the community, including support for the institution itself. Interestingly, in comparison to other public and private institutions, this assumption holds true with the Carnegie Classified Engaged category trending higher in the number of donors and the total dollars given (Figures 9.1 and 9.2). When it comes to average giving by faculty and staff individuals, however, those at private institutions, baccalaureate institutions, and research/doctoral institutions gave more than at the engaged institutions (Table 9.1). Also, participation in giving at Carnegie Classified Engaged institutions was lower than at the other institutions except public institutions and research and doctoral universities. Naturally, some of these findings relate to the mixture of institutions that have chosen to be classified as engaged and completed the VSE (public 55%; private 45%; associate's 1%; bachelor's 22%; master's 38%; research/doctoral 39%), but this does not explain all of the differences. There is a subset of highly generous faculty and staff at Carnegie Classified Engaged institutions. The overall population at these institutions, however, is not notably participatory but is slightly more inclined to give than research university and public institution peers.

That the VSE serves as the lone national database of its kind suggests the need for greater analysis of faculty and staff giving as an important—and growing—component of institutional support. From the data, we can hypothesize that different kinds of colleges and universities have different cultures of giving, perhaps fostered with unique, institution-specific strategies. We can, furthermore, augment our understanding of the VSE figures by exploring the strategies, institutional practices, and cultivation of faculty donors recorded in a small series of studies directed at enhancing faculty and staff fundraising efforts

Research on Faculty and Staff Giving

> *I think that the faculty who have made larger gifts are primarily citizens of the campus more than of the discipline, who see the potential of [the university] to make a difference, who see the potential of gifts to make a difference.*

—Faculty major donor

Based on a survey of fundraising personnel from public universities across the country in the middle-2000s (n = 164), March (2005) discovered that 76.8 percent of the institutions solicited faculty and staff as a part of annual fundraising campaigns. Faculty and staff were likely to give when solicited by their peers, department chairs, campaign volunteers, or university leadership. Giving was most frequent for restricted purposes including academics, scholarships,

TABLE 9.1 Faculty and Staff Giving in 2011 by Institutional Type and Classification with Information on Number of Institutions Reporting, Average Number of Faculty and Staff Donors, Participation Rates, Individual Gifts, and Institutional Totals *

Institutional type / classification **	Total number of institutions ***	Average number of faculty and staff employees	Average number of faculty and staff donors	Median number of faculty and staff donors	Participation rates	Average faculty and staff gift	Median faculty and staff gift	Average total given by all faculty and staff per institution
All higher education	664	1,194	289	142	24.2%	$766	$477	$252,385
All private higher education	351	748	193	111	25.8%	$826	$482	$183,553
All public higher education	313	1,746	393	204	22.5%	$701	$458	$328,228
Associate's institutions	63	425	125	107	29.4%	$283	$252	$35,534
Baccalaureate institutions	185	407	100	84	24.6%	$875	$453	$72,383
Master's institutions	222	805	198	156	24.6%	$562	$412	$99,958
Research/Doctoral institutions	153	3,706	719	433	19.4%	$1123	$748	$808,378
Carnegie Community Engaged institutions	168	2,323	539	233	23.2%	$790	$520	$431,219

Source: CAE VSE Data Miner

Most of the data in this table were drawn directly from variables available within the VSE. A few of the figures (average number of employees) were extrapolated from VSE-provided data. Across the categories, institutions report some figures but not others, resulting in figures within this table that are not always in alignment with one another. A zero value is a default setting when an institution does not provide a particular data point. In order to reflect what is available to others within the VSE and without secondary calculations across the data, the values in this table include the zero values.

** In the VSE, institutions are not required to select a classification or to indicate whether they are public or private; therefore there are disparities in this column. Additionally, Carnegie Community Engaged Institutions span the other Carnegie Classifications and are also included in those data, just as associate's, baccalaureate, master's, and research/doctoral institutions also are within the public and private categories in most cases.

***This column reports the number of institutions that reported any data for the VSE less those institutions which were eliminated due to significant data problems.

and special projects rather than for unrestricted purposes. Three million dollars was the largest individual gift reported in the survey with 75 percent of the institutions reporting that gifts from faculty and staff averaged more than $100. Notable variations were evident in giving by regional groupings (employees of midwestern institutions were more likely to give), Carnegie Classification (faculty and staff at baccalaureate colleges had higher giving levels), and institutional size (employees at institutions of less than 1,000 students gave at a higher level).

In addition to March (2005), several others (Agypt, Christensen, & Nesbit, 2011; Holland, 1997; Holland & Miller, 1999; Knight, 2004) have explored institutional and individual differences in giving by university employees. In a three-institution survey of faculty donors of record (n = 183), researchers (Holland, 1997; Holland & Miller, 1999) found that 86.7 percent of the liberal arts college faculty, 80.5 percent of the comprehensive university faculty, and 61.5 percent of the research university faculty believed that giving was important. Invited to select from a list of 30 motives for giving, the respondents, most of whom were senior, tenured faculty, most often chose altruism, social responsibility to the institution, self-fulfillment, professional attitude, conviction, and institutional loyalty, with institutional loyalty holding most constant across the three institutions. A select group of interviewees (n = 12) cited allegiance and connectivity as reasons for giving in a Bowling Green State University (BGSU) study (Knight, 2004). The quantitative portion of the BGSU study drew together giving and demographic data and found that full-time administrators were more often donors than full- or part-time faculty or hourly staff. High salaries, long institutional employment, previous giving, in-town residence, and alumni status also were characteristics of faculty and staff donors. In Agypt et al.'s (2011) longitudinal study of two annual campaigns at a public university, only salary was found to be an accurate predictor of giving, while length of service was relevant in one campaign but not in another. Unlike the other studies, the latter research focused on external giving of faculty and staff to the United Way and local arts organizations. In the Agypt et al. analysis, hourly staff gave the most, and neither sex nor age significantly affected the giving of any faculty or staff group.

A second group of case studies (Byrne, 2005; Cardon, 2009; Gray & Hohnstreiter, 2012), conducted at public institutions, provides examples of faculty and staff fundraising efforts at single sites through analyses of campaign strategies. All are inspiring success stories and testaments to organized, faculty- and staff-specific fundraising campaigns. An annual campaign initiated in 2001 at the University of Arkansas at Little Rock (UALR) increased participation from 6.5 percent to 42 percent of benefits-eligible employees within three years (Byrne, 2005). A carefully chosen steering committee of faculty, administrators, and staff shaped campaign administration and practices, including a strategy that aligned with the culture of the university and focused on participation goals rather than fiscal ones. Restricted giving, typically back to employees own units, was made easy by a variety of convenient giving vehicles and was encouraged by a friendly sense of competition among areas. Requests for gifts built on the momentum of the academic calendar and existing events. Solicitations spoke to the importance of employee giving for external fundraising. The UALR techniques were also successful at Southern Utah University (SUU) in a 2008 redesign of its faculty and staff campaign that resulted in a participation increase from 27 percent to 85 percent in one year (Cardon, 2009). Mail appeals, one-on-one solicitations, pitches at meetings, and special events formed a strategy for a teaching center campaign emphasizing faculty and staff giving (Gray & Hohnstreiter, 2012). Gray and Hohnstreiter reported that in 2010, 100 donors gave $30,000, one third of that center's budget for the year, and that the staff had come to anticipate this support as part of the center's annual budget. Faculty and staff, Gray and Hohnstreiter concluded, had not been asked for philanthropic support before but were willing to give because they believed in the center's work.

Turning from annual giving to major giving, I conducted a phenomenological study of faculty who had made gifts or planned gifts of $25,000 or more to their academic unit (Shaker & Palmer, 2012). I interviewed six female and four male senior, retired, and administrative faculty about their professional histories, institutional experiences, and philanthropic activities in order to better understand them as "faculty philanthropists." The small sample size and single institutional setting are study limitations that reduce its applicability to practice. The qualitative methodology, however, provides preliminary in-depth understanding of the donors' motivations and experiences that lends insight into the quantitative and case study findings. I discovered that all of these faculty had been administrators who had developed some understanding of fundraising in their careers and had thoughtful views about philanthropy and higher education. They had worked at the study institution for 15 to 20 years and enjoyed successful, respected, and fulfilling careers. All but one of the donors had made annual gifts before making their larger commitment and several had become annual donors almost grudgingly. Over time they underwent philanthropic transformations, and they came to see giving as an outgrowth of their professional commitment. Many were inspired by philanthropic faculty colleagues in deciding to make their own major gifts, all but one of which were estate gifts. The participants were deeply invested in the life of the university, and university life had shaped their private lives, from hobbies and interests to friendships and, obviously, personal philanthropy. Many of the gifts coincided with life events, such as retirement planning, or institutional efforts, such as comprehensive campaigns. For most, the idea of making a significant gift was considered and discussed at home long before it came to fruition. As it turned out, the faculty major donors were not the most highly paid faculty in their unit or on campus, thus salary was not an effective predictor of proclivity to give. It is quotes from this study that you see throughout this chapter, and, together with other literature in this section, it helped shape the subsequent recommendations for fundraisers.

Recommendations for Enhancing Faculty and Staff Giving

> *I think education is one of the most important things that can happen for an individual, to carry them forward, something they can't lose. It makes such a difference in people's lives… So, to me it's a very worthwhile thing to support.*

> —Faculty major donor

Although only a small fraction (1.3%) of individual donations to higher education, giving by faculty and staff not only is relevant for its own sake, it is also widely assumed to send a signal to external donors as an important measure of internal commitment (Byrne, 2005; Dove, Lindauer, & Madvig, 2001; March, 2005; Schroeder, 2002). The most visible signals come from headline-grabbing gifts like the one to SUNY Stony Brook or large collective faculty and staff gifts garnered during major comprehensive campaigns (Eaton, 2011; Palmer, 2004; Pérez-Pena, 2011). All faculty and staff have a key role to play, however, as exemplar donors and "boosters" for their institutions, people who shape the case for support, spread the word, and lend credence to fundraising requests with their own gifts (Collins, 2000; Dube, 2005; Eckert & Pollack, 2000).

Building support among faculty and staff is a process which requires time, commitment, and planning. A series of recommendations developed from the studies cited in this chapter and professional experience follow and will help fundraisers hone their efforts (Table 9.2). The suggestions are certainly not all-inclusive, and because institutions vary in their faculty and staff fundraising strategies and readiness, the perspectives of those raising money at institutional and unit levels may differ. These recommendations are, therefore, framed as broadly as possible to be helpful across the several contexts for fundraising within the academy.

These recommendations apply for both annual giving and major/planned gift fundraising. Research shows that in some combination, those faculty or staff with long institutional histories, knowledge of fundraising and philanthropy, a commitment to engaging with the community in their professional capacity, and deep institutional ties may be good prospects for significant gifts (Shaker & Palmer, 2012). These characteristics of a select group of major faculty donors likely come as no surprise to fundraisers but perhaps they offer a reminder to look to colleagues anew as prospects rather than solely as coworkers. This research also suggests that personalized efforts to woo faculty and staff during comprehensive or capital campaigns and during their pre-retirement planning period can lead to significant gifts.

When faculty and staff (and retirees) become major donors, it raises their stake in institutional success to an even greater level, and it may empower them to take a more vocal role in the institution's future. This can have the positive consequence of increasing the bond of loyalty between faculty and staff and the institution. Alternatively, the depth of donors' institutional knowledge may lead to difficult situations if they choose to use their gifts as leverage to advocate for a point of view or criticize institutional policy. On the other hand, faculty and retirees of long standing can also be encouraged to think of both their legacy and the future of the institution after they are gone as a way of overcoming difficult short-term issues.

Those seeking additional understanding of the overall landscape of research about faculty and staff giving should explore the full studies summarized in this chapter and examine the resources available through the Council for the Advancement and Support of Education website (http://www.case.org), which features a substantial section on faculty and staff fundraising and giving for premiere members (i.e., those who pay a higher membership fee). As this study and review of the literature has intended to show, we have only limited understandings of faculty and staff giving. There is ample opportunity to build new knowledge for both scholarly and practical reasons through qualitative, quantitative, and mixed-method studies at the individual, institutional, and national levels.

Faculty and Staff Giving in the Future

> I've always been a strong believer that wherever you are you participate in what makes it go.
>
> —Faculty major donor

At the most recent reckoning there were 1.5 million faculty working in U.S. postsecondary institutions and 2.4 million non-instructional personnel (including full-time and part-time employees and medical school employees; Knapp et al., 2011). With only 24.2 percent of faculty and staff reported as donors (CAE, 2012b), there is a great deal of untapped potential among the academic ranks. We find ourselves in an era of major upheaval for colleges and universities as institutional budgets are constricting, technology and disciplinary connections are loosening academic employees' institutional ties, the ranks of staff and administrative employees are growing, and the tenure-track and tenured faculty are being replaced by a new majority of part-time and full-time faculty who are ineligible for tenure (American Federation of Teachers, 2010; Burgan, 2006; Schuster & Finkelstein, 2006; Votruba, 1996). Consequences of this turmoil on faculty and staff giving are evident at St. Catharine College where, in an ironic twist of fate, just a year after the 200 employees pledged $200,000 for a new building, the institution announced a suspension in its contributions to faculty and staff retirement funds (Smith, 2012), showing that institutions may not always respond to the generosity of faculty and staff in a comparable manner.

Despite difficult times, faculty and staff giving has been on the uptake over the last decade (CAE, 2012b), demonstrating that forces of change may not have predictable effects when it comes to faculty and staff giving. Fostering the lasting loyalties and commitment that lead to consistent and increasing faculty and staff giving over time (among other desirable institutional consequences including involvement in the life of the institution) may, however, become more difficult both practically and ethically. Building regularized giving campaigns for faculty and staff, reinforcing the outcomes and importance of this support, and encouraging participation at any level will create a culture of giving built on well-established fundraising practices that will in turn create a foundation for the future. One concrete step both academic leaders—among faculty as well as administration—and fundraisers alike can take is to begin to reflect on just how much of academic work performed by all members of the academic community is at least in part philanthropic, what the Indiana University Center on Philanthropy has defined as "voluntary action for the public

TABLE 9.2 Recommendations for Enhancing Faculty and Staff Giving and Strategies for Implementation

Recommendation	Strategies for Implementation
Determine and fine-tune a fundraising strategy that is right for the institution.	• Develop knowledge about faculty and staff giving, past and present, on campus and more broadly through the literature, benchmarking, and conversations with peers. • Build energy around a campaign by being thoughtful in its timing and positioning within the life of the institution. • Consider the strengths and challenges of the particular institution and craft realistic and achievable goals. • Work to overcome institutional challenges in collecting faculty and staff giving data in order to operate from an appropriate and institutionalized baseline.
Faculty and staff are not likely to give if they are not asked.	• Ask faculty and staff to give in a targeted, personal, and direct manner. • Craft messages that are appropriate to the knowledge of faculty and staff as institutional insiders. • Provide ample and easy opportunities for restricted and directed giving. • Develop a regularized cycle and approach for an annual faculty and staff campaign. • Provide multiple avenues for giving using various communication channels. • Encourage giving that makes sense to each person and their capacity. • Develop a clear and convincing rationale for why faculty and staff should give to counter the sentiment that "I contribute enough through my work."

(continued)

TABLE 9.2 Continued

Recommendation	Strategies for Implementation
Treat all faculty, staff, and administrators as prospects with the potential to give a little or a lot.	• Correspond and develop relationships with faculty and staff just as you would with alumni. • Help create the institution or unit as a community with faculty and staff members as participants, rather than employees. • Remind people that all gifts are valued and respect those who proportionately generous from a small income base. • Assume that faculty and staff nondonors can be viable prospects for larger gifts in the long-term. • Be a good steward of faculty and staff donors, realizing a different strategy may be required than with external donors.
Include and educate faculty and staff as volunteers and campaign leaders in fundraising efforts.	• Do not assume that faculty and staff understand anything about institutional fundraising practices or policies. • Dispel myths and misconceptions about the processes and outcomes of fundraising through regular educational programming. • Recruit faculty and staff for institution-wide, internal fundraising purposes. • Include faculty and staff in external fundraising efforts and educate them in the process. • Create allies among the faculty by asking larger donors to talk about their gifts. • Faculty and staff volunteers likely do not how to ask for support; training is a good thing. • Work to overcome faculty biases in relation to administrative practices related to fundraising.
Create messages that build on feelings of institutional loyalty and pride.	• Foster giving by reminding faculty and staff of what they value most about their institution. • Inform faculty and staff about the good effects of their donations. • Help faculty and staff see the long-term impact of their gifts on the institution they care about. • Take advantage of standing events and landmarks at the institution to build momentum and promote fundraising efforts.
Speak the language of philanthropy and serve as a model donor.	• Through words and actions, demonstrate the potential and opportunity of philanthropy. • Use appropriate language and rhetoric to speak of giving and teach faculty and staff to do the same. • As dictated by common wisdom, fundraisers should also be donors and use what they learn from that experience to guide their practice and the development of fundraising systems and structures. • Inspire others with your personal commitment to supporting the institution.

TABLE 9.2 Continued

Recommendation	Strategies for Implementation
Give the faculty and staff avenues for knowing the development staff.	• People give to people; fundraisers should become a part of the institution beyond the development realm however they are able. • Embrace and seek roles within institutional and unit leadership and consider the part that philanthropy can play in shaping and enhancing broader school missions. • Be a presence at events aimed at faculty and staff and on campus in general. • Communicate with (and listen to) faculty and staff on a regular basis and pay attention to what is going on in their corner of the academy; build trust.
Give faculty and staff philanthropy visibility on the campus.	• Tell stories in person, in print, and online about those who make extraordinary gifts either individually or collectively. • Celebrate small gifts by faculty (e.g., adjunct) or staff (e.g., custodial) who might not be expected to care or to contribute. • Make giving a friendly competition by encouraging and recognizing rates of participation among units. • Promote a culture where giving is a natural act and the mentality is that "everyone can contribute." • Instill the belief that philanthropy is part of the institution's culture and is continuous and systematic, not episodic.
Make connections between faculty and staff work and education's purpose in society.	• Help faculty and staff recognize the role of higher education in advancing society and the potential of their philanthropy to further this purpose. • Encourage the role and capacity of philanthropy to serve as a tool for faculty and staff to build on their values and expand on the work to which they are already committed. • Whenever possible, connect giving to the institution to making the community better.

good" (Payton, 1988, p. 3). There are distinct elements of faculty work that are, in fact, philanthropic, and this approach to faculty work is being explored systematically in a forthcoming volume, *Faculty and the Public Good: The Philanthropic Meaning of Academic Work*, which argues that philanthropy and a care for the common good are inherent—but often forgotten—in the work of faculty and their institutions.

Future discussion of faculty and staff as donors will benefit from consideration of the full range of their philanthropic gifts to their institutions and invite even more substantial philanthropy with respect to resources such as time, talent, treasure, and loyalty. Fundraising activities, of course, must accommodate changing times and unique institutional circumstances but with planning, and a deliberate and focused effort, what is put in place now will serve institutions, and higher education, well in an uncertain future.

Notes

1. Although 682 entities submitted some portion of the faculty and staff giving data in 2011, due to reporting errors and complications, for the purpose of the analysis in this chapter, data from 664 institutions were considered.
2. The CAE VSE faculty and staff giving analysis was completed in partnership with Brittany Miller (doctoral student, Center on Philanthropy at Indiana University; graduate assistant, Indiana University Foundation) and with support of the Indiana University Foundation.

References

Agypt, B., Christensen, R. K., & Nesbit, R. (2011). A tale of two charitable campaigns: Longitudinal analysis of employee giving at a public university. *Nonprofit and Voluntary Sector Quarterly*. Retrieved from http://nvs.sagepub.com/content/early/2011/09/02/08997640114 18836.abstract

American Association of University Professors. (2011). *It's not over yet: The annual report on the economic status of the profession, 2010–2011*. Washington DC: Author. Retrieved from http://www.aaup.org/NR/rdonlyres/17BABE36-BA30-467D-BE2F-34C37325549A/0/zreport. pdf

American Federation of Teachers. (2010). *American academic: A national survey of part-time/adjunct faculty*. Washington DC: Author.

Byrne, J. (2005). Forming a culture of giving: A case study in successful university internal fundraising. *Metropolitan Universities, 16*(4), 71–84.

Burgan, M. (2006). *Whatever happened to the faculty?: Drift and decision in higher education*. Baltimore, MD: Johns Hopkins University Press.

Cardon, R. (2009). Developing and implementing a successful employee giving campaign: A case study from Southern Utah University. (Master of Arts Project.) Retrieved from http://www.suu.edu/hss/comm/masters/Capstone/Project/R_Cardon.pdf

Collins, M. E. (2000). Campaign strategies: Drawing together. *CASE Currents, 26*(7), 13–14. Retrieved from http://www.case.org/Publications_and_Products/2000/September_2000/Campaign_Strategies_Drawing_Together.html

Council for Aid to Education. (2012a, February 15). Colleges and universities raise $30.30 billion in 2011: 8.2 percent increase fueled by gifts for capital purposes. Retrieved from http://www.cae.org/content/pdf/VSE_2011_Press_Release.pdf

Council for Aid to Education. (2012b). [Voluntary Support for Education survey data miner]. Unpublished raw data available to survey participants.

Dove, K. E., Lindauer, J. A., & Madvig, C. P. (2001). *Conducting a successful annual giving campaign*. San Francisco, CA: Jossey-Bass.

Dube, S. (2005). *How to engage staff, faculty and alumni as volunteers in fundraising at Royal Roads University*. *Dissertation Abstracts International, 44*(01). (UMI. MR04080). Retrieved from http://proquest.umi.com/pqdlink?did=974437341&Fmt=7&clientId =79356&RQT=309&VName=PQD

Eaton, C. (2011, December 13). $150-million gift to Stony Brook is a record for any SUNY campus. *The Chronicle of Higher Education*. Retrieved from http://chronicle.com/article/150-Million-Gift-to-Stony/130095/

Eckert, G., & Pollack, R. H. (2000). Sowing the seeds of philanthropy. *CASE Currents, 26*(7), 46–49. Retrieved from http://www.case.org/Publications_and_Products/CURRENTS/CURRENTS_Archive/2000/September_2000/Sowing_the_Seeds_of_Philanthropy.html

Gray, T., & Hohnstreiter, M. (2012). Go for the gold: Fundraising for teaching centers. In J. E. Miller & J. E. Groccia (Eds.), *To Improve the Academy, 30,* 262–276.

Holland, A. P. (1997). Faculty motivations for giving to their employing to their employing institutions. *Dissertation Abstracts International* (UMI. 9735711)

Holland, A. P., & Miller, M. T. (1999). *Faculty as donors: Why they give to their employing institutions.* (ERIC Document Reproduction Service No. ED439648)

Knapp, L. G., Kelly-Reid, J. E., & Ginder, S. A. (2011). *Employees in postsecondary institutions, fall 2010, and salaries of full-time instructional staff, 2010–11* (NCES 2012-276). U.S. Department of Education. Washington, DC: National Center for Education Statistics. Retrieved from http://nces.ed.gov/pubsearch

Knight, W. E. (2004). Influences on participation in a university faculty and staff annual giving campaign. *The CASE International Journal of Educational Advancement, 4*(3), 221–232.

March, K. S. (2005). A descriptive study of faculty and staff giving practices at public institutions of higher education within the United States. *Dissertation Abstracts International* (UMI No. 3173632).

Nadolny, T. L. (2012, March 28). NEC faculty donates cash to save jobs. *Concord Monitor.* Retrieved from http://www.concordmonitor.com/article/320059/nec-faculty-donates-cash-to-save-jobs

National Committee for Responsive Philanthropy. (2003). *Giving at work 2003.* Washington DC: Author. Retrieved from http://www.ncrp.org/files/GivingAtWork.pdf

Palmer, T. (2004, January). Advance Work: Giving begins at home. *CASE Currents.* Retrieved from http://www.case.org/Publications_and_Products/CURRENTS/CURRENTS_Archive/2004/January_2004/AdvanceWork_Giving_Begins_at_Home.htm

Penn State University. (2010). Faculty and staff giving boosts programs in college of ag sciences. Retrieved from http://live.psu.edu/story/45593

Penn State University. (2011). Faculty and staff portion of For the Future begins. Retrieved from http://live.psu.edu/story/53087

Pérez-Pena, R. (2011, December 13). Stony Brook University to get $150 million gift. *New York Times.* Retrieved from http://www.nytimes.com/2011/12/14/nyregion/stony-brook-university-given-150-million.html?_r=1

Schroeder, F. W. (2002). The annual giving program. In M. J. Worth (Ed.), *New strategies for educational fundraising* (pp. 75–88). Westport, CT: Praeger.

Schuster, J. H., & Finkelstein, M. J. (2006). *The restructuring of academic work and careers.* Baltimore, MD: Johns Hopkins University Press.

Shaker, G. G., & Palmer, M. M. (2012). The donors next door: Raising funds from faculty for faculty development centers. To improve the academy, The donors next door: Raising funds from faculty for faculty development centers. In J. E. Groccia & L. Cruz (Eds.), *To Improve the Academy, 31,* 85-100.

Smith, M. (2012, March 23). Employees give th. College take th away. *Inside Higher Ed.* Retrieved from http://www.insidehighered.com/news/2012/03/23/kentucky-college-cuts-retirement contributions-delays-raise-announcement

University of Florida Foundation. (n.d.). Two longtime faculty members give to continue their educational legacy at UF. Retrieved from http://uff.ufl.giftplans.org/index.php?cID=196

Votruba, J. C. (1996). Strengthening the university's alignment with society: Challenges and strategies. *Journal of Public Service and Outreach, 1*(1), 29–36.

10

BUILDING A CULTURE OF STUDENT PHILANTHROPY

Lori A. Hurvitz

The concept of involving students in institutional fundraising is not a new idea. Lyman L. Pierce, considered a pioneer fundraiser for higher education, involved students in fundraising endeavors for the first time at Stanford in 1922. After his success in California, Pierce was called to his own alma mater, the University of Minnesota, where he challenged students to raise one quarter of the campaign target. In the end, they raised over 30 percent of the total, more than six times the amount raised by faculty pledges, and almost 70 percent of the amount pledged by all of the institution's alumni (Cutlip, 1965). Since the 1970s, student alumni associations have continued to grow in popularity (Council for Advancement and Support of Education, n.d.), and in the last decade, institutions began to create and implement intentional development initiatives and programs aimed at students in an effort to educate students about the importance of alumni support as well as cultivating a source of sustainable revenue. Modeled after successful strategies utilized by the National Pre-Alumni Council of the United Negro College Fund and private women's colleges, as well as by religiously affiliated colleges, institutions are learning how to better target their messages to what motivates specific alumni populations to give (Briechle, 2007; Drezner, 2008, 2009, 2010). By appealing to their sense of responsibility, preconceived ideas and teachings about philanthropy, loyalty to and bond with their institution, and the desire to help future students, research has found that institutions are getting better at cultivating students for future giving (Briechle, 2007; Drezner, 2008, 2009, 2010; Friedmann, 2003).

While institutions are creating and implementing development initiatives and programs aimed at students to expand their donor base, little guidance exists on the best mechanisms to approach a student population at large about fundraising that will deeply affect a campus. Simply taking what we know about alumni philanthropy and applying it to students seems a rational approach on the surface, however, it does not take into account either the subtle or obvious differences between alumni and students or their frames of reference; however, it should not be assumed we cannot take lessons from established traditional philanthropy programs and apply them to student populations.

Significant research has already proved that the characteristic factors of gender, race, age, and socio-economic status effect alumni giving (Baade & Sundberg, 1993, 1996; Balz & National Institute of Independent Colleges and Universities, 1987; Clotfelter, 2003; Gallo & Hubschman, 2003; Monks, 2003; Young & Fischer, 1996). Going beyond these basic characteristics, institutionally controlled factors can also influence alumni's tendency to give. Two independent studies of multiple institutional members of the Council for the Advancement and Support of Education (CASE) found that the resources and money spent on alumni activities most aptly explain successful fundraising programs (Harrison, 1995; Harrison, Mitchell, & Peterson, 1995). The reason behind this phenomenon is that attending programs and events as an alumnus/a indicated a feeling of connectedness between a person and his or her alma mater. And those alumni who feel a connection with their alma mater are much more likely to be supportive (Conley, 1999; Gallo & Hubschman, 2003; Mael & Ashforth, 1992).

New research is beginning to focus on alternative explanations for alumni's propensities to give, which lends theory to student cultivation. Clotfelter's (2003) research found that "alumni donations made to their alma maters were highly correlated to their expressed satisfaction with their own college experience and other measures of satisfaction with the institution" (p. 119). Institutions must face the fact that the origin of alumni satisfaction begins with the student experience. That satisfaction can also lead to a desire to stay involved with the operations of the institution, such as attending programs and giving, post-graduation. And when institutions efficiently target their resources towards alumni who are known to have graduated with higher satisfaction levels, they find higher levels of success (Monks, 2003). Additionally, for both alumni engagement initiatives and student cultivation programs, money is most wisely spent when it is directed towards programs that attempt to build long-term sustaining relationships (Gallo & Hubschman, 2003). Combining these two ideas, institutions that invest resources wisely on building students' relationships with their institutions, particularly aimed at students who are already engaged and involved with their college experience, thereby indicating that they would already graduate satisfied, can further increase satisfaction and their likelihood of choosing to stay engaged as well as their continued generosity.

What Is Student Satisfaction?

Richard Oliver (1980) contends that satisfaction is a function of the expectations a purchaser has about a product or experience and whether the resulting experience satisfies those expectations. Students enter college with a set of expectations of what they want out of their experience and, as alumni, they can reflect on whether or not those expectations came to fruition, either leaving them satisfied, or not, leaving them dissatisfied. "Satisfaction" here implies that an alumnus/a approved of his/her overall experience as a student and later feels it necessary to show gratitude and appreciation. While giving can be considered an express measure of such satisfaction, it is important to note that there are many other ways to think about satisfaction.

Clotfelter's (2003) study found two relevant factors having significant and positive relationships with satisfaction: whether the college attended was the first choice institution during the admissions process and whether someone at the institution took an interest in the individual. Baade and Sundberg (1996) found the quality of the overall educational experience and institutional quality generally influential. Alexander Astin (1993), in his study of the college student experience, explored satisfaction of students entering college and found satisfaction to be most influenced, not by the entering student's characteristics, but by environmental experiences while in school. Astin's (1993) study suggests there are two categories where student satisfaction can be measured: subjective value of the student experience and the perception of that experience. His study examines five satisfaction categories: relationships with faculty, curriculum and instruction, student life, individual support services, and the availability of facilities. His findings indicate that the highest levels of satisfaction stem from academic courses in a student's major, extracurricular involvement, and overall satisfaction with the college experience. Additionally, studies consistently show students more involved and engaged in their education will be more satisfied with their overall experience (Astin, 1993; Kuh, 1991, 1995, 2005; Tinto, 1993). Furthermore, experiences students have while enrolled in school have a positive influence on their likelihood to continue their participation, including giving, post-graduation (Gallo & Hubschman, 2003).

Since satisfaction is a key motivation for giving, it is essential to understand the benefits of satisfaction with the college experience, and also what specifically leads to that satisfaction, particularly because students who are not satisfied with their overall experience are unlikely to become future supporters (Johnson & Eckel, 1998). Additionally, once they graduate unsatisfied, it is nearly impossible to turn around their negative feelings (Johnson & Eckel, 1998). Astin (1993) and Tinto (1993) each report that out-of-class experiences which support the educational process significantly influence persistence and satisfaction. Chickering's (1969) seminal research finds that institutional commitment to the well-rounded student will generate similar feelings of commitment of students to the institution. Students will feel more connected and more motivated. Ideally, the increased motivation will ultimately extend to giving both at the time of graduation and throughout the alumnus/a's life. Therefore, it is imperative to encourage involvement and satisfaction with the student experience to start a trend that will continue past graduation.

Several problems exist with basing future giving solely on satisfaction. First, it relies on the idea that students already view their experience, whether positive or not, as worthy of support. Second, while students may be satisfied with their experience, since many institutions are so decentralized, students may compartmentalize that satisfaction toward a specific unit or department (Clark, 1971). And finally, while students may be satisfied with their overall education, they have no means to connect it with support for the institution. To compound the issue, Johnson and Eckel (1998) find that most students do not really understand the role of alumni and hold many misconceptions about alumni associations. Students simply do not know the different ways alumni benefit their education or how alumni can be involved with their alma maters. Even if students are seeking involvement both in college and after they graduate, they do not understand how their relationship with the institution will change over time and the different ways they can sustain their involvement, particularly after leaving campus.

Satisfaction to Action

In order to rectify the lack of understanding about philanthropy for students, Baade and Sundberg (1993) suggest starting early and teaching students the different avenues for involvement: "Given the importance of graduate's attachment and pride in their alma maters, a comprehensive fund-raising strategy ideally would begin at the time students are recruited" (Baade & Sundberg, 1993, n.p.). Institutions need to treat their students as if they were "alumni-in-training" (Pumerantz, 2004). Strategies must include ideas about what purpose alumni associations serve, provide clear and intentional messages about involvement, and combat the myths that institutions only value large donors (Gardner & Van der Veer, 1998). Creating structures and programs similar to those that are currently available to alumni but directed at students is inexpensive and extremely effective (Gaier, 2001). Since students are on campus and a captive audience, institutions can easily create new programs and alter existing programs to drive up student satisfaction, focus on creating a holistic student experience, and include involvement in traditional alumni functions to support the concept of sustained involvement and giving.

Mulugetta, Nash, and Murphy (1999) built a model of environmental influence for college students based on Alexander Astin's (1993) model of Input-Environment-Output (IEO), which can be applied to this case. Astin's developmental model for students follows the principles that: (a) students enter college with a set of characteristics, "inputs"; (b) their college experiences and environment including policies and practices of their institutions affect their development, "environment"; and (c) they depart the institution with reformulated characteristics, "outputs." Mulugetta et al. add an environmental module of "Institutional Commitment" into Astin's framework. Their argument is that institutions can alter student outcomes by "creating and reinforcing particular environmental circumstances" (p. 63). Their research differentiated between the learning outcomes students acquired on their own versus those that were "largely created and reinforced by the institution" (p. 63). Their model, I-C-E-O, was tested through the Cornell Traditions Program and offered "striking" results.

The model suggests that reinforcing the importance of student philanthropy on college campuses will create a culture of its own importance and the concept is spreading fast. Many institutions are already embarking on initiatives to teach the imperative lessons of institutional commitment. CASE (2009) reports over 300 members to the Affiliated Student Advancement Programs (ASAP) implementing programs designed to create a culture of philanthropy amongst their students. Most existing programs focus on senior class gift campaigns and transitioning students to alumni roles. One of the benefits to the institutions offering these programs includes more satisfied graduates who later become donors, recruiters, mentors to younger students, and ambassadors for the needs of their institutions in the private and public sectors (Johnson & Eckel, 1998). However, waiting until graduation nears to transition students might not be the most advantageous approach. A study of Boston College sophomores and seniors found that seniors already feel overwhelmed by the decisions and "real world" experiences they are preparing to confront. When waiting to educate students until right before they graduate and leave campus, Boston College experienced a "certain backlash among graduating seniors who had worries of their own financial survival after graduation" (Utter & Noble, 1999, p. 35). On the other hand, the study found sophomores more receptive and positive to the idea of giving back even though they had not yet been exposed to fundraising initiatives (Utter & Noble, 1999).

Prior research on student philanthropy education focused on specific programs like class giving campaigns or the advent of student alumni associations. While the findings in studies of these programs have been no less then startling with involvement in programs increasing student's emotional attachment to the institution and satisfaction, both found to increase the likelihood of giving (Conley, 1999), very little guidance existed on the best mechanisms to approach a student population about fundraising. This fact prompted a research study to look beyond programs that only engage a select group of students to educational initiatives that are offered to a student body at large, both proactively and possibly even passively, through messaging. The research explored how colleges and universities educate their entire student body about the importance of sustained philanthropic support for the institution and how the changes incorporating the philosophies into the environment influence the campus culture as they became instituted. The goal was to provide a framework for institutions embarking on student philanthropy initiatives to learn from a set of institutions already engaging in the practices. A qualitative study of nine of the Ivy Plus institutions (Columbia University, Cornell University, Dartmouth College, Harvard University, University of Pennsylvania, Princeton University, Yale University, the Massachusetts Institute of Technology, and Stanford University) examined the breadth and depth of some of the country's most successful higher education fundraising machines in effort to create a useful framework for practitioners (Hurvitz, 2010). While these institutions only represented a very narrow spectrum of today's higher education environment, they proved interesting for study for many reasons.

Baade and Sundberg (1993, 1996) determined that the higher the public regard for the institution, the more likely alumni are to donate. These institutions are unarguably held in high regard around the world and therefore, in some ways, alumni should already be predisposed towards giving. Student philanthropy education initiatives would therefore show an influence on students and alumni above and beyond the traditional giving and participation rates. Due to their established campus cultures, these particular institutions also provided an overview of the reasons behind whether or not an institution would choose to incorporate student philanthropy into their culture, where they have been successful and unsuccessful, and valuable lessons learned about the process. And finally, these institutions have the resources available to dedicate to programs paving the way to learn what works and what does not.

Action to Results

The institutional review revealed a number of effective mechanisms, initiatives, and best practices employed across the spectrum of institutions that can be applied to all different types of colleges and universities. Additionally, the study also appropriately reflected the barriers and difficulties individuals or departments faced when trying to commence or further develop existing programs that will also be addressed. Overall, the findings indicated the utilization of a number of programmatic initiatives designed to teach philanthropy education including engaging student volunteers, alumni–student interaction and role modeling, events and programs, and online resources and networking opportunities for students, and of course, robust senior class gift drives employing strategies specific to the culture of the institution and purposeful peer-to-peer solicitation techniques. Furthermore, the institutions pay close attention to their campus cultures and unique histories across their planning and strategies. While each campus hosts its own unique array of programs, a common theme throughout is that their strategies are keyed into the needs, desires, and expectations of their own students thereby driving up student satisfaction, and hopefully, those students' propensity to stay involved as alumni and give.

Understanding an institution's population of students and their needs, desires, and areas for improvement is the first step in developing a success-ful student philanthropy education program. A good starting place is to think about students who are already engaged on campus. We know from research on alumni that institutions benefit from targeting their efforts to alumni who are have already expressed their satisfaction with their alma mater and are already engaged and involved (Monks, 2003). Using the same logic, students who are involved on campus or who show an inclination to get involved with philan-thropy are not only a natural target for cultivation, but they are also the people more likely to continue to participate post-graduation (Gallo & Hubschman, 2003). By finding students who are already satisfied with their experience, who are most likely the more involved and influential students on campus as well, institutions can create a core group to lead the charge on spreading the message about the importance of philanthropy. Additionally, these students can provide valuable insight on the student culture to advisors and development profession-als about where the most effective inroads can be made with their peers. Ideas will travel faster student-to-student than a university administration could ever hope to achieve. Students are going to be the best spokespeople for a cause. The institutions in the study went to great lengths to educate their student volunteers and committee members on the institution's messages on the impor-tance of giving with the intention that a small group of students can take that information and act as ambassadors expanding the knowledge to their peers. Researchers and practitioners alike have found that peer-to-peer solicitation techniques are extremely effective. For institutions who do not have existing structures of student leaders with the specific focus of student philanthropy, by reaching out to students in other areas of involvement on campus who are known to be later financial donors such as athletes, Greeks, and student gov-ernment representatives (Monks, 2003), quick headway can be made by target-ing an active group of students to start the education process.

Steps to Success

If knowing the students who need to be targeted is the first step, having access to them is the second. Most alumni and development staff, often those charged with cultivating donors, are secluded from day-to-day student life on cam-pus whether by geography or purpose. It is incumbent on those professionals to build relationships with the people who work most directly with students: student affairs professionals. Involvement by student affairs staff gives programs and messages a more targeted value because professionals in student affairs are trained to recognize the needs of students. Additionally, all students will have interaction with some area of student affairs during their college careers widening their contact points with their potential audience (Kellogg, 1996; Kroll 1991). Development staff need to be prepared for some potential unease from colleagues in student affairs who may be uncomfortable talking to students about fundraising. Addressing their fears head on and aligning the goals of alumni relations and development with those of student affairs will likely break down some of the barriers and hesitations from future collaborations. At the end of the day, both organizations are working towards the same end goal: graduating satisfied students. Realizing this is not an "us versus them" situation and consistency of efforts can breed positive results. In fact, Chickering's (1969) seminal studies of student development suggest that environments that most consistently project objectives through policies, programs, and resource allocations, will generate that same consistency of ideas amongst its students. Furthermore, a collegial relationship can provide benefits to student affairs as well such as increased resources for programming, access to alumni for career development and networking, speakers for campus events, or experts to advise student groups or to teach institutional history at orientation.

There are some downsides to be aware of as well. Clark (1971) warns of students' tendency to compartmentalize their experience and satisfaction with their college experience to a specific department or unit, instead of recognizing the connection to the institutional as a whole. Student affairs administrators can help combat the compartmentalization if they reinforce the same ideas and messages about philanthropy that students will hear from development and alumni relations. Students, while busy with their studies, extra-curricular activities, and friends, are not going to magically understand the point of why their institution is making sure they network with and learn from alumni and understand the value of giving. It is important to offer role models who model the behavior future alumni should emulate.

Finding alumni role models for students and expanding programs to include larger groups of students and more alumni through any number of programmatic initiatives can achieve many goals simultaneously. As mechanisms for role modeling, networking, and learning altruistic behaviors, alumni participating in the lives of students re-enforces the messages student philanthropy teaches (Brittingham et al., 1990; Dovidio, Piliavin, Schroeder, & Penner, 2006; Drezner, 2010). Programs such as alumni mentoring, career networking, and sponsored internships have the added benefit of showing students that their institutions are committed to their being successful and well-rounded, which will be beneficial to the students' overall satisfaction with their experience (Astin, 1993; Chickering, 1969). Furthermore, it is important for students to understand how their experience with their alma mater can change and develop post-graduation (Trice & Beyer, 1993). By providing opportunities for alumni and students to connect with each other, the students, the alumni, and the institution benefit. Ikenberry (1999) and Young and Fischer (1996) established that alumni who stay involved with their institutions post-graduation are more likely to donate as well. The institutions in the study go to great lengths to provide opportunities for students and alumni to interact through programmatic initiatives and events as well as virtual networks. Using their own unique campus cultures, programs involving career planning and exploration, opportunities for free food—the easiest way to a college student's heart is through his or her stomach—and social networking both in person and online, paved the way for alumni-student interaction.

Once students' attention is gained, the messages delivered and how they are being delivered are possibly the most important aspects of a student philanthropy program. Unfortunately, there is not one magic-bullet phrase that will bring a student philanthropy program from start to success, but it might not be necessary to start from scratch either. Once a group of students is identified to work with and a handful of programs that are tied to student philanthropy initiatives are found, simply capitalize on their opportunities presented. Develop a few strategic messages that apply to all different types of situations and repeat them, at every chance available. George Homan stressed the importance of multiple and shared sentiments and their effect of being "emergent and mutually reinforcing" (Beyer, Hannah, & Milton, 2000, p. 327). Applying Homan's theories to student philanthropy education, institutions should use every opportunity, no matter the circumstance, to embed their messages on the import of alumni giving and involvement.

One of the most common starting points of student philanthropy on college campuses is the senior gift campaign. All of the Ivy-Plus institutions in the study have robust senior giving programs often serving as the cornerstone of their philanthropy education programs. The senior gift campaigns exist on the campuses for two over-arching reasons: to begin the tradition of individual annual giving to the institution and to educate graduating students about the importance of giving to the institution. These ideas are certainly not unique from other colleges and universities, particularly private schools. However, the improved results, as a more general student philanthropy program, are significant.

One common theme heard from all of the participants was the importance of paying attention to campus culture and allowing it to influence the kind of senior class gift program the institution engages in. Pumerantz (2004) identified that fitting programs to campus culture was an instrumental component of success. The programs of the Ivy-Plus ranged from pledge programs, to three-week drives, to more traditional, year-long fundraising campaigns. Further probing revealed that a simple explanation of the type of gift campaign the institution has is a clear reflection of the culture of the college or university. Some institutions have also chosen to recognize young donors in their leadership giving programs either by incorporating them into existing alumni recognition programs or by instituting new recognition levels for students. Not only do the leadership giving levels give students important and deserved recognition for their leadership giving, but they also reflect an important aspect of their experience as alumni where giving is recognized at different levels through membership in societies and with different honors.

Measuring Progress

Setting appropriate metrics is a necessary component of student philanthropy education as it is the only way to provide evidence-based results of initiatives; however, measurement was one of the most difficult obstacles participants in the study faced. Best practices indicate that a broader system of measurement to track the changes they see occurring in their culture are the most useful considering the longer-term nature of student philanthropy education. Most simply, measuring event attendance and dollars raised both amongst students and alumni is a quick results–orientated approach, but it is also short sighted of the larger goals. While it is difficult to measure student understanding of philanthropy education, it is not difficult to choose indicators of success that makes sense with distinct campus and alumni cultures. These could include more active young alumni participation and involvement, increased enthusiasm among volunteers, the desire by graduates to stay connected including attending regional events, updating forwarding addresses and online profiles, and volunteering with their local alumni clubs, promoting the institution to prospective students, reading alumni publications, and returning to campus for some of the milestone events that engaged them in the first place. While these goals are non-financial, many are measurable and can show growth over time. Finally, it is important about staying realistic about what you are trying to accomplish. There are both subjective and abstract realities to the work of influencing students. While students may not realize what is happening around them and not completely understand the reason for donating to their senior class gift, if they graduate feeling strongly connected to their alma mater and desire to stay involved post-graduation, they are much more likely to support the institution financially in the future. It is essentially important to realize that long-term success on these initiatives may not be realized for decades, but higher education cannot afford the risk to not implement these ideas.

Call to Action

Now is the time to revitalize student philanthropy as a sustainable revenue source for higher education. While a significant amount of research exists on alumni giving, there is very little information available about how to approach students to instill the ideas of philanthropy. Unfortunately, there is no out-of-the-box program that can create a campus culture where student philanthropy is widely accepted, but this study did present some options for raising the profile of philanthropy for students. Institutions can easily capitalize on the work they are already engaging in to improve results by garnering additional support and resources, increasing collaborations across the university, and being more intentional and strategic in their communication efforts (see Table 10.1). Furthermore, some institutions are starting to recognize where collaborations and partnerships are interconnected in creating a full student experience and play a critical role in student expectations and satisfaction ultimately leading to higher giving levels (Moneta & Kuh, 2005). While the findings of the particular study discussed present some possibilities and options for specific types of institutions and those already engaging in student philanthropy education, there are two fundamental findings that can be applied across the spectrum of institutions wishing to engage their students more in philanthropy efforts. First, in order to design successful programs aimed at changing campus culture, institutions should use their existing culture as the starting point for identifying the most viable programs and initiatives for their student body. Second, plans should be strategic and thoughtfully promote cross-campus collaboration while not ignoring the important communications that must accompany whatever

TABLE 10.1 Recommendations for Starting a Student Philanthropy Program

Recommendation	Strategies for Implementation
Develop partnerships and messages	• Find campus partners who you can educate about why student philanthropy is important and how it can benefit them—a broad spectrum of faculty and staff participation provides access to a wider group of students. • Create opportunities for students to be involved in your planning through advisory boards, student groups, and committees. • Develop messages that speak to your institution's needs and culture and decide the best places to broadcast them. • Convince higher level leadership that student philanthropy is an important investment for future fundraising.
Assess programming needs	• Before developing new programs and events, brainstorm existing programs where the concepts of student philanthropy can be added. • Consider your campus culture and what will appeal most to your students as new ideas develop. • Consider ways to involve alumni in programs with students. • Example: use an alumnus/a instead of an outside speaker at a campus event.
Set metrics	• Set realistic goals and expectations. • Decide how you plan to measure the success of your efforts; using out-of-the-box thinking—simple dollars raised and participation will not tell the same story for this population as for alumni

initiatives the institution chooses to implement. As the Ivy-Plus institutions integrated these programs and initiatives onto their campuses, albeit with potentially different purposes or messages, over the last decade, they undeniably saw the results in their fundraising efforts with their graduating classes and are likely to continue to see the benefits of their work.

References

Astin, A. W. (1993). *What matters in college?: Four critical years revisited*. San Francisco, CA: Jossey-Bass.

Baade, R. A., & Sundberg, J. O. (1993). Identifying the factors that stimulate alumni giving. *The Chronicle of Higher Education*. Retrieved October 8, 2008, from http://chronicle.com

Baade, R. A., & Sundberg, J. O. (1996). What determines alumni generosity? [Electronic Version] *Economics of Education Review, 15*(1), 75–81.

Balz, F., & National Institute of Independent Colleges and Universities, Washington, DC. (1987). *Donors to higher education: A statistical profile of individual giving*. (ERIC Document Reproduction Service No. ED284507)

Beyer, J. M., Hannah, D. R., & Milton, L. P. (2000). Ties that bind: Culture and attachment in organizations. In N. M. Ashkanasy, C. Wilderom, & M. F. Peterson (Eds.), *Handbook of organizational culture & climate* (pp. 323–338). Thousand Oaks, CA: Sage.

Briechle, P. (2007). Does institutional type affect alumnae donating patterns in the United States? In A. Walton, & M. Gasman (Eds.), *Philanthropy, volunteerism & fundraising in higher education* (pp. 648–655). Boston, MA: Pearson.

Brittingham, B. E., Pezzullo, T. R., ERIC Clearinghouse on Higher Education, Association for the Study of Higher Education, & Council for Advancement and Support of Education. (1990). *The campus green: Fund raising in higher education*. Washington, DC: School of Education and Human Development, the George Washington University.

Clark, B. R. (1971). Belief and loyalty in college organization [Electronic Version]. *The Journal of Higher Education, 42*(6). http://www.jstor.org/stable/1979081

Chickering, A. W. (1969). *Education and identity*. San Francisco, CA: Jossey-Bass.

Clotfelter, C. T. (2003). Alumni giving to elite private colleges and universities [Electronic Version]. *Economics of Education Review, 22*(2), 109–120.

Conley, A. T. (1999). *Student organization membership and alumni giving at a public, research I university* (Ed.D. dissertation). Retrieved November 8, 2008, from Dissertations & Theses @ CIC Institutions database. (Publication No. AAT 9944044).

Council for Advancement and Support of Education (CASE). (n.d.). Affiliated student advancement programs. Retrieved January 2, 2009, from http://www.case.org/asap

Cutlip, S. M. (1965). *Fund raising in the United States, its role in America's philanthropy*. New Brunswick, NJ: Rutgers University Press.

Dovidio, J. F, Piliavin, J. A., Schroeder, D. A., & Penner, L. A. (2006). *The social psychology of prosocial behavior*. Mahwah, NJ: Erlbaum.

Drezner, N. D. (2008). *Cultivating a culture of giving: An exploration of institutional strategies to enhance African American young alumni giving* (doctoral dissertation). Retrieved March 31, 2009, from Dissertations & Theses: Full Text database. (Publication No. AAT 3328548).

Drezner, N. D. (2009). Why give?: Exploring social exchange and organizational identification theories in the promotion of philanthropic behaviors of African American millennials at private-HBCUs. *International Journal of Educational Advancement, 9*(3), 147–165.

Drezner, N. D. (2010). Private Black colleges' encouragement of student giving and volunteerism: An examination of prosocial behavior development. *International Journal of Educational Advancement, 10*(3), 126–147.

Friedmann, A. S. (2003). *Building communities of participation through student advancement programs: A first step toward relationship fund raising* (doctoral dissertation). Retrieved November 8, 2008, from Dissertations & Theses: Full Text database. (Publication No. AAT 3081201).

Gaier, S. (2001). *Increasing alumni involvement and alumni financial support through a student alumni association.* (ERIC Document Reproduction Service No. ED451767).

Gallo, P. J., & Hubschman, B. (2003). *The relationships between alumni participation and motivation on financial giving* (Reports-Research (142) — Speeches/Meeting Papers (150) No. HE 035 951) EDRS.

Gardner, J. N., & Van der Veer, G. (1998). *The senior year experience: Facilitating integration, reflection, closure, and transition.* San Francisco, CA: Jossey-Bass.

Harrison, W. B. (1995). College relations and fund-raising expenditures: Influencing the probability of alumni giving to higher education [Electronic Version]. *Economics of Education Review, 14*(1), 73–84.

Harrison, W. B., Mitchell, S. K., & Peterson, S. P. (1995). Alumni donations and colleges' development expenditures: Does spending matter? [Electronic Version] *American Journal of Economics & Sociology, 54*(4), 397–412.

Hurvitz, L. A. (2010). *Building a culture of student philanthropy: A study of the Ivy-Plus institutions' philanthropy education initiatives* (doctoral dissertation). University of Pennsylvania, Philadelphia.

Ikenberry, J. P. (1999). *Alumni institutional commitment: Connecting student involvement with alumni involvement and institutional commitment* (doctoral dissertation). Retrieved October 13, 2008, from Dissertations & Theses @ CIC Institutions database. (Publication No. AAT 9937989).

Johnson, J. W., & Eckel, P. D. (1998). Preparing seniors for roles as active alumni. In J. N. Gardner & G. Van der Veer (Eds.), *The senior year experience: Facilitating integration, reflection, closure, and transition* (pp. 227-242). San Francisco, CA: Jossey-Bass.

Kellogg, K. O. (1996). *An analysis of the collaborative programming between student affairs and alumni relations professionals at select postsecondary institutions in Missouri* (doctoral dissertation). Retrieved November 7, 2008, from Dissertations & Theses: Full Text database. (Publication No. AAT 9717177).

Kroll, D. M. (1991). *Role expansion in student affairs: Student affairs officers and fundraising in selected Midwestern liberal arts colleges* (doctoral dissertation). Retrieved October 4, 2008, from Dissertations & Theses @ CIC Institutions database. (Publication No. AAT 9130503).

Kuh, G. D. (1991). *Involving colleges: Successful approaches to fostering student learning and development outside the classroom.* San Francisco, CA: Jossey-Bass.

Kuh, G. D. (1995). The other curriculum: Out-of-class experiences associated with student learning and personal development [Electronic Version]. *The Journal of Higher Education, 66*(2), 123–155.

Kuh, G. D. (2005). Putting student engagement results to use: Lessons from the field [Electronic Version]. *Assessment Update, 17*(1), 12–13.

Mael, F., & Ashforth, B. E. (1992). Alumni and their alma mater: A partial test of the reformulated model of organizational identification [Electronic Version]. *Journal of Organizational Behavior, 13*(2), 103–123.

Moneta, L., & Kuh, G. (2005). When expectations and realities collide: Environmental influences on student expectations and student experiences. In T. E. Miller, B. E. Bender, & J. H, Schuh (Eds.), *Promoting reasonable expectations: Aligning student and institutional views on the college experience* (pp. 65–83). San Francisco, CA: Jossey-Bass.

Monks, J. (2003). Patterns of giving to one's alma mater among young graduates from selective institutions [Electronic Version]. *Economics of Education Review, 22*(2), 121–130.

Mulugetta, Y., Nash, S., & Murphy, S. H. (1999). What makes a difference: Evaluating the Cornell tradition program [Electronic Version]. *New Directions for Institutional Research, 101*, 61–80.

Oliver, R. L. (1980). A cognitive model of the antecedents and consequences of satisfaction decisions. *Journal of Marketing Research, 17*(4), 460–469.

Pumerantz, R. K. (2004). *Alumni-in-training: Institutional factors associated with greater alumni giving at public comprehensive colleges and universities* (doctoral dissertation). Retrieved November 8, 2008, from Dissertations & Theses: Full Text database. (Publication No. AAT 3133230).

Tinto, V. (1993). *Leaving college: Rethinking the causes and cures of student attrition* (2nd ed.). Chicago, IL: University of Chicago Press.

Trice, H. M., & Beyer, J. M. (1993). *The cultures of work organizations.* Englewood Cliffs, NJ: Prentice Hall.

Utter, D., & Noble, C. H. (1999). Investing in the future: Transforming current students into generous alumni [Electronic Version]. *Fund Raising Management, 30*(9), 31–36.

Young, P. S., & Fischer, N. M. (1996). *Identifying undergraduate and post-college characteristics that may affect alumni giving. AIR 1996 annual forum paper.* (ERIC Document Reproduction Service No. ED397748)

11

THE INFLUENCE OF SORORITY AND FRATERNITY INVOLVEMENT ON FUTURE GIVING

Ryan E. Merkel

For college fundraisers and alumni affairs officers, there is no group more important than the alumni base of the institution. Although much research has been conducted on the giving habits of alumni (Bruggink & Siddiqui, 1995; Mann, 2007; McAlexander & Koenig, 2001; Patouillet, 2001; Weerts & Ronca, 2007), little data has been gathered on the current students of the university (who will eventually become alumni) and their perception of alumni participation and philanthropy to their alma mater.

Research indicates that alumni of fraternities and sororities are particularly engaged as donors (Bruggink & Siddiqui, 1995; Monks, 2003), suggesting that membership in such organizations might be particularly informative to the perceptions current students hold of alumni relations and alumni giving. This chapter will explore how current university students who are members of fraternities and sororities (also known as "Greek life" due to these organizations' use of the Greek alphabet) make meaning of the alumni relations function and how such membership acts as a point around which understanding of alumni relations and alumni philanthropy coalesces.

Data from 17 in-depth interviews with students and alumni relations professionals, as well as documents and publications, was used to answer the following research questions: (a) How do students involved in fraternities and sororities perceive and make meaning of the relationship between alumni and the university? (b) How do students involved in fraternities and sororities perceive and make meaning of philanthropic donations to the university by alumni? (c) How does the fraternity or sorority affiliation of the student influence perceptions of alumni relations and alumni philanthropy at the university?

Within the pool of students interviewed, several were members of Black Greek letter organizations, or historically minority-serving chapters (as the organizations are called on a given campus). For these individuals, alumni connectivity was an especially salient topic and data was plentiful. Because of this, particular focus was paid to these students' perspectives, in the hopes of examining similarities and contrasts in the way that historically White and historically minority-serving fraternities and sororities frame alumni relations activities.

This study used the theoretical framework of relationship management, a perspective which underscores the importance of the mutual benefit of both players in the relationship and the managed perceptions that both parties hold of each other. In the field of managed communication, Waters (2008) applied the framework to donor management, opening the door for research using the principles of relationship management to explore the exchange between a university and its student and alumni publics.

Review of Literature

Relational Perspective

Relationship management is an all-encompassing framework for directing theoretical growth in the area of strategic communications (Ledingham, 2006). Using this approach, the unit of analysis becomes the relationship that exists between the communicators (Seltzer, 1999), allowing the researcher to investigate how two sides of a communication situation perceive the mutual relationship and how power is distributed in that relationship. Research by Waters (2008) showed that the relationship management perspective can have significant applications in donor management and fundraising.

Relationship management scholars use theory from a number of different sources. A primary source is social exchange theory (Broom, Casey, & Ritchey, 2000; Grunig & Huang, 2000; Hung, 2007), which suggests that two parties enter into a relationship when they expect an exchange of resources, which could include information, social status, money, services, intimacy, friendship, etc. (Hung, 2007). If the expectations both parties bring into the exchange are met, identification between the parties in the relationship is increased (Bhattacharya, Rao, & Glynn, 1995). Other sources of theory on which relationship management scholars rely are interpersonal theory (Broom et al., 2000; Dougall, 2005; Hon & Grunig, 1999), inter-organizational theory (Broom et al., 2000; Dougall, 2005; Post, Preston, & Sachs, 2002), and system's theory, which contributes perspectives on how units interact with each other and how interdependencies form between these units (Broom et al., 2000; Dougall, 2005).

Because the benefits received by both parties are significant in the relational perspective, many variables for evaluating relationships have been explored through academic discourse. Through this conversation, trust, control mutuality, satisfaction, and commitment have emerged as the most valuable constructs. These outcomes, theorized by Hon and Grunig (1999) and Grunig and Huang (2000) have been used extensively as a set of variables by which relationships in public relations are measured (O'Neil, 2007; Ledingham & Bruning, 2000; Seltzer, 1999; Waters, 2008, 2009a, 2009b). Trust includes confidence and openness between the parties, and the belief that goodwill will not be exploited. Control mutuality involves the agreement of a power balance between the parties in the relationship, which does not necessarily have to be equal. Satisfaction is the degree to which expectations are met and the parties feel favorably towards one another. Finally, commitment is the extent to which both parties feel that the relationship is valuable, worth maintaining and promoting (Grunig & Huang, 2000; Hon & Grunig, 1999).

Philanthropy

Development practitioners know well the adage that "Fundraising is about relationships" (Klein, 2003, p. 289). Many will go as far as linking relationship management directly to their job description; "Development is not a one-way relationship, it is an exchange" (Elliott, 2006, p. 29). The relationship management perspective offers a way to grow understanding of how to evaluate such relationships, while also directing this understanding in a more focused theoretical framework.

Many practitioners and scholars define the relationship between donors (or prospective donors) and the organization as "involvement." Noonan and Rosqueta (2008) found involvement to be the second highest criterion for giving and suggested that it was an "absolute precondition" for a gift. Investigating the involvement students have with their university, and how this influences the relationship they have with their alma mater as alumni, offers a unique opportunity to advance knowledge of the university-alumni relationship.

Upon their graduation from a university, students are often quickly asked to become active in annual giving programs, and campaigns targeting young donors have become much discussed topics (see Chapter 8, this volume; Drezner, 2009, 2010; Langley, 2010; Masterson, 2010; McAlexander & Koenig, 2001; Monks, 2003). Barack Obama's 2008 presidential campaign showed the potential for significant amounts of money to be raised by collecting small gifts from large groups of people, particularly young people, leading many universities to rethink annual giving programs, especially those aimed at recent graduates (Parry, 2009). Generally, organizations are becoming increasingly strategic in their cultivation of annual donors (Schroeder, 2002; Waters, 2009a), pointing to the increasing importance of annual giving funds and alumni associations (which usually require a yearly dues payment as a form of annual giving).

In addition to sources of annual gifts, these alumni associations offer a means by which interested parties self-identify as potential donors of more significant contributions, thus serving as "building blocks" in the fundraising process

(Rosso & Schwartzberg, 2003; Schroeder, 2002). Waters (2009a) argues that the annual giving appeal is the beginning of what will hopefully be a continuous relationship, and development professionals know that the annual fund offers an excellent pool of prospects for major gift cultivation.

Research exploring the reasons that individuals give to charitable organizations has generally concluded that they do so for a variety of reasons, including: gaining prestige and respect (Mann, 2007), altruism and direct benefits (Bruggink & Siddiqui, 1995; Mann, 2007), religious and philosophical beliefs, guilt, self-preservation, obligation (Elliott, 2006), emotional and economic gain (Merchant & Ford, 2008) and community uplift (Drezner & Garvey, 2012; Gasman & Anderson-Thompkins, 2003; Gasman, Drezner, Epstein, Freeman, & Avery, 2011). Various researchers have come to different conclusions on the most significant motivation, although "passion for the cause" and "direct involvement" with the cause are two criteria for general giving which occur with frequency in the literature and which are particularly appropriate to this study (Conley, 2000; Noonan & Rosqueta, 2008; Seiler, 2003).

Because participation in Greek life and other campus involvement activities represents a great commitment of time and resources on the part of the student, it might play a significant role in the relationship between the student and the university. If involvement with a cause is a significant indicator for giving (Seiler, 2003), a student's involvement in activities such as Greek life while on campus might influence how that individual views giving back to his or her alma mater. Although a student's involvement with his or her university might not be involvement with the cause, per se, it does give the student a unique perspective on the organization. The student experience is a significant variable in predicting educational giving (Sun, Hoffman, & Grady 2007; Monks, 2003), and involvement with Greek life has been specifically singled out as a significant predictor of increased giving (Bruggink & Siddiqui, 1995). Research by Monks (2003) indicates that participation in activities such as intercollegiate athletics, performing arts, student government, and Greek life, all of which require significant investment of time, is correlated to higher levels of alumni giving.

Of such activities, Greek involvement is a major factor in philanthropic giving and volunteerism in the African American community (Gasman & Anderson-Thompkins, 2003; Sanders-McMurtry & Woods Haydel, 2005; Smith, Shue, Vest, & Villarreal, 1999; Winters, 1999). Historically Black fraternities and sororities have strong traditions of alumni connectivity, have traditionally served as catalysts for community involvement, and are also recipients of philanthropic dollars (Gasman & Bowman, 2012; Winters, 1999). Other minority and culturally centered Greek organizations, such as those serving Asian American and Latino/a students, have recently begun appearing more frequently on college campuses. Although they do not yet have such a history of alumni connectivity as historically Black fraternities and sororities, it is reasonable to believe other multi-cultural fraternities and sororities could follow a similar path given philanthropy is often driven by a community association for Asian American and Latino donors (Chao, 1999; Ramos, 1999).

Alumni Relations

The relationship that alumni share with their alma mater is unique and has its beginnings in the time when alumni were students at the institution. Thus, alumni relations programs see their overall goal not as creating, but rather increasing and cultivating a relationship that has already been formed (Dolbert, 2002), perhaps with the assistance of Greek life or other campus activities. Research by Merchant and Ford (2008) suggests that higher education organizations have a closer connection to their giving groups than most institutions because of the shared experiences between the two groups, and that much of this connection is associated with nostalgia.

Research is attempting to better understand the relationship between the educational institution and its alumni groups, especially how the relationship is formed and how it can be evaluated. It is conventional wisdom that alumni bonds to their institution are strongly influenced by the experience the alumni had while a student (McAlexander & Koenig, 2001), which has led researchers at the University of Indiana's Center for Philanthropy (Conley, 2000) to suggest that the emotional connection between alumni and school starts at the student level, and should be studied as such. Work by McAlexander and Koenig (2001) has shed additional light on the nature of the relationship, concluding that alumni form relationships with the institutional identity of their school. They also present evidence that time is a significant factor in the relationships; these bonds will decay as the alumnus grows older if they are not cultivated. Other research shows that students who were involved in a philanthropically-focused group while in college were more likely than non-members to give back to their institution in some way—in some cases the giving rate was six times as high (Conley, 2000).

Forming a significant relationship with students requires a cross-organizational effort. "Making one feel part of the university community is something that is more comprehensive and involves other people than just the top administrator" (Patouillet, 2001, p. 63). McAlexander and Koenig (2001) recommend additional research on how alumni and college representatives view each other, as strong interpersonal bonds can lead to strong institutional bonds.

An additional trend is an increase in the connection between the alumni affairs function of the campus and the current students of the institution. This can be seen in the increase in on-campus programming by alumni associations (Dolbert, 2002). Following calls from practitioners and scholars that institutions should view current students as future donors (Dolbert, 2002; Sun et al., 2007), these tactics are an attempt to create a culture of significant relationships while undergraduates (Sun et al., 2007) and to help them identify with the alumni association early on (Dolbert, 2002).

Relationship management offers a rich and unique perspective from which to conceptualize alumni relations and philanthropy to higher education. By becoming involved in Greek life, especially fraternities and sororities affiliated with minority groups, students have added another facet to their relationship with the institution. This involvement would thus inform the way students construct meaning around alumni relations and philanthropy. Such involvement might also increase the significance of a student's shared experiences while at the institution (Merchant & Ford, 2008) or increase the emotional cost to the student of withdrawing from the relationship with the institution (Weerts & Ronca, 2007). These factors might explain why quantitative analysis has shown a correlation between Greek involvement and increased giving (Bruggink & Siddiqui, 1995; Monks, 2003). However, more research is needed to determine how Greek involvement informs the relationship between the student and the university in the context of alumni relations and fundraising.

Methodology

This research represents a component of a larger qualitative case study which used several channels of data to explore the ways that students make meaning of alumni relations and philanthropy to their alma mater. In the original research, 17 in-depth interviews with current students were conducted to collect data, many of whom were affiliated with fraternities and sororities, and the importance of these affiliations became such a significant theme that it warranted an independent set of conclusions. Although not all the original interviewees were members of fraternities and sororities, they were kept in the data set because so many still referenced the Greek communities in their interviews, and because discussions with such a wide range of students helped establish broad trends in student relationships with the university. Of the 17 participants, four interviewed students were members of fraternities or sororities primarily focused on minority populations. Analysis of documents and external publications were also used as sources of data.

Findings

The Impact of the Greek Experience on Alumni Connectivity

Although few reported it directly, all research subjects cast alumni involvement in a positive light and were able to speak freely on the matter. All participants who were members of a fraternity or sorority were able to discuss alumni relations in the context of their Greek chapters. Several individuals reported that seeing alumni, through their Greek letter organization or otherwise, helped to shape their perceptions of alumni behavior and alumni relations. Moreover, while alumni interactions might take place outside of the sphere of Greek life, these interactions were peripheral. This effect seemed to be stronger for members of historically Black organizations, with a member of one such fraternity stating that "I have met so many alumni of this school through the [Greek] organization and I think that if I wasn't Greek, I would still have some alumni encounters, but I don't think they would be as personal as they are now ..." (Personal communication, November 20, 2009). The fraternity or sorority connection clearly does much to make the alumni interaction unique.

The fraternity or sorority, regardless of the population it served, was clearly cast as a significant factor in bringing alumni back to campus. In one interesting example of what might occur if the Greek component of student life is eliminated, one participant expressed confusion as to how he would stay connected to the university, since the fraternity he was involved with was recently removed from campus. He said, "That's a difficult question [how I will stay connected], because my fraternity just got kicked off, and I always viewed myself as being really active in that aspect of [university] life, so I don't know what's going to happen with that." (Personal communication, December 7, 2009). Many students, even those who were not members of fraternities or sororities, acknowledged the significance such organizations hold in keeping alumni engaged with the institution. Statements, such as, "I think that [the fraternity] is one of the best things that has ever happened to me because I've met so many good people and I've learned about something that is bigger than myself" (Personal communication, December 11, 2009) were commonly heard from research participants who were involved in Greek life.

Many of the positive effects of organizational involvement were summed up by this student, whose biological brother, now an alumnus, was a member of the same Greek organization:

> Every time I see my brother come back, it's for a fraternity event, but he was a [colloquial name of students at the case university] too, and he realizes that it isn't just the fraternity, it's [the case university] too in a bigger picture. But I think it's more possible through smaller organizations to handle alumni ... I get the feel that a lot of alumni who were on the basketball team and football team and whatever come back and watch the games together, but that's the only thing I've seen with alumni that are grouped together at some type of event.
>
> *(Personal communication, December 14, 2009)*

Interestingly, this individual, a member of a historically White Greek organization, acknowledges that fraternity life is only one component of a larger relationship with the university. A different student, a member of a minority-focused chapter, reflected on the fact that the Greek chapter will likely outlast most of her other connections to the institution:

> I feel that because I am Greek, I do always have that connection to the university, and it might not be to everyone, but because I have my chapter here, it's at least something. It might not be a whole lot—you know, people will move and teachers will change, but my chapter will basically, or hopefully, always be here.
>
> *(Personal communication, November 19, 2009)*

The longevity of the Greek chapter seemed to be a source of strength for the relationship and a reason for this individual to put more trust in the relationship.

These participants pointed out that their alumni come back to the university for Greek events, including, but not limited to, recruitment, initiation rituals, and galas celebrating chapter anniversaries. Interestingly, representatives from historically White chapters were generally not able to cite as many examples of alumni involvement. Some students pointed out that to be a member of their Greek organization in good standing, participation in alumni-related events is required. Others mentioned alumni connections as a factor they considered in joining Greek organizations.

Benefits of Effective Alumni Relations

Interviewees associated alumni interactions with a number of benefits. On an institutional level, students across all types of organizations believed that alumni involvement is healthy for the university's reputation and academic standing, as it both provided resources for the institution and a sense of engagement for the individual:

> I think in the history of a lot of these great universities around the country, one of the constants has been strong alumni support. Whether we look at a new facility or a new building, we all know that once a program gains recognition or the program has a huge donor, and the program becomes named after them, then that person has become invested.
>
> *(Personal communication, November 20, 2009)*

Interviewees claimed that alumni can also assist in recruitment, and help mitigate budget cuts on campus. The benefit of university staff members and advisors being alumni was also discussed. Some students pointed out that those alumni who try to help students have the resources that the alumni did not have during their time at the university. Such alumni had gone through their student careers, identified areas at the university which needed improvement, and then devoted resources as alumni to improving such areas so that current and future students could have a better experience. Students also believed that interacting with alumni was beneficial because it broadened perspectives and built knowledge. Communicating with alumni offered the students opportunities learned from individuals who had shared similar experiences but, because of their experiences in the professional world, offered insight not found in a traditional classroom.

Finally, students spoke of their expectations of their own alumni experience. Due to the personal nature of the alumni relationship with the university, themes in this area were not uniform. Several respondents believed that alumni should be given a greater voice in the administration of the university because of their experiences as undergraduates. Several also tied alumni involvement to geographic location, pointing out that it might be difficult to stay in touch with the university if their careers or families took them to other parts of the country. However, because of geographically based alumni groups, individuals might have the chance to become engaged with alumni chapters affiliated with their fraternity or sorority chapters, but in other geographic locations. For members of historically Black fraternities and sororities, these geographic alumni organizations were especially significant. Two students believed that the opportunity to see old friends (not necessarily Greek) would "pull" them back to the university. One individual believed that the responsibility was strongly on the alumnus to cultivate the relationship with the undergraduate chapter and alumni groups.

The Impact of the Greek Experience on Understanding Philanthropy

Students spoke openly about philanthropy in the context of higher education, showing this to be a salient issue for them. Many students reported being involved, in some cases heavily, with philanthropic events through their Greek chapter and other organizations. Many participants stated that they would be willing to donate money to at least one cause in the university community at some point, and some participants even stated that they wanted to serve as role models and "be seen" giving back, as to encourage others to do so. One individual who was not open to the idea of a financial contribution believed that she had invested enough money in the institution by paying for her degree, although she was willing to give back in other ways such as joining a regional alumni association and being a mentor to her chapter or other chapters in the area in which she settles. Possibly because financial resources are limited for many students, many of the participants specifically recognized that alumni "give back" in ways other than donating money. Two participants mentioned their interest in contributing to an area that they were involved with, as opposed to the university as a whole. Two individuals associated with historically Black Greek letter organizations expressed a desire to financially support diversity initiatives.

Making Sense of Philanthropy

Students displayed a lack of understanding of the complexities of educational philanthropy, with several directly admitting that they do not know where money that is donated to the university goes or how it is used. Many of the interviewees representing a range of organizations associated university fundraising and alumni philanthropy with large, tangible items such as buildings and the names on colleges. In some cases, students specifically felt that financial gifts to their fraternities or sororities would achieve greater impact than donations to the larger university. Despite admitting their knowledge was limited, students were able to speak at length on the subject of philanthropy, and also held opinions which seemed to be heavily influenced by their experiences in the Greek community.

One student who was a member of a fraternity claimed he was only able to see the personal benefits of alumni philanthropy within the confines of his student groups, but not the university as a whole. He said, "In the smaller groups of athletics and fraternities and clubs, I can definitely see how graduates have impacted their lives individually. Unfortunately, I haven't been assisted other than in Greek life" (Personal communication, December 7, 2009). According to one student, "But I'm probably going to feel obligated towards the wrestling team and towards [my fraternity] and whatever other organizations I was in because I was a part of them, and they did give me a lot and they helped shape my undergraduate experience" (Personal communication, December 11, 2009), indicating that he might feel greater obligation to the student organizations and team sports he was involved with than the university as a whole.

Although many students reported not feeling the personal effects of alumni giving at the university level, students provided many anecdotes showing the effects of alumni philanthropy on a chapter level: alumni sponsoring trips to leadership conferences, paying for scholarships, etc. However, some participants felt that they were better informed of the effects of alumni giving than the "average member" of their chapter due to leadership roles or special participation in the chapter. A participant from a historically Black chapter discussed feeling that, as an alumnus of a Greek organization, he must work harder and give more back. This was attributed to higher expectations of individuals involved with minority-serving organizations, as well as a feeling that this individual was directly responsible for ensuring the future success of the fraternal organization.

The Reasons that Alumni Give Back

Interesting discussions arose around alumni motivations for giving back to their alma mater, either through volunteering or donations of money. A representative from a historically Black organization believed that alumni give in order to have their voices heard: "They're [the university] going to ask you for money, they're going to ask you for time, so the least they can do is to listen to something you have an opinion of, down the road" (Personal communication, November 20, 2009). The same individual went on to say:

> So, I think when you have a strong alumni involvement, the alumni become invested in making sure their degree continues to mean something. When I graduate from this school, I want to make sure that if I apply [for jobs], I want the university to mean something, so I think that we all, as alumni, look at it that way. We want our degree to mean something when we go into the business world.

This idea of alumni being motivated to donate to the university to increase the value of the degree they received was mentioned by several individuals. Some participants went on to say that they believed that the professional success of alumni, which is what allows them to make such financial contributions, was derived from the degree that they received from the institution.

The Benefits of Being Greek

Interviewees clearly felt a strong sense of connection and commitment to their Greek chapter, and felt that there were many benefits to being a member of that campus community. In the words of one student who did not join a sorority until later in her college career, it is "Better to be Greek than not to be Greek" (Personal communication, November 19, 2009) because she felt that she was receiving more benefits from her college experience now that she was a member of a Greek organization. Although interviewees from minority-focused groups reported joining these groups later in their university careers, they reported the same, if not greater, levels of fulfillment with their decision to join the Greek community as their counterparts in historically White chapters. Many participants talked about how being Greek made them feel like they were part of a community and that it made the size of the university more manageable. Furthermore, many of the same students talked about how being Greek allowed them to meet more people because they were part of such a defined and socially active community.

Almost every participant derived various degrees of satisfaction from being involved with Greek life. Comments regarding involvement opportunities on campus were especially meaningful: "I feel like if I wasn't in a fraternity or on the wrestling team, I probably wouldn't be as happy as I am now." and, later in the interview, he said, "I feel like the university absolutely gives all the opportunities in the world, it's just up to you as to if you take them" (Personal communication, December 11, 2009). One interviewee discussed how alumni give back to the university because of their satisfaction with the experience they had:

> [They] really gained a lot from [their university] experience—[they] found their spouses here, their best friends, fraternity or sorority brothers and sisters and they've been successful. [They] want to give back in some way, and not just by writing a check, [they] really want to impart experience and knowledge on the next generation of students here.
>
> *(Personal communication, December 7, 2009)*

Participants believed they were receiving more than just personal satisfaction from their Greek experience, including greater access to administration, thus allowing their voices to be heard. This was an especially salient finding for members of minority-based organizations. One individual, who was the president of his chapter, said that by being a leader in the Greek community, "You get that personal interaction with administrators that you don't usually find as an undergrad" (Personal communication, November 20, 2009). Several students, including many from the minority-serving organizations, also felt that through their Greek involvement, they were leaving a lasting impression on the campus—a sort of legacy. One interviewee remarked "[Chapter name], it's been keeping me really busy and keeping me involved, and it gives me a sense that I've been able to make a difference on this campus" (Personal communication, November 17, 2009). Several of the interviewees talked about their Greek experience giving them a network that they can take forward into their alumni years.

Alumni Involvement and Greek Life

The comments of all interviewees indicated that alumni involvement was a significant component of the Greek life experience and all participants seemed particularly aware of the relationship between their chapter and the alumni. Representatives from historically Black organizations commented on the high level of alumni involvement in their chapters, and suggested that the mission of their organizations, which focuses on community service and empowerment of minorities, does not end at graduation, thus providing a natural channel for alumni to continue involvement.

Beyond being a part of Greek life, alumni were said to add value to the chapter and the community. One participant noted, "I've noticed that I've picked up a lot more mentors through the process of becoming Greek who were alumni of the university" (Personal communication, November 20, 2009). The alumni pass on the values of the chapter by staying involved, and thus create a cycle which makes the students want to continue their interaction with the chapter after graduation. Two participants reported that alumni of Greek organizations helped recruit them into the Greek community. This concept of alumni adding value to the undergraduate chapter was especially prevalent in interviews with students involved with minority-serving Greek organizations, where alumni serve on multiple committees and participate extensively in the guidance of the chapter.

Possible Dangers of Strong Greek Relationships

A surprising finding was that some students saw certain aspects of their relationship with their Greek chapter having a negative effect on their relationship with the university. Many participants voiced the opinion that since becoming Greek, the relationship with the university has become secondary to the relationship with the chapter. For other students, frustration grew out of issues surrounding fraternity and sorority governance and a lack of control mutuality. A student indicated that when his chapter was dealing with the university, the institution held most of the power and his barriers to action were too high. He said, "… the university, they don't care, once you come here, you can't just transfer just because you are disappointed in [Greek administration], so they kinda have a monopoly on that aspect of my life, and they don't have an incentive to change, really" (Personal communication, December 14, 2009).

For members of minority-serving organizations, some complaints had racial implications. One individual discussed how many alumnae of her organization were at the university at a time when they felt their race inhibited them from receiving a satisfying experience. Because of this, they felt that their sorority was one of the few positive parts of their university career:

> But I will say that African-Americans in general who have graduated from this university, they'll stick to their chapters more, but not necessarily the university, because for a lot of sorors [sic], our charter members in the late 70s … for them, it wasn't like college was so much fun, it was their org that made college fun.
>
> *(Personal communication, November 19, 2009)*

Unfortunately, one interviewee, associated with a similar type of organization, stated: "If I were just a regular old alumna, I would have no connection to this university" (Personal communication, November 11, 2009), indicating that her connection to her sorority is stronger than any other connection she has to the university, and will likely be the only one she maintains after graduation.

Discussion

The Greek experience was found to be a significant influence in the relationship between the student and the university and may go on to shape the alumni-university experience. This is especially true for students involved with historically Black or minority-focused organizations. The relationship between student and Greek organization was, in some cases, the strongest link that the student felt towards the university. The fact that some interviewees expressed displeasure towards how their chapter was treated by the university shows that Greek membership might enhance the relationship with the fraternity or sorority while damaging the relationship with another component (the administration). Since students in Black Greek letter organizations feel such a strong connection to their chapters, which they assume will continue post-graduation, and because they attach so much meaning to their fraternity and sorority experiences, it would behoove development and alumni relations professionals to include membership in these organizations in discussions about alumni relations. These findings suggest that the Greek experience can and should be conceptualized as a tool of alumni relations, and not just as a student involvement activity.

The aforementioned variables of relationship management can be used to analyze how involvement in Greek life affects the overall university experience. Regarding control mutuality, comments by students involved with Greek life indicated that they felt more empowered in their relationship with the institution due to the connection between campus leaders and Greek chapters. This was an especially significant theme for minority student groups who have historically suffered from a notable lack of empowerment. For the students who were highly satisfied with their institution, much of this satisfaction stemmed from the experiences and interactions they were having in the Greek community. Commitment was demonstrated in references to the mission of the organizations and a desire to stay connected after graduation, with special note again being owed to members of Black Greek letter organizations who have well-defined avenues of post-graduation involvement. Themes of trust, dealing with openness and goodwill, were not as prominent, although the massive and continuing devotion of time to the Greek letter organization was evidence that trust exists. While all interviewees seemed to understand alumni relations and philanthropy on a chapter level, they expressed a lack of understanding of these terms on a university level. However, they were able to see the positive effects that alumni philanthropy has on their individual Greek organizations, but in general did not see the positive effects of alumni giving to the university as a whole. This indicates that the university has room to improve in regard to explaining the meaning of these concepts to students, and that trust of the university might be mitigated by this lack of understanding.

If the relationship management theoretical construct is to be used to understand the connection tying students and alumni to their alma mater, the relationship can be conceptualized in terms of smaller units, such as student involvement organizations, Greek societies, sports teams, clubs, etc. It is through relationships with these smaller entities that the relationship with the larger entity (the general university) forms.

The Greek letter system is indeed an important component of the relationship between a member of a fraternity or sorority and the institution. However, data indicate that the relationship between the student and the Greek organization could be stronger than the relationship between the student and the university, which raises a potentially concerning possibility. When students create such a committed relationship with their Greek chapters as undergraduates, the strength of the relationship, upon graduation, may transfer more to the Greek organization than to the university. When graduation occurs, the university and the Greek organization have the potential to diverge even further as entities in the perception of the student. More than just one relationship being stronger than the other, the strength of the relationship between the student and the chapter might be a weakening factor for the relationship between the student and the university, a phenomenon termed "relationship cannibalization" for the purpose of this research. The roots of relationship cannibalization may occur when the individual is still an undergraduate, especially if he or she feels that the university is not treating their chapter fairly. If unresolved, any such tension may fester and cause the individual to take a side, with either the chapter or the university. With such an alumnus/ae feeling that the university is an enemy, alumni relations and philanthropic cultivation of that individual become extremely challenging for the institution.

Implications for Practice

Alumni relations professionals must also acknowledge the opportunities that the Greek system provides due to the strength of the relationships that students and alumni form with their fraternities and sororities. While university Greek systems will likely remain under the umbrella of student affairs offices, it is logical that they should also be reconceptualized as tools of alumni relations. Leaders of Greek organizations deal with alumni on a regular basis, yet they do not think of themselves as being a part of the alumni relations process. By reaching out to assist Greek organizations with their alumni relations work, even in very basic ways, alumni relations professionals at the university level are both assisting the Greek organizations by helping build the strength of their chapter community, and also forwarding the mission of the alumni relations department of the university. Facilitating the connection of graduated members back to the university community, gathering information about the alumni network of the university, and also exposing undergraduate students to alumni and alumni affairs are all objectives that alumni relations professionals could hope to meet by working more closely with student organizations (such as fraternities and sororities), which are already well connected to their alumni networks.

As Greek life is described as such an important part of the college experience and has such an effect on perceptions of alumni relations, involvement in multicultural or historically Black Greek letter organizations can also be seen as a segmentation tool for alumni populations by alumni relations and development professionals. These unique organizations, with their focus on minority empowerment and extremely active engagement with their alumni, attract individuals who want to be active in these respective communities. With minority groups having long been an enigmatic constituency for alumni relations and development professionals (Smith et al., 1999), these student organizations are powerful tools for prospecting and cultivation. Working with any organization that focuses on a specific demographic within the student population might have the benefit of helping the alumni association segment its audience and refine its outreach programming targeted at the corresponding alumni demographic.

Lastly, alumni relations professionals must be sensitive to the effect of administrative action against a Greek organization on the alumni of that chapter. With research participants reporting the possibility that their alumni relationship to their chapter will be stronger than their alumni relationship with the university, it is logical that if sanctions were taken against the Greek organization, the relationship with the university would be greatly affected. However, findings in this area must be viewed critically, as the interviewees are all current students, and it is impossible for them to accurately forecast what their relationship with their university and their chapter will look like in the future. Additionally, as some of these students were all involved in the leadership of their chapters at the time of the interviews, it is possible that administrative sanctions are an especially sensitive topic. Although alumni relations departments should by no means be guiding judicial policy for Greek organizations, actions against the chapters should be monitored by professionals engaged in alumni affairs for the university, as the effects of such judicial policies might be significant for the constituencies that the alumni relations professionals are attempting to engage.

Conclusion

This study explored how undergraduate students involved in Greek life organizations construct meaning around issues of alumni relations and philanthropy, and how their experience in Greek letter organizations informs these constructions. Additionally, the study sought to situate the relationship between the student and the university within the theoretical framework of relationship management (Ledingham, 2006), using the variables of trust, control mutuality, satisfaction, and commitment (Hon & Grunig, 1999). Being involved in Greek life organizations had a significant effect on the relationship between the students and the university, and on how that relationship would evolve into a relationship between alumni and the university. This effect was especially strong for students involved in minority-serving Greek organizations. Alumni affairs professionals would do well to notice and monitor these effects and use Greek affiliation as a tool of segmenting and developing alumni connectivity and effective alumni relations strategies (see Table 11.1).

Alumni relations professionals must also remember that even with so much alumni interaction occurring within the Greek community, the vast majority of students will not be exposed to this, as the Greek community does not represent a majority of the student body at most institutions. Research participants stated that even though they did have experiences with alumni outside of the Greek community, these experiences were generally not as meaningful as those within that community. With that in mind, substitutes must be found for these meaningful experiences for students not affiliated with fraternities or sororities so that they too will foster closer ties with their university, alumni relations, and philanthropy. Following the findings of this study, alumni relations professionals should focus on using clubs, athletic teams, and other smaller units of student involvement to cultivate these relationships. Additional research on student engagement with specific groups while on campus impacts alumni connectivity would undoubtedly yield fascinating and valuable research for academics and professionals who seek to build stronger and more fruitful relationships between alumni and their respective alma maters.

TABLE 11.1 Recommendations for Engaging Sorority and Fraternity Alumni

Recommendation	Tactics for Implementation
Make the Greek System a tool of the alumni relations effort, not just a student involvement activity.	• Monitor Greek life—what chapters are coming and going from campus, etc. • Know the Greek affiliation of key alumni and donors. • Use Greek affiliation as a segmentation tool within the alumni pool.
Assist interested Greek alumni in reconnecting with their chapters.	• Partner with alumni chapters of fraternities and sororities that operate at your institution. • Offer news and information about connecting with the undergraduate chapter to alumni who are already involved with the alumni association. • Host special events or forums for individuals who are alumni of the Greek systems, and invite current students who are affiliated with the system.
Strengthen the alumni relations and philanthropy efforts at the undergraduate chapters of your institution.	• Mentor undergraduate Greek leaders on how to successfully engage alumni. • Offer alumni services such as archiving alumni records or construction of an alumni database to undergraduate chapters. • Offer chapters operating without a "house" (such as many minority-serving chapters who are not large enough to have a facility) the use of facilities of the alumni relations team for meetings and events.

References

Bhattacharya, C. B., Rao, H., & Glynn, M. A. (1995). Understanding the bond of identification: An investigation of its correlates among art museum members. *Journal of Marketing, 59*(4), 46–57.

Broom, G., Casey, S., & Ritchey, J. (2000).Concept and theory of organization-public relationships. In J. A. Ledingham & S. D. Bruning (Eds.), *Public relations as relationship management: A relational approach to the study and practice of public relations* (pp. 3–22). Mahwah, NJ: Erlbaum.

Bruggink, T. H., & Siddiqui, K. (1995). An economic model of alumni giving: A case study for a liberal arts college. *American Economist, 39*(2), 53–61.

Chao, J. (1999). Asian-American philanthropy: Expanding circles of participants. *Cultures of caring: Philanthropy in diverse American communities.* Retrieved from http://www.cof.org/files/ Documents/Publications/Cultures_of_Caring/asianamerican.pdf

Conley, A. (2000). Breaking away in the race for donors. *Philanthropy Matters, 10*(2), 3, 10.

Dolbert, S. C. (2002, October). *Future trends in alumni relations.* Paper presented to the 16th Australian International Education Conference, Hobart, Australia.

Dougall, E. (2005). *Tracking organization-public relationships over time: A framework for longitudinal research.* Gainesville, FL: Institute for Public Relations Research.

Drezner, N. D. (2009). Why give?: Exploring social exchange and organizational identification theories in the promotion of philanthropic behaviors of African American millennials at private-HBCUs. *International Journal of Educational Advancement, 9*(3), 147–165.

Drezner, N. D. (2010). Private Black colleges' encouragement of student giving and volunteerism: An examination of prosocial behavior development. *International Journal of Educational Advancement, 10*(3), 126–147.

Drezner, N. D., & Garvey, J. C. (2012). "(Un)Conscious queer identity and influence on philanthropy towards higher education." American Educational Research Association, Vancouver, B.C., Canada.

Elliott, D. (2006). *The kindness of strangers.* Lanham, MD: Rowman& Littlefield.

Gasman, M., & Anderson-Thompkins, S. (2003). *Fundraising from Black college alumni: Successful strategies for supporting alma mater.* Washington, DC: CASE Books.

Gasman, M., & Bowman, N. (2012). *Understanding, cultivating and engaging college alumni of color.* New York, NY: Routledge.

Gasman, M., Drezner, N. D., Epstein, E., Freeman, T. M., & Avery, V. L. (2011). *Race, gender, and leadership in nonprofit organizations.* New York, NY: Palgrave Macmillan.

Grunig, J. E., & Huang, Y. (2000). From organizational effectiveness to relationship indicators: Antecedents of relationships, public relations strategies, and relationship outcomes. In J. A. Ledingham & S. D. Bruning (Eds.), *Public relations as relationship management: A relational approach to the study and practice of public relations* (pp. 23–54). Mahwah, NJ: Erlbaum.

Hon, L. C., & Grunig, J. E. (1999). *Guidelines for measuring relationships in public relations.* Gainesville, FL: Institute for Public Relations Research.

Hung, C. F. (2007). Towards the theory of relationship management in public relations: How to cultivate quality relationships? In E. Toth (Ed.), *The future of excellence in public relations and communication management challenges for the next generation* (pp. 443–476). Mahwah, NJ: Erlbaum.

Klein, K. (2003). Fund raising at the grassroots level. In E. R. Tempel (Ed.), *Hank Rosso's achieving excellence in fund raising 2nd edition* (pp. 289–300). San Francisco, CA: Jossey-Bass.

Langley, J. (2010, July 30). Listening — really listening — to alumni. *The Chronicle of Higher Education,* A26.

Ledingham, J. A. (2006). Relationship management: A general theory of public relations. In C. H. Botan & V. Hazelton (Eds.), *Public relations theory II* (pp. 465–483). Mahwah, NJ: Erlbaum.

Ledingham, J. A., & Bruning, S. D. (2000). A longitudinal study of organization-public relationship dimensions: Defining the role of communication in the practice of relationship management. In J. A. Ledingham & S. D. Bruning (Eds.), *Public relations as relationship management: A relational approach to the study and practice of public relations* (pp. 55–70). Mahwah, NJ: Erlbaum.

Mann, T. (2007). College fund raising using theoretical perspectives to understand donor motives. *International Journal of Educational Advancement, 7*(1), 35–46.

Masterson, K. (2010, July 18). Appeals to college loyalty are not enough to engage younger alumni. *The Chronicle of Higher Education*, A1.

McAlexander, J. H., & Koenig, H. F. (2001). University experiences, the student–college relationship, and alumni support. *Journal of Marketing for Higher Education, 10*(3), 21–43.

Merchant, A., & Ford, J. (2008). Nostalgia and giving to charity: A conceptual framework for discussion and research. *International Journal of Nonprofit and Voluntary Sector Marketing, 13*(1), 13–30.

Monks, J. (2003). Patterns of giving to one's alma mater among young graduates from selective institutions. *Economics of Education Review, 22*(2), 121–130.

Noonan, K., & Rosqueta, K. (2008). *"I'm not Rockefeller": 33 high net worth philanthropists discuss their approach to giving.* Retrieved July 18, 2009, from http://www.impact.upenn.edu/

O'Neil, J. (2007). The link between strong public relationships and donor support. *Public Relations Review, 33*(1), 99–102.

Parry, M. (2009, April 24). Colleges weigh 'yes we can' approach to fundraising. *The Chronicle of Higher Education*, A1.

Patouillet, L. D. (2001). Alumni association members: Attitudes towards university life and giving at a public AAU institution. *The CASE International Journal of Educational Advancement, 2*(1), 53–66.

Post, J. E., Preston, L. E., & Sachs, S. (2002). *Redefining the corporation stakeholder management and organizational wealth.* Stanford, CA: Stanford University Press.

Ramos, H. A. J. (1999). Latino philanthropy: Expanding U.S. models of giving and civic participation. Retrieved from http://www.cof.org/files/Documents/Publications/Cultures_of_Caring/latino.pdf

Rosso, H. A., & Schwartzberg, R. (2003). The annual fund. In E. R. Tempel (Ed.), *Hank Rosso's achieving excellence in fund raising 2nd edition* (pp. 71–88). San Francisco, CA: Jossey-Bass.

Sanders-McMurtry, K., & Woods Haydel, N. (2005). The links, incorporated: Advocacy, education, and service in the African American community. In M. Gasman & K. V. Sedgwick (Eds.), *Uplifting a people: African American philanthropy and education* (pp. 101–118). New York, NY: Peter Lang.

Schroeder, F. W. (2002). The annual giving program. In M. J. Worth (Ed.), *New strategies for educational fundraising* (pp. 75–88). Westport, CT: Praeger.

Seiler, T. L. (2003). Developing a constituency for fund raising. In E. R. Tempel (Ed.), *Hank Rosso's achieving excellence in fund raising 2nd edition* (pp. 41–48). San Francisco, CA: Jossey-Bass.

Seltzer, T. (1999). *Measuring the impact of public relations: Using a coorientational approach to analyze the organization-public relationship.* Gainesville, FL: Institute for Public Relations Research.

Smith, B., Shue, S., Vest, J. L., & Villarreal, J. (1999.) *Philanthropy in communities of color.* Bloomington: Indiana University Press.

Sun, X., Hoffman, S. C., & Grady, M. L. (2007). A multivariate causal model of alumni giving: implications for alumni fundraisers. *International Journal of Educational Advancement, 7*(4), 307–333.

Waters, R. D. (2008). Applying relationship management theory to the fundraising process for individual donors. *Journal of Communication Management, 12*(1), 73–87.

Waters, R. D. (2009a). Measuring stewardship in public relations: A test exploring impact on the fundraising relationship. *Public Relations Review, 35*(2), 113–119.

Waters, R. D. (2009b). Comparing the two sides of the nonprofit organization-donor relationship: Appling coorientation methodology to relationship management. *Public Relations Review 35*(2), 144–146.

Weerts, D. J., & Ronca, J. M. (2007). Profiles of supportive alumni: Donors, volunteers, and those who "do it all". *International Journal of Educational Advancement, 7*(1), 20–35.

Winters, M. F. (1999). Reflections on endowment building in the African-American community. Retrieved from http://www.cof.org/files/Documents/Publications/Cultures_of_Caring/africanamerican.pdf

12

FOSTERING STUDENT AFFAIRS AND INSTITUTIONAL ADVANCEMENT PARTNERSHIPS

Michael Puma

Introduction

Over the last 20 years, a combination of rising costs and diminished public support of higher education has made institutional fundraising efforts an increasingly important source of funding (Miller, 2010). One has to no look no further than President Obama's 2012 State of the Union speech or debates taking place in countless state legislatures to understand that this trend will continue. Reducing costs for students and improving accountability is the new normal. Colleges and universities continue to explore ways to expand the scope of comprehensive campaigns, annual funds, and planned giving in order to maintain and enhance the academic quality, co-curricular activities, and prestige of their institutions. However, challenges remain, and in an age of austerity, departments and programs that some constituents view as ancillary to the primary educational aims of higher education will have to explore new approaches to fund their various initiatives. In this environment, student affairs programs may be one area deemed on the periphery, and therefore, at risk for budget cuts and downsizing. At the same time, the work of Student Affairs divisions offers some of the greatest opportunities for growing fundraising efforts and expanding the donor base.

Rissmeyer (2010) contends that "the daily work of student affairs lies the groundwork for successful fundraising" (p. 22). To that end, collaboration between institutional advancement and student affairs is imperative and worthy of further exploration. What was called an "untapped resource" by Gold, Golden, and Quatroche (1993) is now a necessity for institutional and Student Affairs divisional growth. This chapter reviews the evolution of student affairs and institutional advancement partnerships over the last 30 years. A small, but growing literature in the area provides insights into how to approach collaboration and strategically create partnerships. Additionally, the chapter offers suggestions and best practices to implement and refine current student affairs and institutional advancement collaboration. Factors such as institutional type, organizational structure, monetary and human resources and the scope of the partnership will all shape how collaboration is imagined and experienced day to day. A proactive and inclusive approach maximizes the opportunities for success and sustaining collaboration over time. Beyond raising additional money, both divisions can benefit by understanding the work of the other division in an effort to develop ongoing, positive relationships with students, parents, donors, and alumni.

The Evolution of Student Affairs and Institutional Advancement Partnerships

The prevalence of student affairs involvement in development work has grown over time. Literature and research from the 1990s revealed limited perspectives and practices regarding student affairs and development collaboration. A 1993 study of Senior Student Affairs Officers (SSAO) found that the majority of them have not been asked to assist in soliciting funds and most seem ambivalent about fundraising as an aspect of their job. However, the overwhelming majority thought that they should be involved in fundraising (Terrell, Gold, & Renock, 1993). Writing from the perspective of a college president, Shay (1993) warns that some college presidents may view SSAO involvement in fundraising as a "diversion from primary responsibilities" or a "misguided incursion" (p. 17). Fygetakis and Dalton (1993) conducted an educational fundraising survey and found that over 85 percent of respondents did not have an institutional advancement officer assigned to student affairs. While there was little tension between offices, most student affairs administrators and fundraising officers reported that the other office either had helped or had no effect on educational fundraising for cocurricular activities and that student affairs efforts tended to me be independent of institutional advancement (Fygetakis & Dalton, 1993). For the most part, Student Affairs fundraising efforts were not embedded within a greater institutional advancement strategy and the practice depended on the efforts of a few key individuals rather than cross-divisional partnerships.

In 2001, National Association of Student Personnel Administrators (NASPA) published a resource for student affairs administrators entitled *Dollars for Dreams: Student Affairs Staff as Fundraisers*. This resource was one of the first nationwide attempts to educate student affairs administrators about the principles and practices associated with campus fundraising efforts. Penney and Rose (2001) report the results of the 1997 National Association of Student Personnel Administrator (NASPA) Survey on Fundraising for Student Affairs, a limited survey of 150 member institutions. Of the 72 NASPA member institutions who responded, 85 percent of their student affairs divisions were involved in fundraising on their campus and 4 percent were considering or were in the process of establishing a fundraising function for student affairs. Thirty percent already had a full-time person dedicated to the student affairs division, with over half of people reporting to student affairs. Parents and targeted alumni groups constituted the main donor group for this collaborative fundraising approach that addressed a variety of funding opportunities from special needs to capital campaign priorities (NASPA, 1997, as cited in Penney & Rose, 2001). The NASPA effort to provide professional development to all of its members signaled the growing importance of fundraising in student affairs.

More recent literature documents the continued institutionalization and strategic advantages of collaborative efforts. Miller (2010) views student affairs and development as "natural partners" and "powerful allies" in the identification and cultivation of current parents of students and alumni donor prospects, especially for targeted programs for first generation college students and enhancing student wellness. As part of her dissertation research, Crowe (2011) found growth in the number of institutions who employ a staff member in the student affairs division responsible for fundraising. Crowe (2011) also found that student affairs divisions within larger and more research-oriented institutions were more developed in their advancement efforts. Drawing from the professional experiences as student affairs development officers, Morgan and Policello (2010) surmise that it takes three to five years for an institution to develop the organization and infrastructure necessary for a successful student affairs fundraising effort. As the number of fully-dedicated student affairs development officers increases, additional resources for professional development and best practices will be necessary. Additionally, a clear articulation of goals and processes increases the chance for success. The following sections highlight some of the considerations and conditions necessary to start, refine, and sustain collaboration between institutional advancement and student affairs.

Support for Student Affairs and Institutional Advancement Collaboration must be Embedded in the University-Wide Strategic Approach to Fundraising

The first critical steps to encourage collaboration include taking stock of the role of student affairs plays at your institution and gauging the climate for collaboration. Are there examples of collaboration already occurring? If so, who has championed those efforts? Depending on how developed institutional advancement is across campus divisions, precedents may already exist for expanding collaboration such as with individual academic schools or colleges within the institution. In most cases, the senior student affairs officer should be the one of the earliest supporters for a divisional fundraising plan as they will be one of the primary players in cultivating gifts. SSAOs must be aware that committing their division to a more robust fundraising operation will also require additional personal time and attention. SSAOs are also best equipped to advocate for the division if questions arise from other divisions. Gordon, Strode, and Brady (1993) warn that at some institutions a new approach to collaboration has the potential to create tension and mistrust between student affairs and established campus fundraising operations. The addition of student affairs priorities to comprehensive campaign and annual giving initiatives may be viewed as competition for donors and their scarce resources. Therefore, it is important for the SSAO to frame the rationale for collaboration beyond the acquisition of monetary resources. Gold et al. (1993) suggest the mission and values of the institution must be "the backdrop against which all student affairs functions are actualized" (p. 99). Furthermore, the mission and values should guide the fundraising objectives. Articulating a vision for collaboration that benefits the strategic goals of both divisions and the institution is crucial.

One important rationale for collaboration is the connection between the experience of current students and their potential to become engaged alumni donors. SSAOs should point out that today's students are the donors of the future. A study by Sun, Hoffman, and Grady (2007) utilizing a two-year alumni survey at a Midwest public university suggests that working collaboratively across divisions could create a comprehensive communication strategy to reach alumni. Based on the result, Sun et al. believe that a focus on current students as future funders, providing quality educational experiences to students, encouraging and supporting relationship building between faculty and current students and graduates, and enhancing alumni services based on stakeholder needs would all strengthen future collaboration. In particular, the authors describe quality student experiences as student extra-curricular activities and career counseling—two areas in which student affairs administrators work closely with students throughout their time at college and develop deep relationships.

Beyond providing a clear rationale, buy-in from the president and others responsible for institutional decision making is also critical. If the president is not amenable to the inclusion of student affairs, it is highly unlikely institutions will be able to sustain their efforts over time. In a qualitative study of presidents and vice presidents of development and student affairs at comprehensive colleges, Arminio Clinton, and Harpster (2010) found that a university's strategic plan, institutional mission, the president's leadership style, a student-centered philosophy, and value of partnerships all influenced the process and priorities of collaboration. Other considerations that will impact buy-in include the institution's size and current capacity for fundraising efforts. Miller (2010) contends that large institutions have an advantage in establishing and supporting a student affairs development function since the costs can more easily be absorbed by a large budget. For smaller institutions and those who historically have lagged behind in fundraising initiatives, institutional leadership teams may have concerns about whether the amount that can be raised from donors will justify the personal and staff energy required to raise the money (Shay, 1993). In these cases, focusing on smaller, more targeted and realistic projects may provide a strong foundation for success that can later be expanded. In summary, institutional buy-in and right-sizing the enterprise will set the appropriate groundwork for collaboration.

Determine How the Collaboration Will Be Organized and Assessed

Beyond committing to collaboration, institutions should decide how to organize and assess their collaborative efforts. Unless the initiative is embedded in a larger plan to shift strategic priorities, the organization of the initiative should stem from the model set forth by the Chief Advancement Officer (CAO). Frameworks for organization range from a centralized model to a decentralized model depending on the size of the institution and historical precedent. In a centralized model, the institutional advancement office mobilizes an institution-wide program designed to raise funds for all initiatives ranging from endowment growth, capital projects to department specific programs. Additionally, institutional advancement officers work closely with specific divisions to set priorities and conduct needs assessment (Miser & Mathis, 1993). Ultimately, the CAO controls the priority setting and decision making for the entire institution. If operating in a centralized model, it is important that the development officer have a close relationship with a liaison from student affairs to gain knowledge and expertise on specific needs and priorities (Miser & Mathis, 1993). In lieu of direct involvement by student affairs administrators, the ability of the development officer to articulate the vision for student affairs fundraising is pivotal.

In a decentralized model, each school, college, or division has a dedicated advancement officer who coordinates fundraising specific to that area (Shea, 1986). The institutional advancement office sets the ground rules for donor solicitation, record keeping and ways to navigate conflict of interest between decentralized areas (Gold et al., 1993). If fundraising for student affairs is new for your campus, intentional conversations should take place to ensure that pre-existing fundraising guidelines set forth from institutional advancement address nuances or special considerations of fundraising for student affairs. For example, student affairs and institutional advancement need to agree on how they will address proposed gifts that do not hold true to the goals of a specific program. Political, religious, and social beliefs of donors may be at odds with student affairs best practices and fundraising priorities. Therefore, institutions and divisions should understand what expectations (if any) come along with the donations they accept.

Additionally, institutional advancement should seek ways to educate other units about the inclusion of student affairs as a decentralized fundraising area. Proactively anticipating questions and seeking solutions reduces the probability of conflict during the initial collaboration. The decentralized model combined with collegial relations help student affairs development officers "shape an integrated system of interdependent components" (Gordon et al., 1993). In this model, senior level administrators should advocate for conditions that allow for horizontal information sharing and the development of professional relationships between members of both divisions.

Determine the Facilitators of Collaboration— The Boundary Spanners

Once the organizational structure is determined, attention should be paid to selecting the individuals best suited to do the work of student affairs development. These individuals will be called on to learn the existing structures and cultures of two divisions and determine how best to communicate across divisions. The role may require strong collaborations between multiple professionals who work primarily with one division or the creation of new professional positions with a boundary-spanning role reporting primarily to one division. Fortunately, similarities in work styles and work environment of student affairs and institutional advancement may help establish collaborative structures. Penney and Rose (2001) assert that student affairs administrators and development officers have parallel skills sets. Professionals in these areas are dedicated, self-motivated, understand the needs of their constituents, and are willing to try new ways of doing their work. Furthermore, Morgan and Policello (2010) emphasize that relationship building is the central characteristic of the work of both student affairs and institutional advancement. Transferable skills may also help professionals being asked to step outside their comfort zones to develop new collaborations. Gold et al. (1993) write, "Transferable talents from Student Affairs work to educational fundraising activities include people skills, community-building skills, personal growth orientation, leadership capability, counseling and mediation skills and ability to convey enthusiasm for the institution" (p. 106). In general, enthusiasm combined with a love of working with students helps to convey authenticity and integrity—important qualities for the work of both divisions. Given the importance of authenticity and integrity, professionals who have attended or worked at the institution for a number of years may be best equipped to combine knowledge and enthusiasm in ways that will resonate with donors. In some cases, alumni donors may remember their personal relationships with student affairs professionals who later become involved in development work. This pre-existing relationship helps the donor envision the stewardship of their gift.

The combination of personal skills sets, transferable skills, and previous knowledge of the institution and work of both divisions situates those who engage in student affairs development work as boundary spanners. Toffler (1970, as cited in Gordon et al., 1993) describes boundary spanners as "skilled in understanding jargon of different groups and can communicate them across groups by translating and interpreting the language of one into the language of another" (p. 144). The idea of boundary spanning appears to be central to the work of student affairs development work. Pruitt and Schwartz (1999) write, "Successful student affairs work requires constant boundary spanning to stay connected to events, activities, and actions, in, across and outside the institution and to interpret constantly the changing environment both inside and outside the institution" (p. 63). The boundary spanners, therefore, are central to setting and monitoring the climate for collaboration and keeping up to date on activities across campus. As such, it is important that both divisions feel comfortable with the people tasked to do the boundary spanning work.

Through her survey research, Crowe (2011) found that a majority of institutions have both student affairs and institutional advancement weigh in on hiring decisions of student affairs development professionals. Furthermore, the number of fully dedicated professional responsible for student development work has increased significantly over the last 20 years. They are usually housed in student affairs divisions and report to the SSAO. In some cases, they may report to both divisions. Based on the length of the initiative, student affairs development officers may be asked to create structures for collaboration or to maintain a pre-existing model. The length of time a school has been engaged in student affairs fundraising will dictate how the job description is crafted and how the majority of day-to-day work time is spent. Professionals working with newer initiatives will spend more time developing new relationships and cross-divisional training. Undoubtedly, "patience is a key attribute for development officers in student affairs" (Morgan & Policello, 2011, p. 11), and perseverance will be necessary as new collaborations evolve.

Set the Scope and Priorities of Student Affairs Fundraising Efforts

If student affairs development work at your institution is still in a primary phase, you will need to decide the scope and types of projects that you hope to fund and who will be the primary donors of interest. In the era of billion-dollar comprehensive campaigns, where does fundraising for student affairs fit in? There is a difference between sponsoring an event or giveaways and funding a million-dollar strategic initiative. For example, many campuses already engage in capital campaigns for new residence halls or student centers. A structure may already be in place to cultivate gifts for large building projects. Therefore, this may not fall in the purview of student affairs fundraising. Instead, student affairs development efforts may focus on sharing the stories and needs of the programs and offices that will populate a new building. In the past, women and minority student, career planning and development, alcohol and substance abuse, and creative arts or performing arts programs, as well as building projects and recreation related activities tended to be the areas where joint fundraising appeared most feasible (Terrell et al., 1993; Fygetakis & Dalton, 1993). Crowe (2011) reports that from 2002 to 2007, priorities most frequently reported by NASPA affiliated institutions participating in her survey were scholarships, leadership programs, and diversity programs. For most campuses, targeted priorities will stem from a student affairs strategic plan. If possible, priorities should be tested as part of feasibility studies or pre-campaign planning studies to get a sense of what types of giving opportunities would resonate with alumni and donors who have contributed in the past.

Determine the Primary Constituents for Student Affairs Fundraising

Part of developing the scope of collaboration is deciding which types of potential donors will be of primary interest. Student affairs fundraising presents a particular challenge in that everyone and no one may have a primary affinity with the student affairs division as compared to a specific academic program, athletic team, or campus initiative (Henry, 2012). As institutions add more decentralized units to their fundraising initiative, the risk of asking the same set of donors to contribute to multiple areas of the institution increases. For example, how will an institution decide who gets to solicit a donation from an influential alumna who was a student athlete, a graduate of the business school, and participated in a women's leadership program? In the end, all three units may obtain a donation, but the overall amount of the gift may be reduced. Additionally, donor fatigue may set in, which will impact future solicitations. The answer to this dilemma lies in a well-coordinated effort and clear guidelines set forth by institutional advancement as to the appropriate donor base for student affairs initiatives in relation to other needs of the campus and the capacity of individual donors. Morgan and Policello (2010) urge that "coordination of donor relations is as important as asking for the gift" (p. 17). Therefore, student affairs development officers should be fully integrated into the record keeping structures so that all contact with donors is documented. As institutions expand the scope of interdisciplinary and cross-divisional collaborations, a well-coordinated donor relations effort will maximize to link prospective donors with initiatives that are salient to who they are or their experience while on campus.

One of the great benefits of including student affairs in the work of institutional advancement is the potential to expand the donor base to include new constituents or reacquaint alumni who have not donated over time. The Fundraising School at the Center for Philanthropy, part of Indiana University-Purdue University Indianapolis, developed a constituency model for student affairs division development model (Penny & Rose, 2001). Visualized as a set of concentric circles, the core of the student affair model includes parents, grand-parents, and corporations with an interest in employing students. The next layer includes more traditional constituents such as alumni and past donors, but also includes foundations and vendors that primarily work with student affairs divisions. Within these two circles, institutions can craft a strategy or develop a list of potential donors that is primary to student affairs.

Student affairs fundraising can be a way to connect donors who have never donated or have lapsed in their donations by viewing them as affinity groups. Similar to the ways in which Greek organizations organize their philanthropic efforts, institutions can look to alumni who participated in specific student leadership groups, multicultural clubs and service organizations. Student affairs administrators have knowledge of young alumni, levels of involvement, areas of satisfaction, and contributions to the institution while they were students. Additionally, Rissmeyer (2010) points out that student affairs administrators' training in human development theory can be particularly effective when working with young alumni. Including administrators from across the division in the fundraising process may provide the impetus that compels young alumni to donate to the institution by providing reassurance that their donation will make a difference to something they believe in and want to support.

Burdened by loans, graduate school costs, or a tough job market, young alumni may feel like they cannot support a donation to the institution. How-ever, young alumni may be more agreeable to targeting a smaller donation to an organization or initiative they recently engaged with or benefited from. Sun et al. (2007) contend that those treated favorably as students, were satisfied with their academic experiences, and believed their college education contributed to their career success, are more inclined to give. Maintaining a connection with young alumni through small donations of money or time creates a culture of giving that may translate into larger donations as they develop the capacity to give (Drezner, 2011).

Some special considerations exist when expanding the donor groups to include constituents such as parents, grandparents, and vendors. Soliciting par-ents and grandparents of current students has the potential to blur boundaries and create a perception of preferential treatment. Any effort to expand this strategy should be carefully considered in the context of the divisional prin-ciples that guide work with individual students and parents. Offices that are responsible for the day-to-day welfare and support of students such as residen-tial life, student conduct, the counseling center, and career services should be prepared for parents inquiries that reference donations.

A potential exists for parents to connect their donation to a specific request for their child such as more desirable housing accommodations or an appeal of a student conduct decision. At smaller institutions, it may be possible to antici-pate issues and adjust parent solicitations accordingly. It is also important that institutional advancement and student affairs be aware of dual roles that new constituents have with the institution. Parents may also be alumni or vendors who do business with the institution. The potential for these issues to arise will vary campus to campus. However, safeguards should be put in place to uphold the integrity of both divisions in their solicitations and commitment to student learning, so that no particular group of students whose families have the capacity to give receive undue advantage.

Support Cross-Divisional Collaboration through Relationship Building and Professional Development

A student affairs development professional cannot cultivate a culture of collaboration in isolation. Once the scope of collaboration is decided, those responsible for implementing the plan need to develop partnerships and educate their colleagues about the initiative. Education helps colleagues understand priorities, clarify needs, and understand specific roles they can plan in the solicitation process (Arminio et al., 2010). In addition, increased informal and formal training for both institutional advancement and student affairs officers would help counteract any stereotypes that may exist. For example, student affairs professional may have a skewed view of the cultivation process and may minimize the efforts that development officers make to develop ongoing relationships. Conversely, development officers may not appreciate the diversity of functions student affairs professionals participate in on campus and the theories that drive the work. Initial trainings would provide an overview of the day-to-day work of each division, the professional standards that guide the work and how each division's work contributes to the mission of the institution. In other words, the process of learning (and perhaps, unlearning) about the "other" increases understanding and leads to the development of new skill sets. While many pre-existing skill sets will translate well between the two divisions, others may not. For example, evaluation of job performance and how success is measured look and feel very different for a student affairs administrator and institutional advancement professional. An honest and transparent assessment of the most fulfilling and challenging aspects of the position serves to humanize the collaboration.

Depending on the expectations for collaboration and the integration functions, more intensive training may be warranted. If student affairs development officers expect divisional colleagues to meet with donors, more detailed information and one-on-one preparation meetings will be necessary. For example, a student affairs professional will need to understand how donor meetings typically unfold and what role they will play in the meeting. In some cases, a student affairs professional will be asked to attend because he or she knows more about the program or initiative under consideration and will be able to speak about it with enthusiasm, passion, and conviction. However, speaking about it in front of a donor may cause added pressure. Additionally, they will have to find ways to translate program specifics and student affairs lingo into language that an outside donor can follow. In some cases, student affairs colleagues should practice the development of "an elevator speech," which aims to succinctly explain the program goals, aspirations, and benefits in less than a minute. Beyond brevity, the elevator speech should also be compelling so that the donor can visualize how their donation will make a difference. Finally, student affairs professionals should know whether or not "an ask" will be part of the meeting and if they play a role in that process. While there may be transferable skills sets, student affairs administrators may have difficulty actually asking donors for money (Arminio et al., 2010). Ultimately, this level of involvement may be unnecessary given the expertise and training of the development officer. The overall purpose of training and preparation is to make them comfortable with the process and understand their role as the champion of the specific initiative.

Development officers can also benefit from information about specific fundraising initiatives. If development officers are assigned to assist with student affairs fundraising, they should be able to articulate the goals of the program as well as the larger learning outcomes of the division. If possible, they should spend time discussing or shadowing the administrators or students involved in the program or initiative. The more personal they can make the experience, the more compelling they will be when meeting with donors. Better knowledge of the initiative will also reduce the chance that the program is being misrepresented (Gordon et al., 1993). Throughout the fundraising process and at the completion of the fundraising effort, professionals from both divisions should come together to debrief the effort, address issues, and hopefully, celebrate successes.

Involve Students and Connect Them with Alumni

Including students in fundraising efforts may provide an even more compelling argument to sway donors than incorporating administrators. Involving students serves multiple purposes. Beyond making giving a much more personal experience for the donor, students learn the importance of philanthropy (Drezner, 2009, 2010), especially in regards to programs that are important to them. Drezner found that involving students in current fundraising sets the groundwork for cultivating those same students when they become alumni. Students who participate in philanthropy will have a context for giving. Much like the student affairs professionals, students will need targeted training and preparation for their donor interactions. Training that addresses fundraising can be infused into pre-existing leadership workshops for club and organizations. If students are communicating with donors, they should be encouraged to speak freely, but appropriately. Most students, if selected and trained carefully, will rise to the occasion.

Beyond donor meetings with individual students, alumni may have an interest in participating in student events, lectures, sporting events, and programs as guests or active participants. Conversely, student affairs professionals may enjoy attending alumni reunion events and parent receptions. These types of collaborations may be especially important to multi-cultural affinity groups. Research in giving among minority communities highlights the importance placed on sharing time and wealth with family, extended families, and their communities (Drezner, 2011). Connecting alumni with communities they were apart of in college can benefit both the alumni and current students. Promoting volunteerism and mentoring opportunities will benefit both student affairs and institutional advancement as well as the young alumni. If you are considering events involving donors and students, do not underestimate the planning and coordination of the events. Both divisions should be represented and feel comfortable with the planning to mitigate unanticipated issues. For example, the presence of alcohol at events in which underage students attend warrants an intentional conversation in advance of the event. Successful events have the potential to be held annually and therefore, all parties should work to make sure that the event is successful for reasons consistent with the mission and goals of the institution.

Develop a Technology Infrastructure that Supports the Collaboration

Harnessing the power of institutional technology can assist in both the internal and external facilitation of fundraising for student affairs. Internally, student development fundraisers should take an assessment of the types of information that the institution collects about donors, current students, and alumni. While most institutional advancement offices have databases that track donors, the types of information regarding interest in the areas of student affairs are limited and most times, woefully incomplete. Therefore, new strategies and data points should be identified so that data from current students follows them when they become alumni. Rissmeyer (2010) points out keeping records of students' co-curricular affiliations and key events during their matriculation can help build and maintain meaningful relations with alumni well after their graduation. Similarly, parent data should be linked with the activities that their students engaged in while at the institution. Most student affairs development professionals will need to engage in retroactive process of data mining to retrieve records of student involvement. Yearbooks, student newspapers, annual reports, membership list from clubs and organizations, and rosters of student employees such as resident assistants can provide good leads on alumni who may be likely to donate to a specific student affairs initiative (Rissmeyer, 2010). The data may also provide evidence of groups who historically do not give to the institution. This information can be shared with student affairs offices as a way to review and perhaps, improve their services (Drezner, 2011). Data collection and sharing is an added-value benefit of student affairs and institutional advancement collaboration. Beyond digging into historical records, development officers can work with veteran administrators to identify students they have kept in touch with over time. This more personal approach contextualizes the data and may lead to more successful and targeted cultivation efforts.

External uses of technology can vastly expand the pool of potential donors and the ease in which they can make donations. Many institutions with a dedicated student affairs officer have developed websites detailing the student affairs oriented strategic initiatives and provide a link to an online giving page. In addition to stand-alone pages for development efforts, individual offices affiliated with fundraising initiatives can include the donation links on their office webpage. Once the initiative or program is underway, information can be added to the website that highlights the impact that donor money has had on its success.

The use of social and digital media is another area in which institutions span divisional boundaries. Given the wide array of social media options, student affairs development officers should collaborate with colleagues in marketing and communications areas of the institution to determine which social media outlets are most utilized and what level of interactions is optimal to effectively communicate with broad audiences and individual donors alike. An initial step may be to develop a content calendar that is connected to other areas of the institution in order to have communications coincide with yearly events or timely accolades (Rushton, 2012). Embedded videos that highlight successful initiatives or positive student experiences can serve similar purposes to face-to-face meetings or presentations. Given the speed in which popular social media websites and apps come and go, the institution should choose carefully where and how they dedicate time and money to digital communications (Rushton, 2012).

Anticipate the Needs of Future Growth

As fundraising for student affairs initiatives becomes more the expectation than exception, it will be important to imagine future needs and directions for the collaboration. Sustained collaboration will take up more time. In a study of student affairs professionals Terrell et al. (1993) found that lack of time was the primary objection to being involved in fundraising. Therefore, it will be important to build fundraising responsibilities into job descriptions and to shift other responsibilities to free up time for strategic priorities. For example, student affairs offices and administrators will need to take time to report the impact and outcomes of donor gifts so relationships can be maintained and strengthened. Building fundraising into job descriptions will also allow for better recruitment efforts and will minimize lapses in sustained collaboration. Commitment to strategic student affairs fundraising and cross-division collaboration should anticipate departmental and divisional turnover. Another way to expand the influence of fundraising efforts is to create and independent advisory board for the student affairs division comprised of alumni, students, parents, employees, and former employees (Miller, 2010). This board can help guide future growth opportunities and share the responsibilities of identifying and cultivating donors.

A professional development community has emerged as the field of student affairs fundraising work has become more prominent. The American College Personnel Association (ACPA) recently created the Task Force for Alumni Relations and Development. Similarly, NASPA now sponsors a knowledge community dedicated to student affairs development and fundraising work. The mission of the NASPA Student Affairs Fundraising and External Relations knowledge community is to provide development professionals a "home" within NASPA, to provide SSAOs a place to connect for latest fundraising strategies and to enhance connections between different NASPA regions, institutional types, and functional areas (NASPA, 2012). Additionally, NASPA sponsors an annual conference for professionals to share best practices. Over 60professionals attended the 2012 conference held in Louisville, Kentucky. Participants were able to network and attend a variety of sessions focusing on cultivating parents as donors, fundraising with a non-traditional student body, diversity in fundraising, and asking for major gifts. The Council for the Advancement and Support of Education (CASE) has also offered webinars on forging partnerships between student affairs and alumni relations. These opportunities bring fresh, new ideas to campuses and provide a community for professionals to hone their skills and train the next generation of student affairs development professionals.

Acknowledge Hard Work, Recognize Donors, and Celebrate Successes

A final consideration for advancing student affairs development work may seem like common sense, but is often lost in the fast-paced day-to-day work environment. Both divisions value recognition of their constituents. For institutional advancement, thanking donors is commonplace, and for student affairs, recognizing student and staff contributions is considered a best practice. These isolated recognition practices should become a shared expectation of cross-divisional collaboration. A coordinated recognition effort demonstrates the strength of the collaborative endeavor and shows the importance of continued relationships. Finally, creating a culture of collaboration is reinforced by taking time to celebrate successes and thanking colleagues for their hard work and effort. For many, a simple "thank you" may be the only formal recognition they receive for their involvement in sustained fundraising efforts. A healthy and supportive work environment where people feel valued will lead to quality collaboration and more authentic encounters with donors.

The Future is Collaboration

As these practices become more prevalent, there is a potential that fundraising will become the expectation not just to start or enhance student affairs program offerings, but to maintain program offerings. Competition for resources will become fiercer within the institution and between institutions. However, student affairs fundraising can offer donors an opportunity to support initiatives they are passionate about and that will have a direct impact on the defined outcomes of the student experience (Rychner & Clement, 2012). Colleges and universities must be prepared with a long-range plan to sustain programs that advance the mission of the institution and student affairs division (see Table 12.1). Furthermore, preparation programs in student affairs and institutional advancement have to anticipate the need for scholarship and theory that informs student affairs development practice. Future professionals in both areas need exposure and competencies in cross-divisional collaboration and fundraising practices. Working better together strengthens both divisions and improves the experience of current and prospective students and demonstrates to alumni and donors that the institution is a good steward of their philanthropic giving.

TABLE 12.1 Recommendations for Starting and Enhancing Student Affairs and Institutional Advancement Collaboration

Recommendation	Strategies for Implementation
Initiate strategic implementation of collaboration efforts	• Encourage senior leadership to set parameters and goals of collaboration and identify a structure that aligns with institutional goals. • Dedicate resources to student affairs fundraising—especially when starting a new initiative. • Align fundraising efforts with student affairs and overall institution's strategic plan.
Provide ongoing cross-divisional training opportunities for administrators and students	• Expose and educate both divisions on the values and professional standards that guide day-to-day work. • Participate in national conferences and share best practices with colleagues. • Address misperceptions and stereotypes between the two divisions. • Find ways to involve parents, students, and young alumni in fundraising training and practice.
Develop an infrastructure that supports sustained collaboration	• Collect student participation data and share with development once the student graduates. • Build in fundraising and collaboration between divisions into job descriptions. • Utilize technology and social media to continue to evolve efforts. • Recognize and celebrate successful partnerships between administrators, students, and donors alike.

References

Arminio, J., Clinton, L. F., & Harpster, G. (2010). Fundraising for student affairs at comprehensive institutions. *New Directions for Student Services, 130,* 31–45.

Crowe, P. A. (2011). Development and fundraising practices in divisions of student affairs at 4-year public universities. Graduate College of Bowling Green State University. Retrieved January 14, 2012, from http://etd.ohiolink.edu/senddf.cgi/Crowe%20Peggy%20A.pdf?bgsu 1294342953

Drezner, N. D. (2009). Why give?: Exploring social exchange and organizational identification theories in the promotion of philanthropic behaviors of African American millennials at private-HBCUs. *International Journal of Educational Advancement, 9*(3), 147–165.

Drezner, N. D. (2010). Private Black colleges' encouragement of student giving and volunteerism: An examination of prosocial behavior development. *International Journal of Educational Advancement, 10*(3), 126–147.

Drezner, N. (2011). Who is Philanthropic? Philanthropy by non-traditional donors. In *Philanthropy and fundraising in American higher education* (pp. 27-40). ASHE Higher Education Report: Volume 37, No.2. San Francisco, CA: Jossey-Bass.

Fygetakis, E. C., & Dalton, J. C. (1993). The relationship between student affairs and institutional advancement offices in educational fundraising. *New Directions for Student Services, 63,* 51–61.

Gold, J. A., Golden, D. C., & Quatroche, T. J. (1993). The challenge of chief student affairs officers: Planning for the future. *New Directions for Student Services, 63,* 95–107.

Gordon, S. E., Strode, C. B., & Brady, R. M. (1993). Student affairs and educational fundraising: the first critical step. *New Directions for Student Services, 63,* 5–15.

Henry, R. (2012, July). The advancement building blocks and challenges for student affairs. Paper presented at the NASPA Student Affairs Development Conference, Louisville, KY.

Miller, T. (2010). The context for development work in student affairs. *New Directions for Student Services, 130,* 3–8. doi:10.1002/ss.355

Miser, K. M., & Mathis, T. D (1993). Creating a student affairs institutional advancement program: Strategies for success. *New Direction for Student Services, 63,* 29–39.

Morgan, M. F., & Policello, S. M. (2010). Getting started in student affairs development. *New Directions for Student Services, 130,* 9–18.

National Association of Student Personnel Administrators. (2012). Knowledge communities: Student affairs development and external relations. Retrieved January 14, 2012, from http://www.naspa.org/kc/sader/default.cfm

Penney, S. W., & Rose, B. B. (2001). *Dollars for dreams: Student affairs staff as fundraisers.* Washington, DC: National Association of Student Personnel Administrators.

Pruitt, D. A., & Schwartz, R. A. (1999). Student affairs work as boundary spanning: An exploratory study. *College Student Affairs Journal, 19*(1), 62-87.

Rissmeyer, P. A. (2010). Student affairs and alumni relations. *New Directions for Student Services, 130,* 19–29. doi:10.1002/ss.357

Rushton, J. (2012, July). *Digital/social media and fundraising.* Paper presented at the NASPA Student Affairs Development Conference, Louisville, KY.

Rychner, J., & Clement, L. (2012). Emerging roles and the responsibilities of the student affairs development officer/director of development. In A. Tull & L. Kuk (Eds.), *New realities in the management of student affairs* (pp. 58-67). Sterling, VA; Stylus.

Shay, J. E. (1993). The president's perspective on student affairs and educational fundraising. *New Directions for Student Services, 63,* 17–28.

Shea, J. M. (1986). Organizational issues in designing advancement programs. In A. W. Roland (Ed.), *Handbook of Institutional Advancement* (2nd ed., pp. 31–43). San Francisco, CA: Jossey-Bass.

Sun, X., Hoffman, S., & Grady, M. (2007). A multivariate causal model of alumni giving: Implications for alumni fundraisers. *International Journal of Educational Advancement, 2007, 7*(4), 307–332.

Terrell, M., Gold, J., & Renick, J. C. (1993). Student affairs professionals as fund-raisers: An untapped resource. *NASPA Journal, 30*(3), 190–195.

13

CREATING AN ENGAGEMENT MODEL OF ADVANCEMENT FOR YOUNG ALUMNI

Luke Greeley

Public funding for higher education has declined substantially over the last 30 years in terms of both direct contributions to students through grant aid and indirect contributions to institutions through state aid (Cheslock, 2009; National Center for Public Policy and Higher Education, 2002). As governmental support has declined for students and universities, professional fundraising efforts have become a feature of nearly all colleges and universities, public and private alike. To balance tight budgets and keep the skyrocketing cost of tuition in check, competition for public and private funds amongst higher education institutions in the United States has become more intense than ever before.

Successful fundraising is necessary for institutional success, and, for an increasing number of colleges, is necessary for survival (Gasman & Drezner, 2008). Money from fundraising comprises approximately 10 percent of higher education expenditures (Council for Aid to Education [CAE], 2007). Of the $27.85 billion that was donated to higher education by all sources in 2009, $7.13 billion, or 25.6 percent, was donated by alumni (Drezner, 2011). Despite this substantial support from alumni, according to the Council for Aid to Education (2010), the percentage of alumni giving was at an all-time low in 2009 at 10 percent and declined further to 9.8 percent in 2010. Even when considering the downturn in the economy, CAE reports that alumni participation has trended downward for many years. Colleges and universities face an imperative to engender support from their graduates, not only to balance their budgets but also to successfully pursue missions of providing reasonably priced and high-quality educational opportunities.

The basic approach of college and university fundraising have changed little in previous decades, yet fundamental shifts are occurring in who donates to higher education and their motivations for donating. Cook (2008) writes that the Smith (1975, 1977, 1993) "Five I's" model (identification, information, interest, involvement, and investment) has served as the standard for college development offices for over three decades. At the heart of this model are two beliefs. The first is that fundraising efforts targeted at the larger population of alumni are inefficient because the majority of funds raised come from a small population of wealthy individuals (Cook, 2008; Melchior, 1988). The second is that the goal of development in higher education is to raise money for a particular institution. But what if the traditional pool of wealthy donors (i.e., older, heterosexual, White men; Drezner, 2011) is evolving into something else? And what if an unselfish approach to development in higher education benefitted a larger community in which college and universities were a part of, and somehow that unselfish action reaped greater benefits for the institutions involved? In the following chapter, I will argue that the alumni landscape in higher education is changing and that the most successful response of the higher education community will to be to alter the fundraising paradigm from which it currently operates.

Considering the size and scope of the non-profit sector in the United States, fundraising is highly understudied and under theorized (Cook & Lasher, 1996; Kelly, 2002; Merkel, 2010). As previously mentioned, development efforts and resources at colleges and universities tend to focus on primarily on older, wealthy alumni as research has demonstrated the vast majority of funds raised come from a small and wealthy percentage of the population (Cook, 2008; Cherish, 2008). Yet diverting efforts from younger, less-established alumni may by extremely unwise, as some scholars have found past giving to be one of the strongest predictors of future giving (Lindahl & Winship, 1992; Okunade & Justice, 1991). Based on this predictor, college fundraising and development offices face an imperative challenge to reverse the declining alumni participation trend, especially amongst young alumni who are the potential big donors of the future. The level of connection recent graduates still have with their alma mater gives universities a unique opportunity to still shape their perceptions of the undergraduate experience, as Merkel (2010) writes, "Young alumni are still in the formative stages of their relationship with the University and are still highly active in receiving and providing benefits to the institution" (p. 28). In this way, within the age groups containing tomorrow's big donors, a significant amount can be done to increase the chances of future giving.

A number of higher education fundraising studies address alumni giving by focusing on the influence of academic and extracurricular satisfaction. Involvement with student clubs and organizations, such as student government, activities committees, sports teams, and Greek life, and positive relationships and interactions with faculty and staff are demonstrated predictors of future donations (Clotfelter, 2003; Monks, 2003). The unique personal connection alumni feel with their college or university is identified as one prerequisite for successful fundraising (Cook & Lasher, 1996), and development professionals attempt to build on this relationship to encourage higher levels of giving in the future (Mann, 2007). Understanding the ways in which fundraising professionals can acknowledge and celebrate each alumnus' connection to various components of and more specifically, the way in which institutional advancement can transform those meaningful connections into involvement and engagement, are critical components to evolving development practices.

Raising funds from recent college graduates, however, could be a serious challenge according to current research. For example, McDearmon (2010) found that young alumni often refuse to give because they would like something in exchange for their gift. The study also found that alumni may hesitate to give because they only have interest in helping very specific facets of their alma mater and are unaware of restricted gift opportunities (i.e., gifts that go to a particular student organization, academic department, etc., of a donor's choosing). Additionally, the fact that more college students are graduating with significant amounts of student loan debt (National Center for Public Policy and Higher Education, 2002) is problematic for fundraisers as studies show that alumni who received financial aid in the form of loans are less likely to donate their university (Monks, 2003; O'Malley, 1992). Weerts and Ronca's (2007) study of one particular public research university indicates that young alumni are significantly less likely to volunteer for their alma mater, which is relevant to this review because of the demonstrated link between volunteering for an organization and donating money (Wang & Graddy, 2008). From the literature, one begins to get a sense that the college fundraising process is interconnected with many aspects of university activities outside of the development office.

Vast changes are taking place amongst tomorrow's university donors in relation to their demographic background as well their motivations. Donors are becoming younger and more ethnically diverse (Elliott, 2006; Nichols, 2004). The rapidly growing and changing technology sector has allowed some innovative young people to become extraordinarily wealthy. Despite these changes, many studies have found that as alumni age, they tend to give more than younger counter parts (Bruggink & Siddiqui, 1995; Okunade & Berl, 1997; Weerts & Ronca, 2007; Willemain, Goyal, Deven, & Thukral, 1994). This may reflect higher levels of discretionary income that increase with age, or as Clotfelter (2008) seems to suggest, that older generations of alumni are more willing to donate to their alma mater than younger ones.

The long-established image of the university donor as an older, White, male is no longer applicable to today's changing alumni base. The National Center for Education Statistics (2009) reports that, in 1976, 15 percent of college students were minorities, compared with 32 percent in 2007. A large portion of that growth can be accounted for amongst the Latino/a and Asian/Pacific Islander student populations that grew from 4 to 11 percent and 2 to 7 percent, respectively, over the same time period. Black student populations have also risen from 9 to 13 percent of the total enrolled college population. Traditionally, non-profit organizations have not bothered soliciting from groups such as African Americans and Latinos because they are viewed as recipients of services rather than providers (Gasman, 2002; Newman, 2002). This has proved to be a foolish assumption as minority communities have been shown to have a rich history of philanthropic endeavors (Carson, 2008). Further, African Americans tend to demonstrate a greater commitment to organizations they participated in while in college than do their White counterparts (Gasman, 2002), and African Americans have been found to regularly volunteer time more than Whites (Mesch, Rooney, Chin, & Steinberg, 2002). Important motivational factors for racial minorities in participating in philanthropic efforts are the concepts of giving as part of a community effort, racial uplift, giving back for aid previously received from others, and helping others help themselves are reflected in multiple studies on African American giving (Gasman, 2002; Newman, 2002; Scanlan & Abrahams, 2002; Smith, Shue, Vest, & Villarreal, 1999).

Another dramatic demographic shift in America's alumni base is related to gender. According to the National Center for Education Statistics (2009), women accounted for 57 percent of enrolled college students, and that percentage is expected to rise to approximately 60 percent in the coming decade. This is vitally significant to the study of fundraising, as an increasing number of studies are finding that women tend to be more generous than their male counterparts. Rooney, Mesch, Chin, and Steinberg (2005) found in a national study consisting of 4,200 individuals that single women were significantly more likely to give at all to philanthropic causes than single men, and gave more money than single men. Sun, Hoffman, and Grady (2007) reaffirmed the findings in Rooney et al. (2005) in analyzing survey data from approximately 1,800 alumni from a Midwest university and found that women were more likely to donate to their alma mater than men. There are differing opinions on why female alumni are motivated to give, but Capek (2001) and Briechle (2008) seem to draw similar conclusions about the desire of women to give out of a sense of identification with the goals of the institutions they support.

With so many factors of the college experience influencing an alumnus' decision to give, a successful fundraising process should incorporate a holistic educational perspective. Yet this is certainly not the case as shortfalls exist both in the scholarly literature and development practice. For example, the use of programmatic efforts, such as reunions, networking events, athletic competitions, and community service initiatives as a donor cultivation tool are discussed only briefly in studies such as Harrison (2008) and Holmes (2009) that utilize unclear categorizations of these events. Though fundraising literature provides ample evidence linking volunteerism amongst alumni to their willingness to give (Clotfelter, 2003; Taylor & Martin, 1995), one is hard pressed to find research on what, if any, community-based volunteering efforts universities offer to engage alumni.

Clearly, many scholars are studying the dynamics of fundraising amongst evolving demographic groups, but the extent to which practitioners are adapting their fundraising strategies is not known. Today's recent college graduates differ tremendously from their earlier counterparts in that they are more likely to be female, increasingly come from minority ethnic and racial backgrounds, engage in different modes of relationship building, utilize new forms of communication, and engage in alternative forms of philanthropy. As such, there is a great need to study effective fundraising strategies amongst younger cohorts of college alumni. College professionals have made efforts to market to younger generations of alumni through social media, yet development offices have been only marginally successful in communicating with the younger audience (Stevick, 2010). Despite the lack of success, the level of connection recent graduates still have with their alma mater give universities a unique opportunity to still shape their perceptions of the undergraduate experience (Merkel, 2010). By tapping into the transformative power of involvement and engagement, a significant amount can be done by development offices to influence the behaviors of tomorrow's donors.

Theoretical Framework

An objectivist or rational epistemology is one that views knowledge as something derived from logical thinking but that exists independently of the human mind. In other words, as humans, we are able to observe the world around us, make measurements or assessments of what we experience, and draw conclusions about the nature of reality based on our observations. Weerts, in his 2007 article "Toward an Engagement Model of Institutional Advancement at Public Colleges and Universities," argues that universities traditionally have viewed their role in society as producers of knowledge, which is consumed by the public. Furthermore, in upholding that understanding, fundraisers for universities have viewed their role as unilateral communicators of the university's activities and mission. Operating from the objectivist epistemology, or what I will refer to as the "traditional" paradigm, development officers seek to sell the interests of the institution to external constituencies. Weerts (2007) contrasts this with a constructivist paradigm, which asserts that knowledge lies both inside and outside of traditional boundaries and that the creation of knowledge is a collective process. From the constructivist paradigm, development officers engage community partners with the inner workings of the institution and promote a mission that is beneficial to society as a whole. In order to successfully engage alumni as partners in a university's future, a close critique of the assumptions held in the development field is necessary. I will demonstrate that development in higher education is self-serving and discuss the ways in which a paradigm shift can potentially increase support for colleges and universities from not only young alumni, but society as a whole.

In practice, the traditional framework operates with a specific formula for raising funds. Cook (2008) identifies the Smith (1975, 1977, 1993) model of fundraising as the most widespread and "unofficial" standard of the fundraising industry. The Smith model is based on the "Five I's," which are steps in the fundraising cycle that include *identification* of potential donors, gathering personal *information* about those donors, gauging the level of *interest* the donor has in an organization and its goals, encouraging *involvement* in the organization, and finally soliciting an *investment* in the organization. The Smith model has been adapted and tweaked over time to include more particular aspects of donor research, cultivation techniques, and stewardship, but in essence still provides the fundamental model for college development offices (Cook, 2008). This traditional approach to fundraising promotes self-centered strategies that ensure the donors pursued have an interest in the institution's goals and have a high capacity to give.

Traditional fundraising tactics focus the majority of efforts towards the top 10 percent of potential donors. This "90/10 Rule" is based on the fact that 90 percent of support for colleges and universities comes from 10 percent of the donors (Sturtevant, 2002). At the heart of this model is the belief that fundraising efforts targeted at the larger population of alumni are inefficient because the majority of funds raised come from a small population of wealthy individuals (Cook, 2008; Melchiori, 1988). Research demonstrates that focusing fundraising efforts toward the most affluent alumni is not misguided; Clotfelter (2008) writes, "every empirical study of charitable giving confirms the existence of a strong positive income effect on charitable giving" (p. 661). Thus, the main objective of many advancement offices at colleges and universities is to identify alumni who are the most "financially and politically able to help an institution achieve its goals" (Cabrera, Weerts, & Zulick, 2003, p. 16). This framework explicitly ignores individuals with low financial capacity and positions the needs of the institution as paramount to the desires of the donor. The factors that motivate an individual to donate in this context are secondary, in that it does not matter what inspires one to give to an institution so long as they give.

Schervish (2008) writes, "Generosity of time and money derives not from one's level of income or wealth but from the physical and moral density of one's associational life and horizons of identification" (p. 747). This suggests, unlike the traditional model, that individuals should be screened both on their motivation to give as well as their capacity. Several theoretical frameworks exist for explaining donor motivation. Because of the many fields of study that can be used to understand philanthropy, such a economics, sociology, and psychology, attempting to conceptualize fundraising within a single one of these models would not only be difficult, but would likely ignore some of the important nuances of donor relations. Mann (2007) provides a concise summary of six prevalent theories. They include charitable giving, organizational identification, social identification, economics, services–philanthropic, and relationship–marketing.

The charitable giving framework is based on three main principles: altruism, reciprocity, and direct benefits (Drezner, 2011). Bruggink and Siddiqui (1995) describe altruism as a sense of obligation to give towards the collective good of society, and that, in the case of colleges and universities, development offices work to remind alumni of how their institution is worthwhile. Reciprocity is the idea that giving will result in some benefit. This benefit is often perceived and abstract and not restricted to time. For example, one might give because of a belief that he or she will be included in a sense of community in the future or one might give to repay the perceived benefits already received such as economic success. Direct benefits are tangible and usually immediate, such as having a building named in one's honor or being invited to a dinner. Problematic to the charitable giving framework is that it does not address the varied aspects of personal experience, especially in relation to reciprocity. As Mann (2007) points out, one's allegiance to his or her alma mater can vary substantially based on factors such as economic circumstances, proximity to the university, and the quality and type of relationships built while in college.

The five remaining theoretical frameworks for considering donor motivation offer some merits in understanding the college-alumni relationship. For example, the organizational and social identification theories highlight the ways in which alumni may intertwine the success of their alma mater with their own personal well-being. The services–philanthropic, economic, and relationship-marketing perspectives converge on how alumni perceptions of the institutional "product" are important in encouraging donations (Mann, 2007). Despite these benefits, however, all of Mann's frameworks are guided by similar underlying assumptions. These assumptions fall into the traditional perspective: that fundraising amongst alumni is about getting the motivations of the donor to align with the goals of the institution.

Many of the motivational frameworks laid out by Mann (2007) have been contested by newer theories related to institutional communication and marketing. McAlexander and Koenig (2001) suggest that the complex nature of the donor–organization relationship makes traditional marketing metrics such as brand loyalty and customer satisfaction no longer appropriate. Cook (2008) writes that the development of Kelly's (1995) two-way symmetrical view of philanthropy is significant because it negates the "common misperception that fundraising is a marketing or sale function" (p. 739). Kelly (1995) made an effort to move past the unidirectional emphasis of traditional philanthropy. In the two-way symmetrical model, fundraisers act a "mediators" between the institution and the public to ensure that there is a mutual understanding of needs and desires amongst all parties (p. 107). The key difference for Kelly's (1995) model is that persuasion is not the ultimate goal of fundraising, but rather understanding.

This latest model uses formative research to balance the needs of the charitable organization and its donor publics (i.e., research is used to identify opportunities for private funding and issues that the charitable organization is not addressing). Its practice is based on principles of negotiation, compromise, and conflict resolution. The effectiveness of this model is evaluated by its contribution to enhancing and protecting organizational autonomy through the fund-raising process.

(p. 109)

The inherent problem with Kelly's (1995) two-way symmetrical model is two-fold. The first problem is that the research being conducted to identify opportunities and the problems within the fundraising organization is being conducted by the fundraising organization, rather than by, or in collaboration with, outside constituencies. The second problem is that Kelly defines the ultimate goal of "mutual understanding" in relation to how well it advances the fundraising institution. Though the efforts of the two-way symmetrical model are on the surface nobler than traditional fundraising efforts, they still operate from the same paradigm.

The traditional approach to philanthropy operates under a positivist paradigm that asserts knowledge is objective and value neutral. Colleges and universities create knowledge independently of the outside world and disseminate it to consumers (Weerts, 2007). In this context, advancement offices attempt to market to external stakeholders what is created within the wall of the university. Cook (2008), operating under the traditional schema, writes about the ways in which donors can "purchase" varying "commodities" from colleges such as prestige, social status, pride, gratitude, immortality, and a sense of satisfaction (p. 743). Fundraisers attempt to match the interests of potential donors with the interests of the institution.

As mentioned previously, Weerts (2007) uses a constructivist paradigm to shape a new fundraising perspective. Gasman and Anderson-Thompkins (2003) used a constructivist paradigm to look at fundraising among Black college alumni. Drezner and Garvey (2012) and Garvey and Drezner (2012) did the same when looking at giving in the lesbian, gay, bisexual, transgender, and queer communities. The constructivist paradigm is similar to Kelly's (1995) two-way symmetrical approach in that it argues for multidirectional dialogue, but it also calls for shared creation of knowledge and shared creation of community goals. Weerts (2007) frames what he calls an engagement model of fundraising,

In the model, external stakeholders are not merely consumers and supporters of knowledge producers, but partners in the creation, dissemination, and implementation of knowledge. Simply put, the engagement model expands traditional university teaching, learning, and scholarly inquiry to include external stakeholders in a community of learners. The ultimate goal of this model is not knowledge distribution, but systemic change in communities and society at large.

(p. 87)

The benefit of Weerts' (2007) model is that it allows the university to be a centralized location for collective action in addressing community and societal problems. Rather than seeking independent and self-centered goals, that university must be convinced that outside constituents are worthwhile; the engaged university shares common goals with outside constituents and benefits from combined efforts.

Weerts (2007) provides six distinct reasons why the engagement model, founded in a constructivist paradigm, would be successful. The first reason is that engagement enhances teaching and learning. This is poignantly demonstrated through the successes of the service-learning model, which provide students with enhanced critical thinking skills, communication skills, and civic responsibility while simultaneously providing a benefit to the community (Learn and Serve America, 2006). Second, engagement enhances research and scholarship in that it opens diverse lines of inquiry and provides an expanded opportunity to test theory in practice. Third, with what Weerts calls "porous" structures, academic disciplines can effectively serve the public good by operating in a community of knowledge rather than in walled off hierarchies. Building on the previous sentiment, the fourth benefit of engagement is that it supports the "emerging interdisciplinary culture unfolding on campuses" and creates increases opportunities for funding due to the demand for creative, cross discipline research (p. 89). Fifth, Weerts (2007) cites his previous research demonstrating that institutions that are following a true engagement model are receiving greater funding from the state. Finally, engagement can help leverage major private gifts for higher education. New generations of donors seek acceptance of their ideas and opinions, "not just their money" (p. 90). Because donors are increasingly motivated by opportunities that make a tangible impact on society, fundraisers can begin view donors as long-term social investors (Grace & Wendroff, 2001).

Operationalizing Engaged Fundraising Practices

In the 1990s, the National Association of State Universities and Land-Grant Colleges sponsored the Kellogg Commission to reform and reinvigorate the democratic and service mission of public universities. As a product of the Kellogg Commission's recommendation, the Committee on Institutional Cooperation (CIC), an advisory group made up of scholars and administrators from the Big Ten Conference schools, decided to establish a working definition of institutional engagement for themselves as the general tenets of teaching, research, and service no longer seemed adequate enough in addressing societal issues. The definition the CIC (2005) came up with is as follows:

> Engagement is the partnership of university knowledge and resources
> with those of the public and private sectors to enrich scholarship, research,
> and creative activity; enhance curriculum, teaching and learning;
> prepare educated, engaged citizens; strengthen democratic values and
> civic responsibility; address critical societal issues; and contribute to the
> public good.
>
> *(p. 6)*

Many of the crucial elements found in Weerts' (2007) description of an engaged
institution such as collaboration, citizenship, and social responsibility are found
in this definition. Most importantly the CIC definition of engagement and
Weerts' definition agree that the paramount goal of colleges and universities is
to contribute to the public good.

How exactly do institutions of higher education put such unselfish aspirations as bettering the world into practice, and in the context of fundraising
how do such actions increase university donations? Weerts' (2007) theory of
engagement is extremely useful in providing a theoretical framework for which
to ground fundraising practices. Its practical focus, however, is quite limited,
especially in the discussion of drawing students and alumni into the engagement culture. Weerts' suggestions for cross-functional, issue-focused working
groups seem to focus heavily on university faculty and outside constituents,
leaving students and their experiences as a small component of the entire picture. It will be important for universities to recognize that their value to society
is in educating an informed and engaged citizen as much as it is to do research
and provide service. The Truman Commission Report of 1947 nicely articu-
lates the ideals of engendering students with the ability and desire to contribute
to the greater good:

> Today's college graduate may have gained technical or professional train-
> ing in one field of work or another, but is only incidentally, if at all,
> made ready for performing his duties as a man, a parent, and a citizen.
> Too often he is "educated" in that he has acquired competence in some
> particular occupation, yet falls short of that human wholeness and civic
> conscience which the cooperative activities of citizenship require.

Today's young alumni care about their economic and career success more than
any other factors (Higher Education Research Institute, 2011). A university
operating out of the constructivist paradigm described by Weerts (2007) would
utilize engagement as a central educational force in transforming the lives of
students and imparting civic values.

Student Development as Alumni Development

The more college students are given opportunities and encouragement to be
involved, and if they take advantage of those opportunities, the more they

learn and mature (Astin, 1984, 1993; Friedlander, 1980; Pascarella & Terenzini, 1991). Tinto (1997) writes, "The greater students' involvement in the life of the college, the greater their acquisition of knowledge and development of skills ... That engagement, both inside and outside the classroom, appears to be especially important to student development" (p. 600). An influential and widely cited scholar, Alexander Astin, studied and articulated a theory of student involvement nearly 30 years ago that still holds acclaim for many higher education scholars and practitioners. In the context of this review, Astin's (1984, 1999) theory of involvement merges quite nicely with the constructivist engagement paradigm proposed by Weerts (2007). In contrasting what he calls "traditional pedagogical theories," in which students are simply exposed to information, with his own theory, Astin (1999) writes, "The content theory, in particular, tends to place students in a passive role as recipients of information. The theory of involvement, on the other hand, emphasizes active participation of the student in the learning process" (p. 522). Using Astin's student involvement perspective as a basis, I will attempt to tie together important aspects of student affairs, classroom experiences, alumni relations, and fundraising in the discussion of fundraising amongst new generations of alumni.

Astin's (1999) model has five main components: (a) Involvement refers to an investment of energy, physical and psychological energy in various efforts, and these efforts can be specific (studying for a test) or generalized (the student experience). (b) Involvement occurs along a continuum with different types of engagement and in different degrees varying at the individual level. (c) Involvement has both quantitative and qualitative elements, for example, the amount of hours spent doing community service is a quantitative measure and whether the individual feels engaged in the cause being served or is learning from the experience are qualitative measures. (d) Student learning and personal development is proportionate to the quality and quantity of involvement. (e) Effective educational policies or practices increase student involvement. Astin's assertions regarding involvement are simple, straightforward, and allow for easy measurement of a program's effectiveness. There may certainly be some weaknesses to his assertions. For example, a student can put all the energy, effort, and commitment he or she is capable of into involvement, but if that student is not self-reflective of the experience, there is likely less learning occurring. As Astin (1999) points out, however, too often educators focus on content and method of their work and not on the individual efforts of the student to achieve a goal (p. 526).

In a related parallel, much of traditional college fundraising practices have focused on how to get specific (wealthy) donors to align with the goals of the institution and not on increasing the efforts of the alumni base as a whole. For this reason, Astin's (1999) framework is quite appropriate for understanding development literature, though it was intended primarily for understanding student development. (a) Alumni involvement is an investment of energy. (b)

Academic literature demonstrates that levels of involvement for young alumni often depend on personal capacities and emotional connections to the institution (Clotfelter, 2003; Monks, 2003). (c) Alumni involvement can concretely be measured in an amount of money or time donated by alumni or, more abstractly, by examining the level of caring or compassion displayed (Weerts, Cabrera, & Sanford, 2009). (d) In many ways donors can "get back what they put in" through rewarding relationships with individuals at the college or university and "warm glow" feelings of being a significant part of a good cause. (e) Finally, the ultimate goal for effective development practices is increasing alumni involvement. Especially unique and useful in using Astin's model is the ability to bridge the "involvement continuum" from student involvement to alumni involvement. In fitting within the larger framework of engagement, the last component and goal of Astin's model should be altered so that the goal of an educational institution should be to increase both student and alumni engagement with the larger societal picture.

Engagement in Practice

The first step in reaching an engagement model of fundraising would be to adopt an institutional mission that focuses on the production and dissemination of knowledge in partnership with the larger community, similar to the CIC (2005) statement, and commits to increasing student and alumni involvement as lifetime partners in the process. Given the demonstrated importance of overall quality in the undergraduate experience (Clotfelter, 2008), interaction with faculty and staff mentors (Monks, 2003), and involvement in volunteerism and service activities (Wang & Graddy, 2008) in relation to later giving, it is clear that nearly all aspects of a university's operations have a direct or indirect impact on fundraising success. As Weerts (2007) writes, "In the traditional model, advancement, academics, and external constituents are distinct entities and look after their own interests" (p. 92). This is contrasted with an engaged institutional environment in which advancement staff, alumni relations, community relations, faculty, students, and student affairs staff work together to "facilitate an interactive process of teaching, learning, and problem solving in which institutions and external partners exchange perspectives, knowledge, materials, and resources" (p. 93). Without establishing clear objectives in which these ideals become goals and strategic priorities for the entire institution, the development office would certainly be less successful in utilizing an engagement model of fundraising. It would also be important to create an incentives system within the institution to reward faculty and staff for increasing involvement amongst student, alumni, and community groups.

After the goals of engagement have been established, the next logical step is to ask individuals to become engaged. This seems fairly obvious and simple, but the truth is that it is a component of development that is not given enough attention. Schervish (2008) writes that for, the majority of donators and volunteers, "being asked" is cited as a major reason for participation. Perhaps the reason studies are finding that younger alumni volunteer less for the their alma mater than do older generations (Weerts & Ronca, 2007) is because no one is asking them to help. Schervish (2008) notes that impersonal solicitations, such as phone calls and mail requests, are only moderately effective in garnering support from volunteers. He writes, "… being asked directly by someone the contributor knows personally or by a representative of an organization the contributor participates in is a major mobilizing factor" (p. 843). Some research seems to suggest that college mass-marketing efforts are not effectively utilized by development offices (Stevick, 2010), and even if online modes of communication were mastered, they still lack the personal approach recommended by Schervish (2008). Whether it is a community group, faculty, students, or other university staff being asked to help, an essential component of engagement for development and communication offices is to personally solicit volunteers or train, empower, and facilitate ways for other volunteers to make solicitations.

The final step is putting institutional advancement within an engaged university into practice. Drezner (2010) offers a great practical example of how the engagement continuum is bridged. Based on the idea that engagement in pro-social behavior as a college-aged adult increases the likelihood of financial giving later in life (Kang, 2005), Drezner (2010) gathered qualitative data on how students at historically Black colleges and universities (HBCUs) were socialized through the United Negro College Fund's (UNCF) Pre-Alumni Council (PAC) to understand the importance of service for their universities and the larger community. Embracing the importance of educating students prior to graduation about the benefits of philanthropy, the PAC employs several methods to educate and engage college students. These methods include educating students specifically how UNCF funds are used to support programs and scholarships, educating students about how UNCF funds impact them personally even if they are not the beneficiaries of a particular scholarship, encouraging involvement in the fundraising process through engagement at alumni relation events and in solicitation efforts, and encouraging participation in community service projects.

Drezner (2010) outlines how the UNCF utilizes extrinsic and intrinsic motivational factors to get students involved. Extrinsic motivators include networking opportunities with alumni that can allow students to meet esteemed community members or possibly learn of a job opportunity. The PACs include in their mission a desire to connect students with their surrounding communities through service. Programming opportunities are provided to college students to "adopt a class" of local school children, participate in health forums, and establish of on-campus high school visitation days. This blending of mixed motivational factors is important to the students' personal development. Drezner writes, "College aged young adults are at a stage in their development where intrinsic motivations to help others in an altruistic way are beginning to develop while extrinsic motivations—such as peer approval and recognition with gifts and awards—are still important" (p. 141). Fitting perfectly into Weerts' (2007) engagement model, the UNCF understands that though community service projects might not provide direct benefits to the organization, it builds a culture of philanthropy that increases the chances of future support. In the direct words of a student involved in PAC programming, "If you're involved with their institution and you generally have a love for your institution then you're going to be involved as an alum [*sic*]" (as quoted in Drezner, 2010, p. 138).

Another example of an engagement model in practice comes from some of the initiatives put forth by CIC institutions. For over 15 years, the Michigan State University department of Mechanical Engineering has been partnering with community, regional, and national businesses to bring practical and hands-on engineering experience to high school and college students through a Design Day program. Students choose a semester-long project that interests them, are paired with a business or non-profit entity, and given a group of high school students to advise and work with in the creation of a product or device. The actual Design Day takes place at the end of the semester when teams of students present their products to panels of teachers, professors, and businesses and compete for a myriad of prizes and scholarships. Each year, one team in particular is encouraged to design a device to aid those with physical disabilities. There are multiple benefits to the Design Day program. The college students gain valuable experience in leadership and advising, hands-on research, and able to expose their talents to the private sector who may be looking for interns or entry-level candidates. Thousands of high school students are given an opportunity to engage in exciting projects that challenge their math and science knowledge as well as exposure to college student mentors and role models. The companies involved gain excellent public relations exposure and an opportunity to recruit new talent. The university gains hundreds of corporate sponsorships, as well as a chance to dialogue with those sponsors about other opportunities for collaboration on campus. Finally, the larger community benefits from new products and technologies that can address human service needs as well as spark economic growth (CIC, 2005). While the Design Day website does not specifically solicit alumni support for the program, and lacks much of the intentional civic education of the UNCF, it is easy to imagine that as the pool of alumni who participated in the programs grows, some of them are likely to encourage their own companies or organizations to get involved in sponsoring a Design Day project.

The key to these examples is the focus on providing modes for undergraduate engagement and the need to encourage a continuation of that engagement as alumni. Note that both programs are not confined within the walls of any particular department, division, or even university. While the PAC program is developed specifically with fundraising efforts in mind and Design Day was developed with research efforts in mind, both were willing and able to incorporate student involvement into benefitting the university staff, students, campus, and larger community simultaneously.

This continuation of this shared commitment between students and the university after graduation is by no means an easy feat, as young alumni are often extremely busy working long hours with relatively low incomes in "entry level" positions, financing new cars or homes, and paying off student debt. These challenges are not insurmountable. Alumni can still receive guidance and support from faculty, they can maintain contact and even participate with student groups with which they were involved, they can utilize the career center, and they can be given information about university affiliated service efforts. These methods of involvement can be streamlined into the alumni transition and be measured according to an adaptation of Astin's student involvement framework. In this way, within the age groups containing tomorrow's big donors, a significant amount can be done to increase the chances of future giving.

Conclusions

The higher education community faces an imperative to increase financial support amidst a poor economic environment. Alumni have traditionally been, and continue to be, the greatest mode of private support for America's colleges and universities. Unfortunately, research demonstrates that alumni participation in development efforts has been dwindling, especially amongst the most recent cohorts of college graduates.

Given the declining rates of participation amongst alumni in development efforts, it is evident that the current paradigm for fundraising is not engendering support from recent graduates. Increased attention on major donors and attempting to align the efforts of alumni with what the institution wants will not be effective in developing new generations of alumni donors. Alumni want to support causes they care about and organizations they identify with. Supporting an involved and engaged undergraduate experience is the first step supporting an engaged alumni experience. It is recommended that to achieve engaged advancement work, the entire university structure and community must support open and collaborative learning processes. Students and alumni should be viewed as life-long partners in the process and invited to uplift society in any capacity in which they are able.

There are several directions in which future research can take on engaged advancement amongst alumni. As Weerts (2007) suggests, organizational structures and incentives that allow for porous, cross-disciplinary activity within the university should be evaluated. A key component to such a study would be an assessment of how involved alumni were in engaging through those structures. On a more micro level, qualitative studies are needed that evaluate current engaged young alumni and how their relationship with their alma mater was shaped through the student/alumni involvement continuum. The benefits of service learning for current students have been extensively documented, but exploratory studies must be done of university service projects that involve alumni. Finally, attempts should be made to continue to track the changing motivations, demographics, and characteristics of recent alumni.

Researchers and universities must never forget that recent graduates who are involved and engaged are the future's biggest supporters of higher education (see Table 13.1). The education community has a duty to mold and empower engaged citizens. When engaged colleges and universities produce individuals who strive to better their local, national, and global communities, they are producing alumni who will strive to better their alma mater.

TABLE 13.1 Recommendations for Increasing Alumni Involvement in an Engaged University

Recommendation	Strategies for Implementation
Establish the goals of engagement for your institution	• Make the process democratic and cross functional, include community partners, faculty, students, alumni, and administrators. • Focus on how the public good and institutional well-being intersect. • Consider the ideals of engagement (collaboration, resource sharing, citizenship) when establishing objectives. • Create incentives for university constituents to pursue established goals.
Students and alumni are not likely to give if they are not asked	• Ask alumni to participate in a targeted, personal, and direct manner. • Solicit involvement before soliciting money. • Provide multiple avenues for giving using various communication channels. • Develop a clear and convincing rationale for why alumni should give despite competing demands such as jobs or family.
Create programs that bridge the student & alumni involvement continuum	• Consider both intrinsic and extrinsic motivating factors for student and alumni involvement. • Establish partnerships and programs that compliment educational goals and that benefit the community. • Assume that participants in a beneficial program will be more willing to participate again in the future and perhaps donate in the future. • Make the transition from student to alumni participant seamless. • Stay values and vision oriented—remember the goal is to encourage involved citizenship.

References

Astin, A. W. (1984). Student involvement: a developmental theory for higher education. *Journal of College Student Personnel, 25*(4), 297–308

Astin, A. W. (1993). *What matters in college? Four critical years revisited.* San Francisco, CA: Jossey-Bass.

Astin, A. W. (1999). Student involvement: a developmental theory for higher education. *Journal of College Student Development, 40*(5), 518–529.

Briechle, P. (2008). Does institutional type affect alumnae donating patterns in the United States? In A. Walton & M. Gasman (Eds.), *Philanthropy, volunteerism, and fundraising* (pp. 648–656). Upper Saddle River, NJ: Pearson..

Bruggink, T. H., & Siddiqui, K. (1995). An econometric model of alumni giving: a case study for a liberal arts college. *The American Economist, 39*(2), 53–60.

Cabrera, A. F., Weerts, D. J., & Zulick, B. J. (2003, June). *Alumni survey: Three conceptualizations to alumni research.* Paper presented at Métodos de Análisis de la insercriónlaboral de los universitarios. Universidad de León, España

Capek, M. E. S. (2001). *Women and philanthropy: Old stereotypes, new challenges.* Retrieved April 1, 2011, from http://www.wfnet.org/sites/wfnet.org/files/old_stereotypes_new_challenges_capek2001_0.pdf

Carson, E. (2008). Black philanthropy's past, present, and future. In A. Walton & M. Gasman (Eds.), *Philanthropy, volunteerism, and fundraising* (pp. 774–777). Upper Saddle River, NJ: Pearson.

Cheslock, J. J., Gianneschi, M. (2008). Replacing state appropriations with alternative revenue sources: the case of voluntary support. *Journal of Higher Education,79*(2), 208–229.

Committee on Institutional Cooperation (CIC) Committee on Engagement. (2005). Engaged scholarship: A resource guide. Committee on Institutional Cooperation. Retrieved from http://www.scholarshipofengagement.org/benchmarking/FINAL.doc

Cook, B., & Lasher, W. F. (1996). Toward a theory of fundraising in higher education. *The Review of Higher Education, 20*(1), 33–51.

Cook, W. B. (2008). Surveying the major gifts literature: Observations and refections. In A. Walton & M. Gasman (Eds.), *Philanthropy, volunteerism, and fundraising.* Upper Saddle River, NJ: Pearson

Council for Aid to Education. (2007). Contributions to colleges and universities up by 9.4 percent to $ 28 billion strong growth driven by personal giving. Retrieved March 15, 2011, from http://cae.org/content/pdf/VSE.2006.Press.Release.pdf

Council for Aid to Education. (2010, February 3). Contributions to colleges and universities down 11.9 percent to 27.85 billion greatest decline ever recorded. Retrieved November 22, 2010, from http://www.cae.org/content/pdf/VSE_2009_Press_Relsease.pdf

Clotfelter, C. T. (2003). Alumni giving to elite private college and universities. *Economics of Education Review, 22*(2), 109–120.

Clotfelter, C. T. (2008). Who are the alumni donors? Giving by two generations of alumni from selective colleges. In A. Walton & M. Gasman, M. (Eds.), *Philanthropy, volunteerism, and fundraising* (pp. 657–671). Upper Saddle River, NJ: Pearson.

Drezner, N. D. (2010). Private black colleges' encouragement of student giving and volunteerism: An examination of prosocial behavior development. *International Journal of Education Advancement, 10*(3), 126–147.

Drezner, N. D. (2011). *Philanthropy and fundraising in American higher education.* New York, NY: Wiley.

Drezner, N. D., & Garvey, J. C. (2012, April). *(Un)Conscious queer identity and influence on philanthropy towards higher education.* Presented at the Annual Meeting of the American Educational Research Association, Vancouver, B.C., Canada.

Elliott, D. (2006). *The kindness of strangers: Philanthropy and higher education.* New York, NY: Rowman & Littlefield.

Friedlander, J. (1980). *The importance of quality of effort in predicting college student attainment* (doctoral dissertation). The University of California-Los Angeles.

Garvey, J., & Drezner, N. D. (2012, April). *Advancement staff and alumni advocates: Leaders in engaging LGBTQ alumni.* Presented at the Annual Meeting of the American Educational Research Association, Vancouver, B.C., Canada.

Gasman, M. (2002). An untapped resource: Bringing African Americans into the college and university giving process. In A. Walton & M. Gasman (Eds.), *Philanthropy, volunteerism, and fundraising* (pp. 778-787). Upper Saddle River, NJ: Pearson.

Gasman, M., & Anderson-Thompkins, S. (2003). *Fund raising from Black college alumni: Successful strategies for supporting alma mater.* Washington, D.C.: Council for the Advancement and Support of Education.

Gasman, M., & Drezner, N. D. (2008). Fundraising as an integral part of higher education. In A. Walton & M. Gasman (Eds.), *Philanthropy, volunteerism, and fundraising* (pp. 595-600). Upper Saddle River, NJ: Pearson.

Grace, K. S., & Wendroff, A .L. (2001). *High impact philanthropy: How donors, boards, and nonprofit organizations can transform communities.* New York, NY: Wiley.

Higher Education Research Institute. (2011). *The American freshman: Nation norms fall 2010* [policy brief]. Retrieved from http://www.heri.ucla.edu/PDFs/pubs/briefs/HERI_Research-Brief_Norms2010.pdf

Holmes, J. (2009). Prestige, charitable deductions and other determinants of alumni giving: Evidence from a highly selective liberal arts college. *Economics of Education Review, 28*(1), 18–28.

Kang, C.H. (2005, October). *An exploration on individual giving and volunteering in Korea.* Paper presented at colloquium of the University of Pennsylvania School of Social Work, Philadelphia, PA .

Kelly, K. S. (1995). Utilizing public relations theory to conceptualize and test models of fund raising. *Journalism and Mass Communication Quarterly, 72*(1), 106–127.

Kelly, K. S. (2002). The state of fund-raising theory and research. In M. J. Worth (Ed.), *New strategies for educational fundraising* (pp. 39–55). Westport, CT: Praeger.

Learn and Serve America. (2006). What is service-learning? Retrieved from http://www.learnandserve.gov/about/service_learning/index.asp

Lindahl, W., & Winship, C. (1992). Predictive models for annual fundraising and major gift fundraising. *Nonprofit Management and Leadership, 3*, 43–64.

Mann, T. (2007). College fund raising using theoretical perspectives to understand donor motives. *International Journal of Educational Advancement, 7*(1), 35–46.

McAlexander, J. H., & Koenig, H. F. (2001). University experiences, the student-college relationship, and alumni support. *Journal for Marketing for Higher Education, 10*(3), 21–43.

McDearmon, J. T. (2010). What's in it for me: a qualitative look into the mindset of young alumni non-donors. *International Journal of Educational Advancement, 10*, 33–47.

Melchiori, G. S. (1988). Applying alumni research to fundraising. In G. S. Melchiori (Ed.), *Alumni research: Methods and applications. New Directions for Institutional Research, 60*, 51–66. San Francisco, CA: Jossey-Bass Publishers.

Merkel, R. E. (2010). *Managing the relationship between the student and the university, a case study in the context of development and alumni relations* (doctoral dissertation). University of Maryland, College Park;.http://hdl.handle.net/1903/10479

Mesch, D. J., Rooney, P. M., Chin, W., & Steinberg, K. S. (2002). Race and gender differences in philanthropy: Indiana as a test case. *New Directions for Philanthropic Fundraising, 37*, 65–77.

Monks, J. (2003). Patterns of giving to one's alma mater amongst young graduates from selective institutions. *Economic of Education Review, 22*(2), 121–130.

National Center for Education Statistics. (2009). *Digest of education statistics.* Retrieved March 26, 2011, from http://nces.ed.gov/pubsearch/pubsinfo.asp?pubid=2009020

National Center for Public Policy and Higher Education. (2002). *Losing ground: A national status report on the affordability of higher education.* San Jose, CA: Author.

Newman, D. S. (2002). Incorporating diverse traditions into the fundraising practices of nonprofit organizations. *New Directions for Philanthropic Fundraising, 37*, 11–21.

Nichols, J. E. (2004). Repositioning fundraising in the 21st century. *International Journal of Nonprofit and Voluntary Sector Marketing, 9*(2), 163–170.

Okunade, A., & Justice, S. (1991). Micropanel estimates of the life-cycle hypothesis with respect to alumni donations. In *Proceedings of the Business and Economics Statistical Section of the American Statistical Association* (pp. 298–305). Washington, DC: American Statistical Association.

Okunade, A., & Berl, R. L. (1997). Determinants of charitable giving of business school alumni. *Research in Higher Education, 38*, 201–214.

Pascarella, E. T., & Terenzini, P. T. (1991). *How college affects students*. San Francisco, CA: Jossey-Bass.

Rooney, P. M., Mesch, D. J., Chin, W., & Steinberg, K. S. (2005). The effects of race, gender and survey methodologies on giving in the US. *Economics Letters, 86*, 173–180.

Scanlan, J. B., & Abrahams, J. (2002). Giving traditions of minority communities. In M. L. Worth (Ed.), *New strategies for educational fundraising* (pp. 197–205). Westport, CT: ACE/Praeger.

Schervish, P. G. (2008). Major donors, major motives: The people and purposes behind major gifts. In A. Walton & M. Gasman (Eds.), *Philanthropy, volunteerism, and fundraising* (pp. 747–760). Upper Saddle River, NJ: Pearson.

Smith, G. T. (1975). Developing private support: three issues. In F. W. Ness (Ed.), *The president's role in development*. Washington, DC: Association of American Colleges.

Smith, G. T. (1977). The development program. In A. W. Rowland (Ed.), *Handbook of institutional advancement* (pp. 142–151). San Francisco, CA: Jossey-Bass.

Smith, B., Shue, S., Vest, J. L., & Villarreal, J. (1999). *Philanthropy in communities of color*. Bloomington: Indiana University Press.

Sturtevant, W. (2002). *Major gifts fundraising: the mission and promise*. Keynote address at the annual Association for Arts and Sciences Advancement Professionals meeting. Pittsburgh, PA.

Stevick, T. R. (2010). Integrating development, alumni relations, and marketing for fundraising success. *New Directions for Higher Education, 149*, 57–64.

Sun, X., Hoffman, S. C., & Grady, M. L. (2007). A multivariate causal model of alumni giving: implications for alumni fundraisers. *International Journal of Educational Advancement, 7*(4), 307–333.

Taylor, A. L., & Martin, J. C. (1995). Characteristics of alumni donors and nondonors at a research I, public university. *Research in Higher Education, 36*(3), 283–302.

Tinto, V. (1997). Classrooms as communities: Exploring the education character of student persistence. *The Journal of Higher Education, 68*(6,) 599–623

Truman Commission. (1947). Higher education for democracy: A report of the president's commission on higher education. *Vol. 1: Establishing the Goals*. Retrieved from: http://www.ed.uiuc.edu/courses/eol474/sp98/truman.html

Wang, L., & Graddy, E. (2008). Social capital, volunteering, and charitable giving. *Voluntas: International Journal of Voluntary and Nonprofit Organization, 19*(1), 23–42.

Weerts, D. J. (2007). Toward an engagement model of institutional advancement at public colleges and universities. In D. J. Weerts (Ed.), *Transforming campuses and communities through public engagement: Emerging roles for institutional advancement* (pp. 79–103). Special issue of *International Journal of Educational Advancement, 7*(2).

Weerts, D. J., Cabrera, A. F., & Sanford, T. (2009). Beyond giving: Political advocacy and volunteer behaviors of public university alumni. *Research in Higher Education, 51*, 346–365.

Weerts, D. J., & Ronca, J. M. (2007). Profiles of supportive alumni: Donors, volunteers, and those who "do it all". *International Journal of Education Advancement, 7*(1), 20–34.

Willemain, T. R., Goyal, A., Deven, M. V., & Thukral, I. S. (1994). Alumni giving: the influences of reunion, class, and year. *Research in Higher Education, 35*(5), 609–629.

AUTHOR BIOGRAPHIES

Meredith S. Billings is a doctoral student in the Center for the Study of Higher and Postsecondary Education at the University of Michigan. She received her M.A. in higher education from the University of Maryland and her B.S. in neuroscience from the College of William and Mary. Before coming to Michigan, Meredith was the senior research analyst in the Office of Institutional Research & Evaluation at Tufts University. While she was at Tufts, she was awarded NEAIR's Best Paper award in 2009 for her research on young alumni giving behavior. Primarily, her research focuses on utilizing quantitative methodology to solve higher education problems and how colleges and universities use data in the governance of their institutions. Meredith's other professional experiences include working at Middlebury College and the University of Maryland in student services and undergraduate admissions.

Nelson Bowman III is the Director of Development at Prairie View A&M University. Along with Marybeth Gasman, he is the author of *A Guide to Fundraising at Historically Black Colleges and Universities: An All Campus Approach.*

José A. Cabrales received his Ph.D. in Educational Leadership and Policy Studies from Iowa State University. Over the past 10 years, he has served as a higher education administrator for different functional areas, including residence life, admissions, Greek life, and career services. José has also served as a chapter leader and volunteer for his alma mater's alumni association. In addition to his volunteer work, José currently serves as the chair of the Sigma Lambda Beta Education Foundation, which supports leadership development and educational initiatives for its members. He is also a constituency engagement manager at *Excelencia* in Education. His current research focuses on Latina/o philanthropy in higher education and college student success.

Noah D. Drezner is assistant professor of higher education and founding faculty member in the new Center on Philanthropy and Nonprofit Leadership at the University of Maryland. He holds his Ph.D. and master's degree in higher education from the University of Pennsylvania and a bachelor's degree from the University of Rochester. In addition, Noah holds a graduate certificate in non-profit leadership from Roberts Wesleyan College. His research interests include philanthropy and fundraising as it pertains to colleges and universities, including higher education's role in the cultivation of prosocial behaviors. Drezner has published numerous articles and given several presentations on related topics. His dissertation *Cultivating a Culture of Giving: An Exploration of Institutional Strategies to Enhance African American Young Alumni Giving*, was chosen as the Outstanding Doctoral Dissertation winner for the 2008 Council for the Advancement and Support of Education (CASE) H.S. Warwick Award for Outstanding Research in Alumni Relations for Educational Advancement. Additionally, Noah is an associate editor of an ASHE reader on *Philanthropy, Fundraising, and Volunteerism in Higher Education* (2007), which was named the 2009 CASE John Grenzebach Award for Outstanding Research in Philanthropy for Educational Advancement. One of his recent books *Philanthropy and Fundraising in American Higher Education* (2011) has been adopted in master's and doctoral programs across the country. Most recently he co-authored, *Race, Gender, and Leadership in Nonprofit Organizations*. Noah is on the editorial board of the *International Journal of Educational Advancement* and the Association for Fundraising Professionals Research Council. Dr. Drezner's professional experience includes serving as a leadership-gifts development officer at the University of Rochester.

Jason C. Garvey is a doctoral candidate at the University of Maryland, pursuing a degree in college student personnel administration with a focus on LGBTQQI college students. He holds his master's degree in school psychology with a concentration in sexuality studies from The Ohio State University and a bachelor's degree in Educational Studies from the University of Delaware. His research interests include examining the experiences of LGBTQQI college students and alumni, with specific foci in philanthropy, fundraising, campus climate, and student development. Jay has worked in higher education across several domains, including academic advising, undergraduate research, and LGBTQQI student services.

Marybeth Gasman is a professor of higher education in the Graduate School of Education at the University of Pennsylvania. She is the author of *Envisioning Black Colleges: A History of the United Negro College Fund*.

Luke Greeley is currently Residential Learning Coordinator at Rutgers University in New Brunswick, New Jersey. Working in a community with a high concentration of first-year and transfer students, one of his main roles is to provide programmatic initiatives that increase opportunities for student involvement and leadership with the ultimate goal of improving retention. He received his master's in Higher Education from the University of Maryland, College Park where his research interests include student and alumni involvement, fundraising, and institutional engagement.

Lori A. Hurvitz earned her bachelor's degree in sociology and political science from the University of Michigan and her master's degree in administration, planning, and social policy with a focus in higher education from the Harvard Graduate School of Education, and her doctorate from the University of Pennsylvania. Her dissertation research examined student philanthropy education initiatives at nine Ivy-Plus institutions for which she earned distinction from the faculty of Penn and was awarded the John Grenzebach Award for Outstanding Research in Philanthropy, Doctoral Dissertation from the Council for Advancement and Support of Education. After completing her master's degree in 1999, Lori began working at the University of Chicago for the Office of the Reynolds Club and Student Activities. In 2004, she moved to the College (of undergraduate studies) where she is currently the assistant dean and director of college programming and holds responsibility for creating a sense of community and institutional affinity through a series of strategic class-based program initiatives.

Sara Kaiser is a doctoral student in higher education at the University of Mississippi. Prior to graduate school she worked in student affairs, enrollment management, and parent programs. Her research interests include women in higher education, deans of women, and history of higher education.

Anita Mastroieni has served as the founding director of the Graduate Student Center at the University of Pennsylvania since 2001 and as the founding director of Penn's Family Resource Center since 2010. Anita earned a doctorate of education in higher education management from University of Pennsylvania in 2010; her dissertation research focused on the motivations of doctoral alumni giving.

Ryan E. Merkel currently works in the Development Office of the National Symphony Orchestra, an affiliate of the John F. Kennedy Center for the Performing Arts in Washington, DC. Ryan's work includes stewarding midrange and major donors to the orchestra, special event coordination, and researching potential institutional partners. Ryan holds a master's degree in communication management from the University of Maryland, where his research focused on the intersection of public relations theory and major giving, alumni relations, and young alumni philanthropy. This research has been featured at the annual conferences of the Eastern Communication Association (ECA) and the Association for Research on Nonprofit and Voluntary Action (ARNOVA). Ryan earned an undergraduate degree in business marketing at the University of Florida.

Michael Puma is a doctoral student in higher education at the University of Maryland College Park. He received his master's in higher education administration from Syracuse University and a bachelor of science degree in psychology and American studies from Fordham University. He currently serves as the co-director of Living Learning Programs at Loyola University Maryland. While at Loyola University Maryland, Puma has also worked in the Office of Student Life developing peer education programs and fostering collaboration between academic affairs and student affairs colleagues. His research interests include student affairs fundraising, living-learning programs, and junior faculty development.

Genevieve G. Shaker is assistant professor of philanthropic studies at the Center on Philanthropy at Indiana University and director of communications and creative services for the IU School of Liberal Arts at Indiana University-Purdue University Indianapolis (IUPUI). A practicing institutional advancement professional with more than 10 years of experience in the field, Genevieve is a long-standing steering committee member for IUPUI's faculty and staff fundraising campaign and leads the effort for her school. She is currently working on an analysis of faculty and staff giving in the Indiana University system as a part of her research agenda on the intersections between philanthropic action, concepts, and the professoriate. Her dissertation was recognized by the Association for the Study of Higher Education as the 2009 Bobby Wright Dissertation of the Year and by the Professional and Organizational Development Network with the Robert J. Menges Award for Outstanding Research in Educational Development.

Kozue Tsunoda is associate director of capital giving at Swarthmore College. Prior to joining Swarthmore, she worked as development coordinator at Johns Hopkins University. She earned her Ph.D. from the University of Maryland, College Park, specializing in Asian and Asian American philanthropy in higher education. She also studied at Hiroshima University where she earned her M.A. in comparative and international education. She completed her B.A. in Chinese from Tokyo University of Foreign Studies while also attending Sun Yat-sen University in China. Over the course of her studies and research in Japan, China, and the United States, Kozue Tsunoda had an opportunity to work with many organizations including: CASE, Asian American Studies Program (AAST) at the University of Maryland, Smithsonian Institution, OCA, and Special Olympics.

Amy Wells Dolan is the associate dean of the School of Education and an associate professor of higher education in the Department of Leadership and Counselor Education at the University of Mississippi. She earned a Ph.D. from the University of Kentucky, a master's degree from Kent State University, and a baccalaureate degree from Transylvania University. Her scholarly focus involves the history of higher education in the South, and especially the South's historical educational context related to race, class, gender, and philanthropy. Her background and contemporary role includes higher education administration with experience in fundraising parent programs, annual giving programs, and capital campaigns. She is on the academic editorial board for the *International Journal of Educational Advancement* and her publications have appeared in scholarly volumes recognized by the Council for Advancement and Support of Education (CASE).

INDEX